CHINA

Yellow Peril? Red Hope?

CHINA

Yellow Peril? Red Hope?

by C. R. HENSMAN

THE WESTMINSTER PRESS · PHILADELPHIA

Standard Book No. 664–24844–6

Library of Congress Catalog Card No. 69–13170

PUBLISHED BY THE WESTMINSTER PRESS®

PHILADELPHIA, PENNSYLVANIA

PRINTED IN THE UNITED STATES OF AMERICA

Contents

Preface

SHORT OF actual war, relations between China, the most important nation in Asia, on the one hand, and Europe and North America ('Euramerica', as it has been termed) on the other, could not be worse than what they are. And it is only wishful thinking that makes some of us act as though they cannot get any worse.

There is no way of explaining briefly and simply what the purpose of the book is. Like everything else trying to make its voice heard it must speak for itself, and be judged by what it says and does rather than by what is said about it. No part of it can be said to stand for the whole. It is hoped that as the book keeps for the most part to the basic issues the whole can be read in as short a time as anyone can afford to give to issues which involve our understanding of the contemporary world and relations with not just a quarter but the greater part of mankind. There is much that is deliberately left unsaid. There are conclusions which need to be drawn and questions to be answered.

What the extent of one's debt is in the making of a book it is not easy to say. If this one is not found to be more wanting in truthfulness and candour, in the relevance and depth of its perceptions, and in the justice of its observations than it is, it is because of the high standards set by other commentators and scholars on contemporary history from whom I have imperfectly learnt. This is inevitably a wide-ranging book about the contemporary world. People in many parts of the world with whom I have lived and worked and talked as a student and analyst of contemporary world politics have contributed to it. Books, articles, reports, photographs and films which have helped (or provoked) my own attempts over the past twenty-five years to understand what is happening in the world as a whole, and in particular the nature and significance of the revolutionary changes taking place among the Asians, Latin Americans and Africans, are numerous; since this does not pretend to be a work of 'objective' scholarship, footnotes have been kept to a minimum.

For the fact that the attempt has been made to discover why so many in Europe and America feel and act as they do about China and the Chinese no one can share the blame with the writer except Pauline Hensman and Rohini Hensman. That this book has been completed at all for publication is due to the latter, whose encouragement and help was not limited to reading and commenting on the drafts, checking the final copy and helping to read the proofs. That in the given conditions the writer, aspiring to write without fear or favour, could have the freedom and the time for research and writing, and the assurance that the material consequences should not be too disastrous, is due to the former.

Finally, this book would show more signs of hasty writing than it does if it were not for Mrs A. C. Russell of the SCM Press and Ross Terrill. I am also grateful to Mrs B. Sivanandan and Miss Margaret Scruton who typed the manuscript.

London C. R. HENSMAN

Acknowledgements

Acknowledgements are gratefully made to the following publishers for permission to reproduce passages from their publications listed below:

Allen & Unwin: *The Asian Century* by Jan Romein
Ampersand: *Land behind Walls* by Lorenz Stucki
Cape (Jonathan): *The Crippled Tree*; *The Mortal Flower* by Han Suyin
Chatto & Windus: *China and the Peace of Asia* edited by Alastair Buchan
Gollancz (Victor): *The Chinese Communists* by Stuart Gelder; *The Road to Survival* by William Vogt
Harvard University Press: *China's Response to the West* edited by Ssu-yu Teng and John K. Fairbank
Herald Tribune
Hutchinson & Co: *Out of a Gun* by Denis Warner
Methuen & Co: *The Centre of the World* by Robert S. Elegant
New Statesman
New York Times
Oxford University Press: *The Rising American Empire* by Richard van Alstyne; *The Role of the Chinese Army* by John Gittings
Penguin Books: *Spotlight on Asia* by Guy Wint
Polish Scientific Publishers: *Agriculture, Land Reform and Economic Development; Planning and Economic Development* edited by Ignacy Sachs
Praeger (Frederick A.): *People's War, People's Army* by Vo Nguyen Giap
Secker (Martin) & Warburg: *The Blue Ants* by Robert Guillain; *Orbit of China* by Harrison E. Salisbury
Sunday Times
The Congress of Cultural Freedom: *China Quarterly*
The Foreign Languages Press: *Long Live the Victory of People's War* by Lin Piao; *On the Correct Handling of Contradictions*

among the People; *Selected Works*, 4 volumes, by Mao Tse Tung
The Guardian
The Monthly Review Press: *Fanshen* by William Hinton
Vintage Books: *The Vietnam Reader* edited by Marcus G. Raskin and Bernard Fall
Yale University Press: *China under Communism* by Richard L. Walker

For Pauline

I

The China 'Problem'

EARLY IN 1966 The *Evening Standard,* which millions of Londoners read, one afternoon startled its readers with this large, extra-bold, front-page headline:

'YELLOW PERIL'
NEW U.S. WARNING

The news item under it referred to what the Defence Secretary of the United States, Mr Robert McNamara, had said at an important meeting in Paris to ministers of countries allied with the United States. The prominent sub-heading read:

That is why
we fight in
Vietnam
SAYS MCNAMARA

The importance of the headline lay in its indication that the term 'Yellow Peril' was in current use. The caption showed how this concept was being used as an explanation for Western policy in Vietnam, where the fighting at this time was costing the Vietnamese as well as the United States and her allies many lives. Ever since China had become a war-time ally of the North Atlantic anti-Fascist powers in the Second World War there had naturally been little use of a term like this, with its unpleasant racialist undertones. It was only in the fifties that fears of the yellow peril began to be revived.

The use of the term by the *Evening Standard* was not an isolated instance. It signified the fairly widespread currency of the ideas behind it. The *Sunday Times,* a sober and respectable 'quality' newspaper, had carried on 19 December 1965 an article entitled:

Yellow
Peril
1975

It was by Malcolm Mackintosh, who was introduced in the newspaper as 'formerly consultant to the Institute for Strategic Studies on Soviet and Chinese Affairs'. This article, too, was about Mr McNamara's grim and 'startling picture of China in 1975 as an aggressive military power of global proportions, capable of offering a serious nuclear-missile threat to Europe and America'.

The Yellow Peril is, of course, China, with its vast population, though, as we shall see, it sometimes comprises also some other East-Asian peoples of similar race to the Chinese. The sense of menace and opprobrium the term conveys is not exactly the same as that which was intended when the term was first (towards the end of the nineteenth century) used in Europe and Australia of China's millions. At that time the hundreds of millions of Chinamen (in the words of an American, 'morally the most debased people on the face of the earth'[1]) seemed to the Westerners, some of whom were anxious about the declining birth-rate among the peoples of European races, to be a potential danger because their rapidly growing numbers could one day overwhelm the positions occupied by the European peoples. But by the fifties and sixties not only was China widely believed to be what Professor John K. Fairbank (the most influential of American China experts) called a 'totalitarian monster'; but the general public in a number of countries where press and broadcast reports about China were becoming frequent had come to believe that highly responsible leaders in Europe and America regard it as a matter of grave urgency for their countries that there is 'a serious nuclear-missile threat' from this monster. In other words, the Yellow Peril is a *present* danger because of China's intention and growing capacity to bring about the nuclear annihilation of all that North America and Europe have built up. If there was neglect in dealing with the Yellow Peril *now* would not all the efforts which have been made to prevent a nuclear holocaust be in vain? Echoes of these doubts and anxieties were heard on 8 February 1966 when *The* (*Manchester*) *Guardian* remarked in an editorial that Mr McNamara

> was reported as saying that the Peking Government seemed to have embarked on a programme of global conquest that could engulf the Western world in the coming decades. If this is so, we should certainly have our attentions drawn to it; no such dire warning has been given since the days of Kaiser Wilhelm II, who was much concerned with the 'Yellow Peril'. Mr McNamara is more sober in his language, but like the late Kaiser he sees it his country's duty to counter the threat, and he seems to want Britain's help in 'containing' the aggression he foresees.

[1] Quoted in Raymond Dawson, *The Chinese Chameleon* (London: Oxford University Press, 1967).

The views of Mr McNamara and others who think like him are heard with increasing frequency nowadays. But not all those who believe in the reality of the Yellow Peril agree with them that it constitutes a present nuclear threat which calls for *immediate* countering action. The *Sunday Times*, in the article 'Yellow Peril 1975' already referred to, expressed the views of those who thought at that time that these warnings and calls to immediate action were not justified, for China's aggressive and evil ambitions were beyond her power to fulfil.

A survey of the debate on what we may call the McNamara thesis on China suggests that in Britain and the United States generally people do not believe that China can achieve her purposes immediately. Countering or preventive action in the form of an attack on China is not generally considered immediately necessary; but the knowledge that action of this nature has seriously been considered by military and political leaders makes vast numbers of people more uneasy than ever about the China problem. *The Guardian*, for example, reasoned thus in the editorial to which we have already referred:

> Things may be different in a few years, when according to Mr McNamara China will have delivery systems for its nuclear bomb. At present it has no long-range offensive weapons. It could not fight an aggressive war far from its frontiers even if it wanted to. All the more good reason for making use of the time that remains . . .

The consensus seems to be that though China has these fearfully aggressive intentions, she yet (in the words of the Washington Correspondent of *The Times* [London]) 'does not now have the means to pursue expansionist policies, except by subversion. But the assumption is that China will be able to flex her muscles more ominously within a decade.'[2]

In the meantime, however, China today represents the growing threat of unprovoked and unmotivated destruction and terror. What is said and is written about her being unready to attack Europe and America with nuclear weapons does not encourage people to relax their vigilance, or to ask if any mistake has been made in the portrayal of the intentions, posture and policies of China as a present peril *in other ways*. As far as we can judge, senior government leaders of the Western world seem to have agreed with a great deal of what Mr McNamara, on behalf of the American government, said. An Associated Press report was published in *The New York Times*[3]

[2] *The Times*, 26 January 1966.

[3] The edition of *The New York Times* referred to here and elsewhere is its international edition.

on 18 December 1965 with the caption 'Ministers Sound Warning on Red China's Global Ambitions'. It said, 'Ministers of the North Atlantic Treaty Organization agreed today that the Western world must be more alert to Communist China's global ambitions.'

But, those who thought that the American government was being unduly alarmist also agreed, for the next decade China's posture and her ambitions and policies were of the kind that posed an immediate threat to her peaceful neighbours. The author of the *Sunday Times* article 'Yellow Peril 1975' put in sober, almost academic language, what hundreds of other newspapers were telling their readers in more sensational language, when he concluded his article as follows:

> Within the framework of conventional limited frontier hostilities, subversion, and intimidation, the traditional Chinese forces still pose a valid threat to non-Communist powers in the area. But China's strategic ambitions require the utmost caution while her advanced weapons installations are so vulnerable.

In other words, whatever she would like to do, China did not yet dare to act in such a way as to provoke the big powers to destroy her nuclear or missile capacity. She would, however, continue with limited attacks across her borders and attempt to get her objectives by subversion and threats. This assumption was strengthened by statements made by the Indian government. The Indian Defence Minister, Mr Chavan, was reported in 1966 to have told the Lok Sabha that 'the threat of an attack by China was real and immediate', but he did not think that 'China had started making use of tactical nuclear weapons'.[4]

All this raised in a serious way the question of the threat represented by China's conventional forces and militia. The United States government had in urging her allies to take joint action with her against China pointed to the possibility that by 1975 China would be ready to use not only medium-range nuclear missiles, but also inter-continental (that is, long-range) missiles and submarines capable of firing rockets. The *Sunday Times* article speculated hopefully that by 1975 the Chinese leaders of 1965 might have been succeeded by a more cautious, less militant type. But those who shared this hope must take it that the Proletarian Cultural Revolution has made that development less probable than ever. Even if the Maoists fail to revive revolutionary ardour, the kind of change which the Western countries hope to see taking place in China's leadership may not take place. Most of us not only remember the implications of warnings like that of Mr McNamara in 1965 that the Chinese

[4] *The Guardian*, 18 May 1966.

had 'the world's largest army amounting to 2,300,000 battle-ready men plus militia and paramilitary organizations', but also probably suspect that the governments of the North Atlantic Treaty Organization have started planning militarily for action against a Chinese peril which they expect will be more dangerous a decade later than it is now. Behind the scenes the first phases of operations against China may already have begun, by virtue of high-level decisions.[5] Hostility towards China is so great that the West may already be moving inexorably towards war with China. Public opinion has been prepared for this, partly through a series of imperceptible escalations of the attacks on Vietnam. According to a poll of public opinion in December 1965 46 per cent of the Americans, who had earlier been told by Secretary of State Dean Rusk that China was blocking a settlement in Vietnam, were in favour of their government's using nuclear weapons on Chinese troops entering the fighting against the United States in Vietnam. All this accounts for the growing sense of fear and unease evoked by the mention of China in the press, radio, television and books.

But there are a few who will not want to believe in China's guilt, who think that all this about China as the Yellow Peril is too bad to be true. They are aware that China's achievements are regarded in much of the rest of the Third World as a sign of hope for mankind. They will be sceptical about the views of Mr Rusk and Mr McNamara, and will want to study the situation more closely for themselves. If they do so, what will they observe? We have, after all, been describing what was being said and discussed by political leaders during a short period, that is, in late 1965 and early 1966. It is true that at moments of great international tension political leaders tend to take up extreme positions, which they later abandon, and it is possible for readers and listeners to exaggerate the significance of the language used about and attitudes adopted towards China by the news media during the period of a few months. Would a wider knowledge of what is said and is written about China dispel the sense of a grave and urgent Yellow Peril?

Further inquiry into the study of China in fact reveals that it is an impressive band of scholars, statesmen, journalists and others with a world-wide influence who bear testimony to the existence in the contemporary world of *the China Problem* as the major issue of our time. Even Adlai Stevenson, a man certainly not given to crude expressions, in a speech published in 1961 by the Chinese government itself described China as 'a massive and brutal threat to man's survival'.

[5] This is the fear of people like Senator Fulbright of the United States. See 'Senator Fears War with China', *The Guardian*, 8 March 1966.

Ours is an age which is highly conscious that war, especially if it involves the big powers, can destroy not only hundreds of millions of lives but also much that human creativity and hard work has built up over the centuries; and which therefore expects of the major nations and states a great sense of restraint and observance of the civilities of international intercourse. It is not only pacifists who hate war. Militarism, love of war, are not generally admired. But can we expect the same of China? As long ago as in 1955, a year after the Geneva Conference had brought the Vietnamese war to an end, when many people were assuming that the Vietnamese had agreed to stop fighting the French and their allies because the Chinese, like the British and the Russians, were keen on promoting peace, a well-known Australian journalist, Denis Warner, who is often quoted as an authority on East Asian affairs published a book the title of which, *Out of a Gun*, was taken from a much quoted sentence, 'All power grows out of the barrel of a gun', from a speech which Mao Tše Tung had made in Yenan in 1938. In the book Denis Warner offered an explanation of the Chinese tactics. After discussing China's calls for peace, Warner ended his book with these words:

> Step by step along the road he so clearly signposted, Mao is advancing into his world of 'peace'. 'We aim at peace not only in one country but also throughout the world and we aim not only at temporary peace but at permanent peace,' he told his earnest students in the far-off days at Yenan. 'In order to achieve this objective we must wage a life-and-death war, must be prepared to sacrifice everything and must fight to the last until our aim is achieved. The sacrifice may be great and the time long but there already lies clearly before us a new world of permanent peace and permanent light.'
>
> Across the map of Asia, bayonets gleaming, doves flying, come the vanguard armies of 'peace'. We may yet live to see the whole Western world become another Dien Bien Phu.[6]

Dien Bien Phu was the scene of the battle in which the French, in spite of all the Western support they got since 1945, were decisively defeated in 1954 by what were then thought to be the fighting forces of the Vietnamese nationalists. At that time it was widely noticed because it appeared to be the decisive defeat by a weak Asian nation of a Western 'big power' attempting to retake their country. But Mr Warner saw it as the completion of a stage in the long-range plan of China to defeat the whole Western world. This was therefore a very powerful early warning about the Yellow Peril, even before her nuclear threat had materialized. And it warned people against being taken in by what had seemed to many at that time to be the un-

[6] Denis Warner, *Out of a Gun* (London: Hutchinson, 1956), p. 232.

Chinese gentleness and rationality of Prime Minister Chou En Lai.

Almost ten years later, C. L. Sulzberger, one of the regular columnists of *The New York Times*, informed its readers:

> Peking sees the Vietnamese war as only the first in its own long-range struggle to achieve a form of global hegemony and therefore a battle that must be won. As far as it can control the situation Peking wants war at any price.[7]

This was a confirmation of what *The New York Times* had said in 1963, when it described China as a constant threat to her neighbours, and spoke of her hatred for those who did not 'accept her grim philosophy of hate and violence'. On another occasion James Reston of *The New York Times* described 'the Chinese line' as 'vicious'. An even more influential, and probably the most highly respected, American commentator on world affairs, Walter Lippmann, indicated the dimensions of the mood about dealing with a militaristic China in 1965-6 in a column which appeared in both The *Washington Post* and The *Herald Tribune* (New York):

> On the question of the need to contain the military expansion of Red China there is virtually universal agreement in this country. The containment of Red China today, like the containment of Stalinist Russia after the World War, is necessary to the peace of the world and is a vital interest of the United States.[8]

A reader of The *Herald Tribune* would have noted that almost a year later the editorial writers Rowland Evans and Robert Novak, in a regular column, datelined Hong Kong, reported that China was already 'half at war with the United States' as it had '40 to 60 thousand Chinese troops working full-time in North Vietnam' and referred to 'Red China's buccaneer foreign policy, especially in Vietnam', her 'shrill and aggressive foreign policy line', and 'dangerous foreign policy adventures such as the one Peking has been sponsoring in Vietnam'.[9]

This characterization of Chinese activities has been the predominant one in Britain and the United States and much of Western Europe, and is implicit in the widely accepted 'domino theory', according to which if Vietnam 'fell', then Thailand and Malaya would fall to the Chinese. Many people who had read Mr Warner's book (*Out of a Gun*) would feel that his fears had been prophetic. For it is not only the newspapers which suggest that the China

[7] *The New York Times*, 3 January 1966.

[8] *Herald Tribune*, 16 February 1966. The edition of *Herald Tribune* referred to here and elsewhere is its international edition.

[9] *Herald Tribune*, 8 December 1966.

Problem is something more than a nuclear threat; there is also the considered verdict of the scholars.

The Institute of Strategic Studies, a serious research organization in London, published at the end of 1965 two books—*The Security of Southern Asia* by D. E. Kennedy and *China and the Peace of Asia* edited by Alistair Buchan – which took it for granted that China was a menace to the security and independence of the countries in her part of the world. One of the contributors in the latter, Morton Halperin, widely accepted in the West as an expert on China, concluded apparently from careful research that one of the Chinese aims is 'the establishment of hegemony in Asia'. He specifically explained, among other things, that while the Chinese would prefer to have the revolutionary wars take place in areas remote from China, they had another strategy for her immediate neighbours:

> In the border areas the major Chinese emphasis is not on revolutionary war, but on the use of military force, combined with political techniques, leading towards a Chinese attempt to dominate the countries on their border, to establish hegemony over them by a combination of military pressure and political gestures, promises and threats. One finds a pattern of policy in Burma, in Nepal, in Cambodia, in which the Chinese go through the stage of concluding a treaty defining the boundary, a treaty of friendship aiming at gradual establishment of hegemony in the foreign policy field over these countries . . .[10]

Major Galula, in the same volume, offered an expert's analysis of China's policy problems in promoting insurgency and subversion in other countries.[11] In the same volume William Bundy, then the United States Assistant Secretary of State for Far Eastern Affairs, also reported that China 'is now active in a large number of countries in Africa and Asia employing rather subtle subversive techniques'.[12] In a study on *The Politics of the Third World* published by The Royal Institute of International Affairs in London, Professor J. D. B. Miller takes for granted as one of the facts of the international situation China's desire 'to embark on military adventures, or even, perhaps, on nuclear war' (p. 123). The experts leave us in no doubt that a quarter of mankind is infected with a love of world domination and of war, even nuclear war. One can only assume that they can provide a great deal of evidence to convince the sceptics. Robert S. Elegant, a

[10] Morton Halperin, 'China's Strategic Outlook', *China and the Peace of Asia, Studies in International Security*, ed. by Alistair Buchan (London: Chatto & Windus for the Institute of Strategic Studies, 1965), p. 106.

[11] David Galula, 'Subversion and Insurgency in Asia', *China and the Peace of Asia*, pp. 175-84.

[12] William Bundy, 'The United States and Asia', *China and the Peace of Asia*, pp. 15-31.

China scholar who has the advantage of watching China from the vantage point of Hong Kong, sums up the view:

> The Chinese, as open about their objectives as Hitler, have proclaimed that Asia is but the preliminary objective of their global strategy . . . But the danger is not Chinese conquest of the world . . . The danger is Chinese incineration of a good part of the world with the nuclear arsenal which China will eventually possess.[13]

There is also world-public opinion. A proposal in the United Nations General Assembly in October 1966 for the seating of the Chinese government delegation in her place in the United Nations was, as usual, defeated. The proposal reflected the strong feelings of those who argued that China had been maligned and ill-treated. But in the United Nations a number of countries supported the argument of Mr Arthur Goldberg of the United States that China was not fit to be a United Nations' member. In November 1965 the same thing had happened, and similar decisions had been made every year since in 1950 China's representatives were not allowed in the United Nations. Representatives of all countries except China heard Mr Goldberg denounce China in 1966 as a power determined to destroy the 'orderly and progressive world', established during the past twenty years, a 'new imperialism which demands conformity and propounds violence and warfare as a principle of international concourse'. The acceptance by a predominantly Afro-Asian forum of the repeated characterization and condemnation of the major nation in Asia as the Yellow Peril is most impressive evidence of the conviction that the West's indictment of China carries.

The references cited are from British and American newspapers, and have been made by commentators and leaders justly considered liberal and progressive and factually accurate in the West. They are not from wildly irresponsible, cheap journals or by doctrinaire anti-communists. Harsh things are said about China by people who almost never use harsh or racialist language. Some of the writers quoted, for example, Walter Lippmann and James Reston, are rightly held in high regard in many countries and can be said to represent the conscience of the Western world. Leading churchmen have endorsed their views on China. The intelligent man-in-the-street searching after the truth would not be inclined to suspect them as war-mongers, or spokesmen for military or commercial interests. Most people would say that if anyone can be trusted to be truthful, factually correct and just in their judgments it is the kind of people who have been quoted. The case against China,

[13] *Herald Tribune*, 24 October 1966.

fantastic though it may seem, appears to be very strong indeed.

And it is not only North Atlantic opinion which is aware of China as a peril. For some years now what the Russians and other East Europeans say about China is even worse than what the Americans say. It was reported from Washington that on 21 November 1966 'Foreign Minister Andrei Gromyko, in talks with United States officials, repeatedly stressed his nation's concern over a China armed with a growing arsenal of nuclear weapons . . .'. The report, which appeared in *The New York Times* on the following day, continued:

> During the talks Mr Gromyko was reported to have implied that, as frictions increased between the Soviet Union and China, a confrontation might develop. Mr Gromyko was said to have indicated concern that the Chinese leadership might be tempted to launch an atomic attack.
>
> While the Soviet Union has no doubt about being able to maintain a vast superiority of nuclear weapons over the Chinese, a factor that should deter any nuclear strike, the account goes, the Russians are not sure that Peking will always be guided by rationality in such matters.[14]

The Soviet characterization of China as a nuclear threat was no surprise. The Soviet Union and the Communist-ruled East-European countries have for some time been portraying a danger from China in terms similar to those used in the West. By 1967 an immediate Chinese threat to the Soviet Union was widely believed to exist; there has been much discussion of China's intention of making a nuclear strike at the Soviet Union. Further, the Russians and East-European communists, who are no strangers to massive purges, appear to be horrified by the repressions and purges they report as going on in China in 1967.

As we shall see later, there are, in the West and elsewhere, totally contrary opinions about China held by scholars, journalists and statesmen, but one hears or reads comments about their objectivity or competence which leads one to suspect their testimony. Their comments and observations are therefore not often published. The overall impression one is left with is that of a China which is a 'problem nation' on a massive, frightening scale. The sense of the dreadfulness of her conduct and ambitions is created and strengthened by the sheer accumulative effect of the news reports, editorial comments, radio and television broadcasts, articles, books, which report, analyse, discuss and warn about China. Most of us only half-assimilate the details, but the impression remains with us. Even if one goes back to the time, 1949, when China was reported to have fallen into her present condition, and, starting from there, follows the literature about her, one is persuaded that the last nineteen

[14] *The New York Times*, 22 November 1966.

years have not provided prospects of change, that the hopes of a thaw in China were illusory. If we take a poll of opinion by sampling what is published or said publicly about China in various parts of the Western world, the impression one is left with is the same: THERE IS AN UNPRECEDENTED, ALMOST INSOLUBLE PROBLEM FOR THE INTERNATIONAL COMMUNITY. IT IS CHINA WITH ITS SEVEN HUNDRED MILLION PEOPLE UNDER MAOIST LEADERSHIP. REASON, DIPLOMACY, CONSIDERATION FOR THE FUTURE OF MANKIND, RESPECT FOR THE RIGHTS OF OTHERS, ETC. HAVE NO PLACE IN CHINA – NOTHING SEEMS TO RESTRAIN THE CHINESE.

A number of people are aware in a vague and general way that this is a vast problem which, if it is not solved, threatens all mankind. It is with confused and perplexed thoughts and feelings that they apprehend the Yellow Peril. Yet China has made a strong impact on the imagination of people in the West. Paul Johnson, editor of The *New Statesman* (reputed in the English-speaking world as a left-wing journal) in 1967 found himself moved to describe in his paper Mao Tse Tung and China in terms of Hitler and the Nazis – the most terrible instance of obscene atrocity, cruelty, oppression, racialism and passion for domination that the world has hitherto known. I. F. Stone in his famous *Weekly* has taken a poor view of China, and called the Maoists by the nasty name of 'neo-Stalinists'. There is contempt and loathing for, as well as fear of China. The film and the book, *The Manchurian Candidate*, probably won popularity and acclaim because the villain Yen Lo, a descendant of Fu Manchu, evokes the fascinated hatred of those whom China appears by all reports to have marked out as her victims. But the China Problem is not just a literary or psychological one; it is a practical one.[15]

[15] Before 1949 it was possible for people to hope that civil war leading to China's break-up and famine would keep the Yellow Peril in check. For example, here are passages from William Vogt's widely read book, in which he quotes from an article by Dr Nathaniel Peffer in *The New York Times*: 'Some population authorities consider that the greatest potential threat to world peace lies in the development of industry – war potential – in India and China. When these spawning millions are considered in relation to their degenerating lands, it is difficult to take such threats seriously . . . (in China) it is more likely that there would be a breaking up into regional segments, each under a warlord as in the past. There would be a return to the state of twenty years ago, with a satrap rule over what was only officially called a single country. It is even possible that Chiang Kai Shek and his circle could remain entrenched in the lower Yangtze Valley, with its rich industrial cities. In one of the regions the Communists would rule. The one certainty is that neither side can win a decisive victory . . . There is little hope that the world will escape the horror of extensive famines in China within the next few years. But from the world point of view, these may be not only desirable but indispensable. A Chinese population that continued to increase at a geometric rate could only be a global calamity.' (*Road to Survival*, [London: Gollancz. 1949] pp. 236-8.)

As the twice-daily, daily, weekly, and monthly reports and comments continue in the same strain, and earlier impressions are reinforced, there seems to be justification to take for granted the Yellow Peril as an unpleasant fact of life. The specific situations, *dramatis personae,* and sequences in the reports about China, if we distinguished them at all clearly in the first instance, recede into the back of our minds. We come to be familiar with this exasperating, intransigent, immature and menacing China, with a power-hungry, scheming and cruel Mao at her head. We even know beforehand, take for granted, what the Chinese are going to do and say. For example, if the chances of peace in Vietnam increase, we know almost for certain that the Chinese are going to do or say something to reduce them. If a gesture of friendship and forgiveness is made towards them, we anticipate a churlish and insolent response. To use the words of a well-known reconciler like U Thant, the mild-mannered United Nations' Secretary General, as quoted in *The Guardian* editorial we have already referred to, we expect from China 'certain strong reactions, certain rigidities, even arrogance and hysteria'.

China has indeed come to be a standard and a criterion of what is bad in the international order. It is common now for nations and even individuals to be judged good or bad according to whether they are hostile or friendly towards China. There are a number of instances – discussions of Indonesia, Cambodia and Pakistan – of the assumption that to be anti-Chinese is to be politically sound.

But if the problem of China is merely a vague and indefinable feeling or impression of anxiety or hatred, which invests with great significance such events as China's nuclear tests, it hardly calls for further discussion. The talk of a Yellow Peril will then, we will have reason to suspect, be crude racialism. In fact the picture is much more specific than that of seven hundred million Fu Manchus armed with deadly nuclear devices and building missiles for them.

Many of the people and journals from which we have quoted examples of what is being thought about China are not only significant because they may be assumed to be well-intentioned, good-hearted and moderate; for it is indeed not enough in these matters that people have their hearts in the right place. Far more important is the fact that those who are warning us about the Yellow Peril have a high reputation as trained, experienced and truthful reporters and analysts of the contemporary world scene. There must be a great deal of historical and factual material on which, in spite of those who see in revolutionary China a great, humane and peace-loving nation, they base their conclusions about China's love of war, her aggressions and her ambition to dominate the world.

What do we learn about the China Problem if we move on from more or less vague and disorganized impressions to specific charges which are made against China? What have the Chinese been saying and doing that they – the contemporary representatives of what some people at least regard as the greatest of the civilized peoples – have qualified to become the world's Public Enemy Number One? Can we by studying in more detail the specific charges against China find some other way of defining the China Problem than that in which some Western political leaders, scholars and journalists now do? Is 'containment', and possibly preventive war, the only way for us to live free of the constant fear of the Yellow Peril?

However depressing a more detailed examination of the charges against China may be for most, we cannot avoid it. For a problem for mankind as a whole demands all the good sense and intelligence that men and women of peace and goodwill can bring to bear upon it. Analysis and solution, as far as the Western world is concerned, cannot be left to intelligence agencies, military leaders and politicians. In any case we need much more evidence than what we have so far noticed before we can intelligently ignore those who are deeply sceptical about and critical of the Yellow Peril arguments. How did this resurgent Asian nation come to be seen as a 'totalitarian monster'?

2

Portrait of a 'Totalitarian Monster'

1. China's Isolation from the Outside World

IT IS one of the chief complaints of China's antagonists that she has cut herself off from the possibility of salvation by refusing to deal with the outside world in what has come to be accepted as the normal and civilized way. She has, especially since 1949, been churlish and provocative in resolutely excluding the rest of the world from her consciousness, and thus from the possibility of civilized intercourse with her. This self-imposed isolation of a large nation is itself a major source of danger to mankind.

Most of us recognize the fact that the kind of world into which we have moved is one in which the dangers of a large-scale nuclear war breaking out are great. The confirmed survival of civilization requires the co-operation of all countries, especially of the major nations. This co-operation presupposes a respect for the international order which has been established as a result of hard work. As befitting a large and historic nation, an important role in the maintenance of this order could have been assigned to China; but, far from co-operating, China is not even in contact with other countries. Those who see her as the Yellow Peril point out that after the second World War there was a period when the Soviet Union was widely reported to be very unco-operative and intransigent, and hostile to the Western powers; for many years before that free contact between her people and those of the West had been impossible; but even in the worst days of the Cold War the Soviet Union acted as a member of a common world order, in which there was a common allegiance to certain basic assumptions and values; more recently she has become more amenable, in spite of the difficulties arising from the international situation. There is continuous and close contact between the Soviet bloc and the Western bloc, and between Moscow and Washington. In the United Nations and other international bodies the two work together, even if they seldom agree. The Soviet Union seeks to emulate and even surpass the

United States in her achievements, but in doing so she also acknowledges the excellence of American standards and achievements in the common fields of endeavour.

China, however, has acted to disrupt the foundations of the world order. She has depreciated and rejected the assumptions and values of the United States, and belittled and derided the fields of achievement in which the United States, Britain, Russia and some other non-Chinese countries excel. She arrogantly proclaims her self-sufficiency. She has thus expressed in contemporary terms her traditional notion of China as 'the Centre Country'. The Chinese have deliberately rejected attempts by outsiders to communicate with them, and do not believe that they have anything useful to learn or receive from Europe and America. They have, in fact, lost touch with reality. It was in the same way that the old Chinese Empire treated outsiders with scant deference and referred to them as barbarians. Chinese newspapers and broadcasts give the impression that the people of the whole world disagree with the attitude of their own governments, and instead look up to China and Chairman Mao with admiration and gratitude. Because of this delusion, China has been less interested in having diplomatic relations with the major European powers and the United States than in establishing them with minor countries in the rest of the Third World.

One example of this which is remembered in Britain was the conduct of the Chinese over the decision of the British government in January 1950 to accord recognition to the new government which had assumed office in Peking the previous year, and to exchange ambassadors with it. In view of the refusal of the United States government to confer recognition, the fact that the British government had made this decision was favourable to China. But after long-drawn-out negotiations the Chinese agreed only to the maintaining by each country of a charge d'affaires in the other's country. This was a discourteous attitude, to say the least, towards a major power, and showed China's inability to act in a manner befitting a major power.

In her attitude to the United Nations, too, China has manifested the same kind of unco-operative, intransigent attitude. Though United Nations' membership is normal for all states, China, we learn, is not even interested in joining this valuable, international peace-keeping organization. The other Afro-Asian countries value the United Nations highly and take an active part in its deliberations and in its decision-making, but China mentions the United Nations only to attack it. China has repeatedly been warned that she must earn her re-entry into the United Nations by good behaviour, but she is so out of touch with world opinion that she has behaved in ways offensive to nearly all members.

In fact the Chinese disrespect for and obstruction of the United Nations – first shown in 1950 – at one time reached the extent of an attempt to set up a rival body in 1965. This action was all of a piece with her active encouragement of and participation in a movement of obstreperous anti-Western Afro-Asian regimes to call themselves the New Emerging Forces against colonialism and imperialism. China has been unable to come to terms with the world as it is and lives in fantasies of her own. She rationalizes this attitude with the delusion, to which reference has already been made, that the *'peoples'* of the Third World, and even of the Western and Soviet blocs, as distinct from their *governments*, are on her side. Hence it gives rise to her fantastic notion that those people who support the so-called 'New Emerging Forces' and 'liberation movements' in the Third World, those who denounce American 'aggression' and 'atrocities' in Vietnam, for example, are in fact the representatives of public opinion in the rest of the world – and to the policy and action based on this notion!

China's intransigence and unruliness is shown not only in her defiant talk, but also in her obstruction of the two super-powers in their role of the world's peace keepers. Both the United States and the Soviet Union have been vilified, and accused of trying to rule the world. China's inability to come to terms with a peaceful international order is also demonstrated in her stirring up of racial feeling at a time when the coloured people were ceasing to be resentful of the white race. China has made wild accusations about Soviet-Western collaboration being an attempt to preserve white domination of the world, and thus tried to provoke racial resentments and enmities. In fact the world has had to be warned of China's own notions of the racial superiority of the Chinese.

One of the people who has done most to alert the world to the insane quality of China's nonconformity and her unshakeable insistence on the rightness of her standpoint is Michael Lindsay who had been in China during the second World War. Lord Lindsay, in his book *China and the Cold War*,[1] pointed out the unreasonable behaviour of the Chinese leaders and gave instances of the behaviour of the Chinese delegations in London in 1950 and the selective character of their outside contacts. Again, in 1962 in an article entitled 'China's Descending Spiral' in *The China Quarterly*, a specialist journal published by the Congress for Cultural Freedom, he discussed China's 'fanatical totalitarianism' and 'the unpleasant

[1] Melbourne: Melbourne University Press, 1955.

realities of (her) political fanaticism', in relation to China's insistence in demanding recognition of her sovereignty over Taiwan, and in opposing any 'two Chinas policy'. Lord Lindsay discussed this in terms of the attitudes of 'people near the borderline of actual insanity'. He believed that China's conduct, – 'the analysis of (their) totalitarian fanaticism' – must be understood partly in terms of a collective psychopathology. The Chinese are not rational, he pointed out. Their conduct could not be explained even in terms of 'an obsessive belief in the inherent superiority of collective or government organization over private enterprise'. Dealings with China do not need the categories of traditional diplomacy but were possible 'only within new categories of applied international psychiatry'. Only then could China's fanatical hatred of the West be overcome.

The Chinese notion that China is the centre-country is criticized on the ground that it is repugnant to the spirit of an age in which no other race or nation thinks of claiming to be superior to or any more important than any other – however much smaller in population. The behaviour of Chinese mobs in 1967 towards foreign diplomats in Peking showed an arrogant refusal to observe the usages of civilized society as practised in the rest of the world. There is not only ignorance, but also an unmotivated hostility to non-Chinese peoples. Even in regard to the few countries which had remained friendly, Chinese arrogance had alienated them. The North Koreans and North Vietnamese, it is reported, also find the Chinese intolerable.

2. *China's Aggression and Expansionism*

Much more serious than her arrogance and isolation is the aggression and expansionism with which China is charged. Towards the Americans in Taiwan and Southeast Asia, towards the Russians, towards India, towards their neighbours in adjacent territories, towards Ceylon, towards Indonesia, towards Australia, towards Africa, towards Cuba and the rest of Latin America, and towards Western Europe and North America, the intentions of the Chinese are reported to be hostile. It is no exaggeration to say that no country's security appears to be assured as long as China continues on her present way.

A close reading of what the experts and other professional authorities say and write about China's outward-directed ambitions, aggressiveness and expansionism reveals a certain degree of disagreement on details. There is also a small handful of observers (whose opinions are rarely published or broadcast) who see no evidence of any

Yellow Peril, and who exonerate China from the charges of expansionism and aggression. But from what the majority of the rest say, a general pattern is discernible.

There is, first, the evidence for speaking of the Chinese intention of attaining in the long run to 'super-power', and asserting, in Mr William Bundy's words, 'a global hegemony'. But evidence has been cited for claiming that it is the Chinese view that until the fire-power adequate for that kind of world power is attained, ideological propaganda, diplomacy, and subversion of democratic and independent countries would see to it that the present centres of wealth and power, 'the towns of the world', would be 'besieged' by the increasingly Chinese-dominated 'countryside'. This could be achieved by the sending of literature, agents and arms to stir up revolts among otherwise contented and happy peoples in Asia, Africa and Latin America. The Chinese in the meantime also use the anti-imperialist and anti-colonialist arguments to make 'claims' on, or take over by force, foreign territory which adjoins China. With a rapidly growing population to feed and keep contented, coupled with the failure to achieve adequate economic growth, the economic need to get hold of more sources of supply is added to the super-power ambitions of her leaders.

This general outline, perhaps, makes interpretations of China's expansionism much more clear-cut and consistent than the details of the reports and analyses warrant. Because of the varying circumstances in the different parts of the world as well as the setbacks, the opposition and the counterpolicies of the world powers, this expansionism has been considerably 'contained' and frustrated. The majority of those who are aware of the menace of China are, as we noticed earlier, agreed that on several occasions China has been forced to restrain or 'contain' herself; she has on occasion been prevented from carrying out her aggressive policies and purposes by the power, vigilance and hostile reactions of the world's policemen – the United States and her allies. The story of her actual aggression against the outside world is therefore only part of what the story might have been if her designs had not on occasion been thwarted and if she had not been threatened with punishment.

When we note in specific terms the range of foreign activities and adventures attributed to the Chinese, therefore, we are still not getting the full dimensions of 'The China Problem'.

(*a*) *The Fall of China to Mao*

The story begins even before the emergence of the New China. Denis Warner, in his *Out of the Gun*, described many of the bloody events which make the history of East and Southeast Asia since the second World War ended. There is a passage at the end of his Chapter One, 'The Man to Watch', which must surely have made the flesh of some of his readers creep:

> . . . Mao, indeed, had become the man to watch.
> He still is. And since the suffering and death I record in these pages would be a pointless tale of horror without at least a nodding acquaintance with this man who is changing the face of Asia, his background, training and ideas, I plead for indulgence while I turn the clock back half a century and for a moment forsake event for cause.[2]

It is the view of this experienced reporter that the *cause* of the bloody events he described is not to be sought indigenously or in Western intervention, but is no other than Mao Tse Tung, and his eventual seizure of power in China.

What has been described as 'the Fall of China' and 'the Communist Conquest of China' took place at a time when the country seemed to have been secure as a well-behaved ally of the West, respectful of the norms and standards of a civilized world order. The establishment of control over all of China by the revolutionaries under Mao led to the expulsion of Europeans and Americans opposed to the new regime. In that sense the new China – which has revived the fears of the Yellow Peril – was conceived in aggression. Beginning with subversion which exploited the grievances of the Chinese masses, this alien seizure of power in that vast country was completed by the power of armed force. The man who had led this take-over of China had successfully practised his doctrine that 'all power grows out of the barrel of a gun'.

Since 1949 the whole of China has become the agency of this militaristic and totalitarian group which the majority of governments still refuse to accept as a normal government with which they can have dealings. The evidence for this is to be found in the reports of people who have expert knowledge of China. As a Swiss journalist who had travelled to China in 1964, fifteen years after the completion of the civil war, put it in the introduction to his book, published in English in 1965 as *Land Behind Walls*:

> A fanatical doctrinaire communist regime has made (China) the most aggressive of all nations, a major hotbed of armed revolutionary upheaval among the nations of the world. There are disputes and conflicts between nations and governments the world over, but communist China is today the only country whose openly pursued policy makes a viable instrument of war and regards it as an essential for the attainment of

[2] Warner, *Out of a Gun*, p. 25.

ideological ends. China's leaders do not intend to engage in 'major' war, for which they lack modern technical equipment, but rather in revolutionary, guerilla combat within the framework of civil war; this makes their aggressive policies all the more formidable, since the form of attack, spreading like an epidemic, undetected at first, cannot be opposed by classic military methods nor by the latest super-weapons.[3]

As Mr Stucki reports here, the new China's aggression is achieved by a sophisticated cunning which enables her to outmatch and outwit the more heavily armed world powers. China is a source of a disease germ whose attack cannot be detected or resisted by conventional means. Mr Stucki's account continues with his first-hand experience of what China has been transformed into:

We in the West know very little about the China which increasingly confronts us. On the map of the world which we carry in our mind's eye we tend to see a vast blank patch and our image is of a rather mysterious, half-smiling, half-snarling face, behind which our imaginations can conceive all kinds of demons. The dragon, symbol of China, takes on a deeper significance; the unknown, when we are suddenly, unavoidably, face to face with it, frightens us; it seems unnatural, irrational, fantastic. What kind of beast is this dragon?[4]

The considered verdict of Lorenz Stucki on China echoes that of many of the China experts. A scholar whose writings on contemporary China carries great authority is Professor Richard L. Walker, who, in his *China Under Communism*, summed up the character of the Chinese regime in these words:

In the first place, it is a regime based upon war, not peace. According to the statements of the top Chinese Communist leaders, warfare – class, civil and international – has been a key factor in all of the major achievements to date. This is one characteristic of Communist China which is unlikely to change, for war and violence pervade what is rapidly becoming the everyday language, the new education, and the whole philosophy of the nation . . . The thesis advanced by the Communist leaders in Peking that China needs peace for reconstruction sounds enticing to a world which longs for peace. Yet the instances in history which argue to the contrary should be remembered; war has frequently served as a method to tap additional reserves of energy . . .[5]

[3] Lorenz Stucki: *Land Behind Walls*, E.T., (London: Ampersand, 1965), p. 1. The book has since then also been published as an American edition.

[4] *Ibid.*

[5] Richard L. Walker, *China under Communism* (New Haven: Yale University Press, 1956), pp. 322-3.

Professor Walker agrees with Mr Warner on how the apparent Chinese longing for peace should be understood. He points out in his book that the whole Chinese nation is being moulded in this aggressive outlook. And on this point the pictures shown in magazines and television portraying Chinese children drilling seem to suggest that the militarization of Chinese thinking permeates the whole of society. This would support the argument that Mao's revolution in China was, as revealed by his background, training and ideas, only a stage on the way to the fulfilment of a more ambitious aim.

(*b*) *The Aggression against Tibet*

The first act of the New China was an act of aggression against a neighbouring foreign state – the invasion of Tibet by the People's Liberation Army under Chang Kuo Hua in 1950. It was reported that resistance put up by the Tibetans was overcome, and Tibet annexed by the People's Republic of China. The Tibetan leaders were forced to sign an agreement in Peking in 1951. A new administration was imposed on the Tibetans regardless of their historic traditions.

Unable to stand the foreign oppression, the reign of terror by the Chinese and the suppression of their ancient customs, the whole people of Tibet rose in revolt a few years later against their Chinese 'overlords'. The revolt was brutally crushed by Chinese troops; the Dalai Lama and other Tibetan leaders were forced to flee to India. The nature of Chinese imperialism was proved by the Dalai Lama's charge that the Chinese had been guilty of rape, deportations, torture and other atrocities. The International Commission of Jurists recorded this in an inquiry headed by an Indian lawyer and accused China, in a report, of genocide. The Chinese government, however, was unmoved.

The annexation of Tibet, moreover, gave the Chinese a base for encroaching farther into the same area. The evidence specifically reveals the Chinese plan. As Dr Robert North, one of the most highly regarded of American China experts, wrote in his *Moscow and the Chinese Communists* . . .

> . . . (there were) reports of Chinese communist infiltration of Nepal from Tibet, of rapid growth on the part of the Nepalese Communist Party, and local estimates of a Chinese Communist takeover within a matter of a few years . . . In August Robert Trumbull, quoting 'unimpeachable sources', in the area, reported systematic Chinese Communist infiltration of Afghanistan, Nepal, Bhutan and Sikkim.[6]

[6] Robert North, *Moscow and the Chinese Communists* (Stanford: Stanford University Press, 1953), p. 273.

The independence of the Himalayan countries was thus in jeopardy. And, as we shall note, the Chinese soon began to occupy part of India itself.

(c) The Korean Adventure

After the conquest of Tibet the next step in aggression was the Chinese crossing of the border into Korea later that year (that is, 1950) in order to support the North Korean, Communist attempt to take over South Korea. North Korea's act of aggression had already been denounced and punished by the United Nations. China's condoning of this kind of foreign military aggression, and her approval of North Korea's stand, was bad enough. (Michael Lindsay in his *China and the Cold War* attaches a great deal of importance to this Chinese support for North Korean aggression.) But in sending her army under Peng Teh Huai into battle against the United Nations' forces and then driving them into South Korea, China was manifesting both her disregard for the United Nations and world peace and her belief in the use of force to impose her power over others.

(d) China's Adventure in Vietnam

For her aggression in Korea China was branded an aggressor by the United Nations. But while engaged in expansion into the Himalayan region and into Korea, she was already involved in her first major action against Western possessions and interests in non-Chinese Asia when she intervened against the French in Indo-China. The French, with British and later American support, had been trying to deal with what purported to be 'the Democratic Republic of Vietnam' which had been proclaimed in her former colonies of Cochin-China and Annam by a revolutionary nationalist movement called the Revolutionary League for National Independence (or Vietminh) who had seized power from the Japanese. The so-called independent Democratic Republic of Vietnam, which had set up her government throughout the country, was not recognized as valid by the Western powers. The Revolutionary League, founded in 1941, was not regarded as representative of the people when it proclaimed independence. China, however, in 1949 'recognized' the independence of Vietnam. According to several scholars the crisis in Indo-China – which has resulted in the long-drawn-out and costly war by the United States and her allies to prevent the Chinese takeover in Vietnam – began because the Vietminh movement was inspired, organized and armed by Mao. In 1954, at the Battle of Dien Bien Phu, the armies of the so-called Democratic Republic of Vietnam under General Vo Nguyen Giap decisively defeated the French and their allies, and demanded and got terms which meant the withdrawal of the Western presence from this key area by 1956. But, as Mr Roger Hilsman, then Director of Intelligence and Research in the United States Department of State, explains in his foreword to the American edition of Giap's *People's War, People's Army*,

> General Giap is actually an 'advance man' for Chinese Communist Power. But he cannot, of course, admit this or make any but token references to the Chinese. Today, he and his doctrines are serving China's purposes by accomplishments that could not be brought about by the Chinese or by open and avowed friends of theirs.[7]

What appears to be the Vietnamese War of Independence is thus revealed to be a victory both for the subtlety of Chinese tactics and for their doctrine of the power of the gun.

Hilsman's authoritative view is supported by the account that Denis Warner in both his books, *Out of a Gun* and *The Last Confucian*,[8] gives of the Vietnamese campaigns against the French in Vietnam in 1949 and 1950. There have been accounts elsewhere of the Battle of Dien Bien Phu in 1954 being won by the Chinese themselves.[9] It is ultimately China, then, which nearly brought about the expulsion of the West from Vietnam during and after the second World War. And, by several accounts, it is China which is obstructing the United States in its attempts to achieve peace in Vietnam. In fact, when, after the Geneva agreements, fighting again broke out in the southern zone of Vietnam in the late fifties, there were reports that Chinese troops were fighting to destroy South Vietnam's independence. Even the aggression by North Vietnam was committed by a country which had been modelled on and controlled by China.

Mr McNamara gave the truth about the Vietnam situation in a speech in March 1964, in which he said:

> First and foremost, without doubt, the prime aggressor is North Vietnam, whose leadership has explicitly undertaken to destroy the independence of the South. To be sure, Hanoi is encouraged on its aggressive course by Communist China. But Peiping's interest is hardly the same as that of Hanoi.
>
> For Hanoi, the immediate objective is limited: conquest of the South and national unifications perhaps coupled with control of Laos. For Peiping, however, Hanoi's victory would be only a first step towards eventual Chinese hegemony over the two Vietnams and Southeast Asia,

[7] Vo Nguyen Giap, *People's War, People's Army*, E. T. (New York: Praeger, 1962), p. xviii.

[8] Published by London: Penguin Books, 1964.

[9] *The Radio Times* (London), 5 March 1966.

and towards exploitation of the new strategy in other parts of the world.[10]

President Johnson himself identified the cause of the trouble in Vietnam in his famous speech at Johns Hopkins University on 7 April 1965, as follows:

> The confused nature of this conflict cannot mask the fact that it is the new face of an old enemy. Over this war – and all Asia – is another reality: the deepening shadow of Communist China. The rulers in Hanoi are urged on by Peking. This is a regime which has destroyed freedom in Tibet, which has attacked India and has been condemned by the United Nations for aggression in Korea. It is a nation which is helping the forces of violence in almost every continent. The contest in Vietnam is part of a wider pattern of aggressive purposes.[11]

China's responsibility for the continued fighting in Vietnam is also something to which Mr Harold Wilson has publicly committed himself. He is reported to have told demonstrators calling for British support for peace in Vietnam on two occasions that it is against the Chinese that they must protest. And when the Commonwealth Prime Minister's Peace Mission was planned in 1965, it was to Hanoi and Peking that it sought to go to press for peace, and not to the South Vietnam National Liberation Front or to Washington. This made it clear where the governments of the Commonwealth countries believe the responsibility for starting or stopping aggression in Vietnam lay.

The assumption that the trouble in Vietnam is due to 'China's aggression against Vietnam' is so widely held, and confirmed by so many reports and analyses, that it can hardly be disputed now. The *Herald Tribune* at the end of 1966 reported that Chen Yi, China's Foreign Minister, had declared that China was paying 70 per cent of the cost of the Vietnam War on the other side.

China's aggressiveness and expansionism in Southeast Asia, we have it on high authority, has not stopped with her involvement in Vietnam. They extend to Laos. Supporting the American government's case in the United States Senate in February 1965, Senator Thomas J. Dodd, who was very close to President Johnson, declared in the course of a major speech:

> I have in my possession a map of Northern Laos showing areas where the Chinese Communists have been building roads that would give China direct access to the borders of Burma and Thailand. The construction of

[10] Marcus G. Raskin and Bernard Fall, *The Vietnam Reader* (New York: Vintage Books, 1965), pp. 196-7.

[11] *The New York Times*, 8 April 1965. See also Arthur M. Schlesinger: *The Bitter Heritage: Vietnam and American Democracy 1941-1966* (New York: Houghton Miffin, 1966) Chap. 6, 'Is China the Enemy in Vietnam?'

these roads bodes ill for the future peace of Southeast Asia. That they are intended for future military use is taken for granted by everyone in the area . . .

In the Congo, the Chinese Communists have launched their first attempt at applying the Vietnamese strategy to Africa . . .

In the Philippines, the Huk guerillas, after being decisively defeated in the early 1950s, have now staged a dramatic comeback . . .

In Thailand, Red China has already announced the formation of a patriotic front to overthrow the government and eradicate American influence.[12]

The speech of Senator Dodd reflects regular news despatches from correspondents and reporters over the years.

(*e*) *Anti-Americanism and Aggression against Taiwan*

While the trouble over her southern borders was growing, China was not quiet on her eastern flank. China's hatred of the United States was not merely emotional; the serious nature of the Yellow Peril is demonstrated in the way this hatred is expressed in hostile moves against an America which desired to live in peace with her. The Americans had legitimately taken up positions on the western edge of the Pacific to safeguard their interests and national security. They had their Seventh Fleet in the waters round Taiwan and the smaller islands of Quemoy, Matsu, and the Tachens off the mainland. But no threat to the mainland was intended. In spite of the pacific intentions of the United States the Chinese had been fiercely hostile, aggressive and provocative in their language about the United States and her positions in East Asia. Furthermore she did not stop with a war of words.

In January 1955 the Chinese started a new phase of aggression and expansion – shelling the Tachens, and attacking and capturing a small island, Yikiang, in the Taiwan Strait. The Americans took alarm at this and tried to deter further aggression. The importance of defending American positions in the west Pacific was made clear in a message by President Eisenhower to Congress, when he declared that the United States 'must remove any doubt regarding (their) willingness to fight, if necessary, to preserve the vital stake of the free world in a free Formosa, and to engage in whatever operations may be required for that purpose'.[13] The President asked for and promptly obtained authority 'to employ the armed forces of the United States as he deems necessary for the specific purpose of pro-

[12] Raskin and Fall, *The Vietnam Reader*, p. 172.

[13] D. F. Fleming, *The Cold War and its Origins* (New York: Doubleday, 1961), p. 707.

tecting Formosa and the Pescadores against armed attack', and also to ensure 'the securing and protection of such other measures as he judges to be required or appropriate in assuring the defence of Formosa and the Pescadores'. The President was therefore armed with wide powers to forestall or repel any Chinese aggression against not only Taiwan but also the other off-shore islands. It is the view of scholars that China's attempt to break out into this area would have been more serious but for the American reaction. But what then Secretary of State of the United States Dulles[14] referred to as China's 'acute and imminent threat' and 'aggressive fanaticism' was not entirely deterred. Preparations for an attack on Quemoy and Matsu, preparatory to the 'liberation' of Taiwan, went on, and so did the war of words against the United States.

(*f*) *China and the Rest of Afro-Asia*

It was not till the Asian-African Conference at Bandung in 1955 that the military confrontation between China and the United States in the Straits of Taiwan quietened down, though it was reported that the virulent anti-American propaganda campaign by the Chinese went on.

Denis Warner remarks: 'It was in character that Chou En Lai, the Tachens safely stowed away, should arrive at the Afro-Asian Conference in April 1955, as a peacemaker.'[15] Participation at the Bandung Conference has been shown by a number of experts to have been a subtle tactic by the Chinese to allay hostility and suspicion among their neighbours. It was a cynical effort to infiltrate Africa and the rest of Asia by winning friends and influencing people among the leaders of ex-colonial countries.

But China's professions of friendship for her neighbours and her canvassing of the Five Principles of coexistence did not, we have been told, prevent her from aggression against the other major Asian nation, India. The unprovoked Chinese invasion of India in 1962 followed a period when she had already occupied by stealth Indian territories. It is believed that the Chinese invasion had a multiple purpose – seizure of Indian territory and the humiliation of India in the eyes of the rest of Afro-Asia. Several writers also explained that seeing that her rival for Asian leadership was thriving and progressing economically while she herself was in a mess, she invaded India in order to disrupt India's economy.

At Bandung China was able to achieve her purpose by getting the Conference to take an anti-imperialist stand. She also made contact

[14] *Ibid.*, pp. 715-6.
[15] Warner, *Out of a Gun*, p. 222.

with Africa through its leaders. Having established, we are told, a kind of bridgehead to Africa by supporting the Algerian insurgents, China took a hand in creating an Afro-Asian People's Solidarity Organization, with headquarters in Cairo. By the early sixties the conditions for what came to be seen as her intrusion into the African continent were favourable. A considerable number of reports and analyses of the current world situation made it clear that until the set-back occasioned by the split in the Afro-Asian People's Solidarity Organization and the overthrow of what was claimed to be the pro-Chinese Nkrumah regime, there was going on in Africa the softening up process of subversion and infiltration by Chinese agents preparatory to a take-over. Evidence of China's evil influence was to be seen in the growing strength and articulateness of the less constitutional-minded, more revolutionary or radical nationalist elements, which tended increasingly to oppose and obstruct capitalism, and what they called colonialism and imperialism. The whole process of peaceful transition to forms of parliamentary democracy for which Africa had been prepared by the West, and the influence of the educated elites, were destroyed by rash demands for socialism, mass democracy, land-reform, and guerrilla war against 'white-dominated' areas, which could benefit only the Chinese. When the Organization for African Unity was formed in May 1963, it set up a Co-ordinating Committee for the Liberation of Africa, and some of the leaders were in favour of preparing for wars of liberation to end white rule or dominance in the continent. Such boldness could not have been African in origin. This extreme attitude, says a writer in a special issue of *Race* (the journal of the Institute of Race Relations) devoted to the Chinese Peril in Africa 'is sufficiently close to China's revolutionary tactics to suggest that these might have been the source of inspiration'.[16]

The ground having been prepared, Chou En Lai made his tour of Africa in 1963-4. In the course of it he is reported to have announced that 'Africa is ripe for revolution', thus issuing a call to China's supporters to overthrow the established governments of the continent. Chou En Lai's interest in more friendly relations between China and the African countries is regarded as a danger not only by Europe and America but also by African leaders and intellectuals who are threatened by China's desire to establish the 'hegemony' that Morton Halperin speaks of (see p. 8 above). This charge and a whole range of other specific charges in the Western indictment of China as a totalitarian and expansionist power are reproduced in a convincing manner by a Ghanaian, Emmanuel J. Hevi, in *The*

[16] *Race*, April 1964, p. 77.

Dragon's Embrace. Mr Hevi expresses a strong dislike for China (though he exempts Chiang Kai Shek's missions in Africa from his attack). He refers to the Chinese as the 'Foreign power that holds (Africans) at gun point',[17] and marshals most of the evidence that has been adduced elsewhere to show that there is a Chinese 'conspiracy' not only in Africa but elsewhere.

But Chinese plans have not worked out. There were reports of Chinese fighting with the Congolese rebels and of Chinese arms supplied to the banned nationalists in Rhodesia. Efforts like these have come to nothing.

The *Sunday Times* on 8 October 1966 in an article written by its China expert and its top foreign staff expressed the view of a good deal of sober Western opinion. It pointed out that by the beginning of 1966 eighteen diplomatic missions had been established in Africa, but three of them had been expelled.

> The defeat of the Congolese rebellion was an important set-back for China; so was the Ghana coup against Nkrumah, which resulted in the expulsion of 200 Chinese technicians; and the removal from office of the pro-Chinese Kenyan Vice-President, Oginga Odinga, was a third blow.[18]

The collapse of the Afro-Asian Summit Conference of June 1965, regarded as a major setback for China, was the most cheering event (or non-event) for the West. But, in the words of the article in *Sunday Times*,

> . . . despite these set-backs, China's subversive intentions in Africa are still strong. The chief centres for these activities are Brazzaville and Dar-es-Salaam. The latter is the chief port of entry for Chinese weapons and trained saboteurs, and China certainly regards Tanzania as its economic showpiece in Africa.[19]

Western public opinion had therefore some ground in regarding in a sinister light the activities of President Nyerere in support of movements allegedly for African liberation in white-ruled Africa: having lost a puppet in Ghana, the Chinese have set one up in Tanzania.

(g) *The Abortive Pro-Chinese Coup in Indonesia*

Considering the opposition which China's actions had provoked all over the world the most audacious example of her expansionist designs was, perhaps, what the *Sunday Times* described, in the article we have quoted above as the 'Chinese-inspired-and-backed

[17] Emmanuel J. Hevi, *The Dragon's Embrace* (London: Pall Mall Press, 1967, p. 116.

[18] *Sunday Times*, 8 October 1966.

[19] *Ibid.*

putsch in Indonesia'. This was not a reference to the seizure of power by the Generals, but to Colonel Untung's abortive counter-coup. Other reports describe these events of October 1965, in the world's fifth most populous country, as an abortive attempt by a pro-Chinese conspiracy to overthrow by force the government of President Sukarno in Indonesia.

Reports of China's objectives in Indonesia had come long before this. In the introduction to a well-known book on the current international situation by four leading experts on China, published by the Council on Foreign Relations (of the United States) in 1957, Arthur Dean had prophesied the pattern of Chinese imperialist expansion:

> Having regained control of Manchuria and taken over North Korea, the Chinese Communists, in cooperation with their ally, Ho Chi Minh, have taken over North Vietnam, are infiltrating Laos and Cambodia, are threatening South Vietnam, Thailand and Burma and have made serious inroads into the political life of Indonesia, where rumours of an impending coup have been frequent.[20]

(*h*) *Other Charges*

A list of all the different aspects of China's aggression and expansionism would be tiresome. We need only note two other important ones: one being the designs that the Chinese have on Russian territory; the other being the Chinese attempt to establish hegemony in Latin America.

One of the countries which for many years has been trying to warn the world against the Chinese as an aggressive and militaristic, even war-loving, nation is communist-led Yugoslavia. But in recent years China's one-time ally, the Soviet Union, has been forced to take a lead in the denunciation of China. It has been pointed out that China owes a great deal to the Soviet Union; yet she has furiously criticized and denounced the Soviet Union as a betrayer of principles, as an expansionist power, and so on. She has also laid claims to vast areas of Soviet territory – about 600,000 square miles across the seven-thousand mile common border – according to reports.[21]

[20] Arthur H. Dean, ed., *Moscow-Peking Axis: Strengths and Strains* (New York: Harper, 1957), p. ix.

[21] See 'Russian Talk of Common Front against China', *Sunday Times*, 21 November 1965; Dennis Bloodworth, 'The Explosive Frontier', *The Observer* (London), 12 February 1967; Kyril Tidmarsh, 'How the Russians View the East', *The Times*, 24 January 1967; 'Russia Builds up Troops on Chinese Border', *The Times*, 5 November 1966; Michael Connock, 'Keeping the Chinese at Bay', *Financial Times* (London), 6 January 1966; Harry Schwarz, 'Soviet Preparing for a War with China?', *The New York Times*, 20 December, 1966.

China's subversive activities in Latin America are related not only to the increase of guerrilla warfare in many countries, but also to the setting up of the Tricontinental Conference of 1966. Even Dr Fidel Castro, it has been pointed out, has supported the Western denunciation of China. China's action in stirring up trouble in a hitherto peaceful continent is part of her plan for world domination.

Before we end this section we might also note another interesting charge made against the Chinese government: that it is carrying on a profitable opium trade, and that opium distributed in South-east Asia earns foreign exchange for China.

3. The Menacing Nature of China's Resurgence

'Communist China,' *The New York Times* warned in an editorial on 14 September 1963, 'has made no secret of its resolve to enter upon a Napoleonic phase of expansionism.' The picture we have of a ruthless and cunning force which since 1949 has moved from the conquest of the world's most populous country to a many-pronged assault on the independence and security of the rest of the world certainly calls for stronger language than this.

Harrison E. Salisbury, a good and experienced journalist, traversed the lands on the periphery of China in 1966, observing what was happening and talking to China's neighbours about China. Early in his book, *Orbit of China*, he described his reactions to the very thought of China.

> China! Was it sheer atavism which sent a chill down my spine as I contemplated the implications of what Peking said and Peking did? It was no longer fashionable to speak of the 'yellow peril'. Indeed, the very phrase seemed like the echo of an earlier, naïve era, of Teddy Roosevelt, the Great White Fleet and the Boxer Rebellion. Yet what of the chauvinistic racism of China's appeals for unity of the peoples of yellow, brown and of black colour? Was this sheer propaganda? I did not think so. Peril stalked the world; it swirled up in clouds from Asia – East Asia. My task was to define its shape and fix its outline.[22]

Towards the end of the book Mr Salisbury communicates the anxiety and alarm he feels when he contemplates the problem of an already highly populated China with a rapidly growing population in a world in which food surpluses for sale in the present food-surplus areas would be reduced. Shortly after the start of the next century, he calculates, there will be nearly two thousand million Chinese – making one third of the world's population. For China

[22] Harrison Salisbury, *Orbit of China* (London: Secker & Warburg, 1967), p. 12.

to continue, as at present, to make up her food needs by purchases from food surplus offered for sale by other countries would become increasingly difficult.

It was this (dilemma), it seemed plain to me, which fired the flames of Chinese aggression, which compelled China's leaders towards a policy of chauvinism, irredentism and adventurism along their frontiers.[23]

China's leaders, in Mr Salisbury's opinion, will not allow their people to starve. If there was not enough food to feed the people or land to grow the food, food and land would be sought beyond the borders, for example, the rich lands to the north, in Siberia, with their great agricultural potential scarcely realized and the rice producing areas in Cambodia, Vietnam, Burma and Thailand. 'Small wonder that there was in China's posture towards the outer world a constant tone of aggression, of hysteria, of menace.'[24]

Solutions must be found to solve the China Problem, as we have labelled it. Mr Salisbury doubts if the massing of Russian troops to protect Russian and Mongolian territory eyed by China, and the barriers of steel and armed power against expansion erected by the United States would provide a solution to the problem.

Was it not like forcing down the lid on a pressure-cooker? Would it not ensure that when the explosion came it would be more violent, more uncontrollable, more destructive? Did we not already see in the violence of the Red Guards, in the savage xenophobia of Chinese policy, in the schizophrenic view which Peking held of the outer world the advance symptoms of precisely such a cataclysm?[25]

The China Problem would seem from Mr Salisbury's account to be something which is growing in intensity partly because of the present attempts by the two major powers to solve it.

To Mr Robert S. Elegant, too, one of the crucial issues is that of food shortage – caused for the first time in China by the Revolution.

The final question raised by the experience of the People's Republic was truly a moral one. The Yellow Peril had finally appeared, though not quite in the manner Homer Lea and William Randolph Hearst predicted. China's sorrows raised humanitarian questions which challenged all humanity . . . Millions of adults were ailing and dying, while tens of millions of children were growing up misshapen and diseased because they did not have enough to eat. Even though their own government had contrived the misery of the Chinese people, men wondered if it was proper for nations which possessed great surpluses to refuse food to the

[23] *Ibid.*, p. 190.
[24] *Ibid.*, p. 193.
[25] *Ibid.*, p. 194.

hungry . . . The mere proposal of the humanitarian question might be denounced as woolly-minded by self-consciously practical men. But the humanitarian dilemma was merely the veneer of a most practical problem. The Yellow Peril did, in truth, exist and the Chinese might yet destroy the world by seeking to conquer the world.[26]

Since even before the time of the long series of what have been reported as acts of foreign aggression by China she has been unacceptable to the rest of the world on the ground that her social system and her government are of a kind to put her beyond the pale. A United Nations, that endorsed the Zionist *coup* in Palestine and the state of Israel created there, that has included in its membership Duvalier's Haiti, South Africa and scores of other dictatorships in Europe, Latin America and Africa formed after military coups, has not been able to accept China in its membership. People have known foreign conquests in the past, but there is a unique reason why people do not want (in the words of a writer in the *Sunday Times* of 4 June 1967) to be 'over-run by the Yellow Peril'.

The sense of 'the Horror that is China' was first renewed when accounts were published in 1949 of a Stalinist-type regime in China. Though Russia had been one of the allies of the West in the fight against Fascism, people sensitive to the human implications of politics could not easily forget that the Communist Parties accepted and justified, sometimes even promoted or collaborated in, the horrors perpetrated in Europe by Stalin and his henchmen from the early thirties – the ruthless and arbitrary elimination of rivals, the creation of a new type of secret police, the massive purges, the concentration camps, the slave labour, the control of Communist Parties in other countries and the disregard of all the norms of civilized life – in order to bolster and expand their own power. The Chinese Revolution of 1949 was a *Communist* revolution, and *therefore* brought to dominance over China Stalin and his hatchet men.

As early as January 1950 those outside China who were wondering what the revolution had meant were left in no doubt by authoritative statements by the Secretary of State Dean Acheson and reports by liberal newspapers like *The New York Times* that China had gone the way of the European countries which had passed into the control of the Soviet Union. The seizure by Russia of Manchuria, Sinkiang and Inner Mongolia was specifically reported.

Mao Tse Tung and his Party colleagues were then opposed and denounced as a puppet government, seizing power in order to alienate parts of China to a foreign country which for a long time

26 Robert S. Elegant, *The Centre of the World* (London: Methuen, 1964).

had been greedy for Chinese territory. After Stalin's death Mao was reported to have put himself in Stalin's place. And accounts, by experts, of Mao's character did not make him any less a tyrant than Stalin. Robert Elegant reflects the views of many people in the West when he sees Mao as a mediocrity who used his power to glorify himself. Speaking of this policy of self-glorification, which was 'greater than was Russian adulation of Josef Stalin at its height', he says,

> Never previously has a single individual been so exalted, for never previously have the myth-makers controlled so efficiently an apparatus of publicity directed at such an enormous captive audience . . . He has repeatedly demonstrated that he will kill to impose his version of truth – or to evoke the adulation which is essential to his assumption of omniscience. Truth, for Mao Tse Tung, is what he makes it.[27]

Mr Elegant also draws a picture of purges, treachery and intrigue to describe the way in which the present Chinese hierarchy was formed. The sordid details of tyranny he evokes have appeared in scores of other accounts, too.

The feelings of horror and disgust evoked by the word 'purges' were roused during the Cultural Revolution of 1966 and 1967, when reports by Europeans and Americans frequently appeared of massive purges, of bloodshed and of other horrors going on in China. The *New Statesman* of 25 November 1966 suggested 'between one and two million "suicides"' that year among Mao's victims. Millions of ordinary people were highly offended by the spectacle of a government which, after eighteen years in power, could not like other countries just dismiss or reprimand, demote and reshuffle, but had to *purge* its leaders. Headlines like 'Peking demands for purges and deaths' (*The Times*), 'Maoist Call for Beating, Killing and Robbing' (*The Times*), 'Death Penalty Threat to Anti-Mao Faction' (*The Times*), all within a short period kept fresh the feeling originally evoked that brutality is commonplace in China. And *The Times* has been one of the most moderate of Western newspapers when dealing with China.

It is no wonder that a recent Gallup Poll in the United States revealed that among Americans the five qualities most commonly associated with the Chinese were: (1) hard working, (2) ignorant, (3) war-like, (4) sly, and (5) treacherous.

(*a*) *The Suppression of Democracy*

The Chinese Revolution meant the overthrow of the democracy

[27] *Ibid.*, pp. 173-4

and modernization which the West by its education, missionary work and influence had established in China. It meant that, whereas China's millions might on a liberal, democratic and westernized basis have lived in peace and in co-operation with their neighbours and the rest of the world, they turned their backs on democracy, with all that this reversal implies for the freedom of the individual and the dignity of the human person.

When he first came to power, Mao, it is said, tried to win support throughout the country by pretending to give all nationalist elements a place in the new set-up. The revolutionaries capitalized on the popular demand for a united and modernized China. They permitted a kind of private capitalism to continue. Even political parties which were willing to accept the overall leadership and direction of the Chinese Communist Party were allowed to function. But even then the democratic polity which had existed before 1949 had been replaced by one in which ultimate political power was concentrated in the hands of a few top Communists.

But once firmly in control the Communist Party of China became more openly totalitarian. Thought control, indoctrination, brain-washing, mutual denunciation of people as enemies of the regime became features of the political scene.

The Agrarian Reform drastically altered a situation which in all democratic countries is accepted as the normal and just basis of land-ownership. Then the 'Three-Anti' and 'Five-Anti' Campaigns of 1951 and 1952 terrorized the bourgeoisie, and particularly the businessmen, into giving up a good deal of the independent resources which originally they had been told they would be able to retain. Just as landlords were arrested and denounced, so wealthy and successful owners of businesses and industrial enterprises were 'investigated' and denounced, fined and imprisoned. The government was thus able to eliminate all independent private elements in the economy. According to some analysts the opportunity was also taken to 'purge' unwanted Party members. Subsequently, there was a clever campaign in 1956, the 'Hundred Flowers Campaign', which deliberately encouraged liberals and anti-Communists to come out into the open, in order that they could be identified, harassed and persecuted.

(*b*) *The Mass Killings*

There was also the savagery and cruelty of the murder of millions of Chinese who were marked out by the new regime for destruction.

Throughout the fifties newspapers and books in the West reported, sometimes with dramatic and gruesome detail, the obscene process by which Chinese who had been denounced or otherwise labelled as enemies of the regime were hauled up before 'people's courts', forced into confessing crimes which they had not committed, condemned to death and then executed. Some of these accounts made a powerful and lasting impression on those who read or heard them. A 'Penguin Special' *Spotlight on Asia* by Guy Wint (then of *The Guardian*) published in 1955 described 1951 in China as 'the year of the great terror. The terror has been one of the outstanding features of the Chinese revolution.'[28]

Guy Wint also spoke of the counter-revolutionaries and secret agents against whom, as 'alleged monsters', a campaign was mounted during the Korean War.

> Landlords, former Kuomintang officers and former officials were the chief target, but the net was cast very widely. The terror was much worse in the villages than in the towns. It was country-wide. On the whole, the further a village from the capital the more savage was the proscription.
>
> All the available large buildings – temples, Christian churches, halls – were filled up with prisoners. The overcrowding and misery has been described in many records. But gaol deliveries quickly began. The law against counter-revolutionaries provided for their trial before people's courts. The process was grim. In a village selected as a centre for trials a large concourse of peasants would be assembled. Skilful propaganda worked up their feelings. The prisoners were then produced before them; many were, in fact, reprehensible characters, local despots under whom the villages had suffered, but there were countless others who had committed no offences which would have brought them before ordinary courts, or even have exposed them to general censure. The organizers of the trial would then read out the terrible crimes of the accused, invite testimony to their offences and, turning to the people, would ask what should be done with them. The usual response, for which the gathering had been coached, was a great cry of 'Kill, kill'; and the demand was usually gratified, often upon the same spot as the trial. Trials, and sometimes even the executions, were broadcast; listeners in Hong Kong heard the shots and screams of the dying. Such a resolve to advertise inhumanity was perhaps without parallel in history.[29]

Mr Wint reported that there was an admission by Po Yi Po, the Minister of Finance in September 1952 that 'two million bandits' had been 'liquidated'. '"Bandit",' Mr Wint explains, 'means anybody who possessed a little land or who was regarded by the Communists as dangerous to the regime.'[30]

The ruthlessness and savagery of a government whose policy was

[28] Guy Wint, *Spotlight on Asia* (London: Penguin Books, 1955), p. 102.
[29] *Ibid.*, pp. 103-4.
[30] *Ibid.*, p. 105.

to promote mass killings of innocent people in cold blood was something which disgusted and enraged people.

(c) *The Ruin of the Economy*

The Chinese regime has been careless of the economic needs and welfare of its citizens, and its claim that the economy in all its aspects has improved since it passed under exclusively Chinese control is an empty one.

Almost from the time of the Revolution there have been reports every year of the terrible suffering inflicted on the Chinese people as a result of the economic policies of China's rulers. Man-made famines and terrible suffering have been reported continually, and most widely in the late fifties and early sixties.

One of the most expert discussions on this appeared in an issue of the Congress for Cultural Freedom publication, *China Quarterly*. In the autumn issue of 1962 the American columnist Mr Joseph Alsop, who had in the previous year reported that the Chinese were rationed to an average of 600 calories a day, worked out in an article that by then 1,300 to 1,600 calories per head daily were what the Chinese were getting out of their allotted diet. This claim was based on data 'collected and analysed with extreme care'. The figures were offered as those 'squarely based on first-hand evidence that exists, and . . . unchallengeable . . . The existence of a descending spiral is seen to be undeniable.' This important *China Quarterly* article referred to the 'nadir of wretchedness which is the present condition of China'.

Several other authorities on contemporary China, commenting later that year on Mr Alsop's arguments, agreed with his assumptions about unprecedented failure and misery in China. Fr Ladislaw la Dany, editor of *China News Analysis*, wrote from the vantage point of Hong Kong: 'The fact is that the regime of Mao has come near to collapse.'[32] Professor Choh-Ming Li, Chairman of the Centre for Chinese Studies at the University of California and one of the most frequently quoted Western authorities on the Chinese economy, agreed about 'the ever-mounting hardship which the government has inflicted on the people'.[33]

Another expert, Rod McLeish, produced detailed clinical evidence of the fate of China's hundreds of millions which left readers con-

[31] Joseph Alsop, 'On China's Descending Spiral', *China Quarterly*, July-September 1962, pp. 21-37.
[32] *China Quarterly*, October-December 1962, p. 29.
[33] *Ibid.*, p. 34

vinced that the Peking government was not only indifferent to the people, but sadistic.

From all available data the physical miseries that Mr Alsop describes are accurate. Collapsed wombs and missed menstrual periods are common among mainland women. Starvation oedema varies, according to intelligence reports, from a dreadful low of 20 per cent in some areas to 60 per cent in others. There are even stories about some parts of China where this grisly affliction of swollen bellies has reached 90 per cent saturation. Hepatitis is on the gallop, coursing even through hospitals where sick doctors lurch about trying to take care of sicker patients.[34]

Discussing Alsop's thesis that a mass revolt against Mao was likely McLeish wrote:

One wonders then, whether a sick, exhausted, fractionalized and heavily guarded class of people like today's Chinese peasants have the ability to kick off a revolution of confrontation against their overlords.[35]

In the course of his article Mr McLeish seriously weighed the possibility that Mao might 'decide deliberately to starve his surplus population out of existence' but decided that in the circumstances it was not likely.

Professor Yuan-Li Wu, another American China scholar, wrote: 'The views expressed in Mr Alsop's penetrating article are largely shared by this writer.'[36]

The expert assessments in 1962 that twelve years after taking office, and after all their propaganda about economic development, the Chinese government had created the immediate prospect of death by starvation for tens of millions, perhaps hundreds of millions, had a profound effect. China seemed to be one vast concentration camp where a vast population was being sacrificed to satisfy the lust for power of Mao and his associates.

(*d*) *The Organization of Slave Labour*

China is a vast camp where forced labour is organized.

One of the agencies of the United Nations, the International Labour Organization, published in 1957 a report asserting that

[34] *Ibid.*, p. 40.
[35] *Ibid.*, p. 41.
[36] *Ibid.*, p. 51.
In order to be just to Dr Kenneth Walker, one of the contributors, it must be said that he regarded Alsop's article as 'arrogant and categorical in tone', 'a series of dogmatic assertions', strung together in a bewildering sequence, without any documentary evidence whatever (p. 45).

there was forced labour on a vast scale in China. Guy Wint, in his book *Spotlight on Asia*, also gives us a description of forced labour, and goes on to quote the American sociologist Karl Wittfogel in support of his view that China was moving towards a state of general slavery.[37] Quite recently, in a note replying to a letter from a reader, the Far Eastern correspondent of *The Observer*, a liberal Sunday newspaper in Britain, suggested that figures of those doing slave labour in China were estimated by the United Nations Secretary General and the International Labour Organization as 'between twenty and twenty-five million'. This certainly confirms Mr Wint's earlier analysis.

Slave labour on any scale is deeply repugnant to all but a few people. To know that a government has condemned about twenty million of its own people to a lifetime of slavery is almost too horrible to contemplate. And when that government is one which claims to be a government of workers and peasants, the cynicism implicit in its policy is even worse.

(e) *The Poisoning and Destruction of the Family*

Family Life as it has been known in all civilized societies has deliberately been destroyed in China.

One of the ways in which the outside world became aware of this was the reports of the forcible creation of communes, with husbands and wives being herded separately into dormitories. The forcible separation of husbands and wives, the forcible deprivation of home life, the loss of contact with children, all these offended against all civilized standards of family life. It was also an example of the kind of coercion which the Chinese government used in order to produce the inhuman type of society which was their aim to create.

This was not all. Robert Guillain, the distinguished French journalist, in his book on China which was published in English with the title *The Blue Ants*,[38] explains how children were persuaded to spy on their parents and to denounce them to the authorities.

(f) *The Destruction of Chinese Culture*

China's rich traditional culture and civilization has been ill-spoken of, neglected and destroyed.

In the course of his account of the horrors of life in revolutionary China Robert Guillain writes:

> A major event of our epoch . . . is that Chinese civilization is dying;

[37] Guy Wint, *Spotlight on China.*

[38] Robert Guillain, *The Blue Ants*, E.T. (London: Secker & Warburg, 1957), pp. 131ff.

in fact, it is practically dead. One of the great civilizations of history, which has illumined the lives of millions, has come to an end . . . (The) philosophical, moral and political values which were the creations of China and made her grandeur in the past – are in their death throes . . . Four thousand years of Ancient China have been relegated to the cemeteries and the museums . . . China is no longer Asiatic. At most she will be Eurasian . . . She is turning aside from nearly all the ideals of Asia.[39]

Many other observers, like Mr Guillain, regret the destruction, by Mao Tse Tung's regime, of the greatness of China's traditional culture – the great Peking Opera, Confucianism, painting and sculpture.

(g) *The Misuse of the System of Education*

The system of education has also been destroyed. Instead of being a means for the modernization of China, the schools have been used as centres of indoctrination, and hardly any time has been given to real teaching or study. During the Cultural Revolution the school system was destroyed, and all schooling suspended. As a consequence, those who leave the schools and colleges have spent most of their time on non-educational activity, and have attained a very low academic standard. The Cultural Revolution helped further to depress educational standards when it successfully attacked the system of recruitment to universities on academic merit. Political conformity, not intelligence or learning, has become the qualification for both students and teachers.

The Western missionaries, we learn, had built up for China educational institutions of high standing. These could have been the foundation on which China built. But the heritage has been repudiated. Ignorance, the inability or refusal to think for oneself, and the giving of assent to wrong notions have ruined intellectual life.

(*h*) *Discrimination against National Minorities*

There was initially the pretence of equality of treatment for all groups, majority and minority, this was because support among the minorities was needed by the new regime. But more recently non-Han Chinese have become 'second-class citizens'. The Chinese government has been accused of colonialism and discrimination in the treatment of non-Han nationalities since 1949. It is said that they are exploited and suppressed, and they are forced to accept Han racial superiority.

The background to this is the fact that though China's population

[39] *Ibid.*, p. 223.

has not been homogeneous or static throughout its history, it is basically composed of people who are described as Han, living predominantly in the central, southern and eastern parts of China, and concentrated in the great river valleys. There are, in the sparsely-populated and undeveloped regions inside China's frontiers, the traditional areas of the most important non-Han Chinese – Mongols in Inner Mongolia, Uzbeks, Kazakhs and others in Sinkiang, and Tibetans in Tibet. Together with several other 'national minorities' in the mountainous and other areas, they make up about 6 per cent of the total population. Since 1949 the economic development of Inner Mongolia, Sinkiang and other such areas has been speeded up, with new industrial centres, modernization of agriculture, dispersal of agricultural settlers from the more urbanized areas, and so on. All this has been hard on the minorities.

There are a number of other vicious features of Chinese life and politics which are also frequently reported and discussed: to name some, the prohibition of religious faith and practice, the exploitation of the peasantry by the exaction of heavy taxes, the Great Leap Forward, the commune system, the insistence on plainness and drabness of living, the rude and inhospitable treatment of foreign visitors, the 'self-criticism' procedures, the hooliganism of the youth, and the suppression of the trade union movement.

(*i*) *Should Such a Nation be Tolerated?*

The picture of a delinquent China which has emerged in these pages is a composite one – more clear-cut and coherent, perhaps, than what is in the mind's eye of most people who have a growing dread of the Yellow Peril. However, there are some who claim to speak with the authority of experience of, insight into and scholarship about the Third World in general and China in particular who, as we shall see later, do not subscribe to the views about China which we have so far reported. But they are in a minority. They are rarely, if ever, given much credit for expertise or honesty in newspapers and broadcasts; and they have limited political influence. There are still others, some of whom like Harrison Salisbury we have referred to, who take a more complex view of China than do those who have seen its resurgence under Maoist leadership as an unrelieved disaster.

But, practically speaking, the continual and purposeful aggression and expansionism of a totalitarian, war-loving and intransigent China has been driven home as a fact of contemporary life, which in turn is the assumption and basis on which urgent political action is being called for by those who hold themselves responsible for seeing that the civilized world does not come to disaster because of appeasement of China by the West.

Some people who were bitterly hostile at the time of the loss of China in 1949 to the West have in the years following testified to some Chinese actions of which they approved. On the other hand, some who in 1949 welcomed the beginning of a new phase in China have been bitterly disillusioned. Michael Lindsay, for example, originally a supporter of the Chinese revolutionaries in Yenan, expressed very strong criticism of China in 1955 in his book *China and the Cold War.* Late in 1966 and in 1967, with Western news-agencies and newspapers describing the horrors of the Cultural Revolution – the bloody street battles, the howling mobs, the brutal purges, and attacks on temples, churches and offices – the picture was still that of the Chinese as people who were as far from respecting the safety or dignity or lives of their opponents and of all foreigners (except the sycophantic admirers of Mao Tse Tung) as they had ever been. Even diplomats could without any provocation be attacked with impunity.

While the xenophobia, the aggressiveness and the fanatical disregard for all kinds of order and civilized values were mounting, communication between China and the rest of the world, with all the possibilities it held of a rational discourse, was virtually non-existent. China has stubbornly refused even to discuss the suggestion that she talk to other powers about scaling down the fighting in South Vietnam. She has not only denounced the widely-hailed 1964 Treaty Banning Nuclear Tests, and all subsequent moves to stop the proliferation of nuclear armaments, but has defied the other powers by speeding up her own nuclear build up. She has created trouble over Hong Kong. She even seems to delight in the fact that, by 1967, she has been left with only one friend or ally – the insignificant totalitarian regime in Albania, as violent, wild and intransigent as herself.

But Albania is a negligible factor, we can argue; she can be contained easily. So can Cambodia, which is pro-Chinese, as Indonesia used to be. But China's vast population, her refusal to accept the leadership of others, and what might be called her demonic energy make her enormities a very serious matter. The cruelties and miseries, and mental and spiritual injuries inflicted internally affect nearly a quarter of mankind. For humanitarian reasons alone the factors which are responsible for the misery of so much of mankind must be done away with.

It is not enough for us to recognize that China is a problem – a problem without precedent. We need to be aware that solutions of the problem are anxiously and urgently being sought, or offered, or considered. Indeed, some partial solutions are even being attempted.

We are all being drawn in one way or another into decisions about what is to be done to deal with this problem nation. We have already been committed to action which our countries and which international organizations have taken or are taking to reduce, or end, the peril. To some the existence of such a monster as we have portrayed is so intolerable that it is worth the risk of another world war to solve the China Problem. This is then a problem of such immediacy that no one, not even people who regard themselves as non-political, could ignore it or leave it to others. China is a problem not only because of her continually reported threats to the security, territory and independence of other countries; an important part of the charges against her is her violation of norms and standards of international conduct which all others agree on as vital for world peace. Respect for the rule of law and the rights of even the smallest nation or state is now the very basis of world peace. No nation, even if it makes up nearly a quarter of mankind, can be allowed to overstep the limits placed on the exercise of its power by its own state boundaries. Especially at this time, when a large number of economically and militarily weak states have recently come into existence and need to have the security to assert the primacy of the interests of their own people, the clear and strict insistence on the containment of each country, especially a large one like China, within its territorial boundaries is vital, if international tyranny is not to result. To put it in another way, if the kind of behaviour which China is accused of had occurred in more barbarous times it might have been less noticeable. But today far too many of the things which are continually reported as happening in China or as being done by China to others outrage some people almost beyond endurance.

Commenting in 1962 on the starvation which the government was reported to have brought on the Chinese, Michael Lindsay proposed two alternative courses of action in the event of an 'economic collapse' in 1963.

> (They were) the rapid replacement of the Communist regime by an efficient new regime with Western support or the shift to a new Communist leadership willing to co-operate with the West and willing to abandon the Communist dogmas which have inhibited the efficient organization of agriculture.[40]

[40] Michael Lindsay, 'On China's Descending Spiral', *China Quarterly*, October-December 1962, p. 38.

Outside intervention of various kinds to solve the China Problem has been proposed from time to time. But the overthrow of the Chinese government has not been achieved after all these years. Are the two types of *coup d'état* which Lord Lindsay suggests adequate solutions for the China Problem? And, further, what if an attempt at them leads to a major war?

'The totalitarian monster', as Professor Fairbank has called it, is portrayed for us as so fantastically evil, vicious and disregarding of all that is human and decent that, as intelligent people, we cannot avoid asking ourselves if it could be fantasy rather than fact that we are dealing with. So much of the intelligence and moral conscience of the West is invested in this view of China that scepticism seems out of place. But even the suspicion that China is too bad to be true must lead us to a closer and harder scrutiny of the contemporary situation. For to talk as we have done so far about the Yellow Peril and the China Problem is to attempt to describe and characterize not just China but the whole world of our time. To talk about the Chinese behaviour that offends us is to posit the kind of international behaviour that delights or satisfies us. To speak in such superlatively condemnatory terms about China is to imply a great deal about our approval of non-China, especially of the standards and conduct of China's chief antagonists and accusers.

Before we can discuss what should be done and what can be done about the China Problem, we need therefore to consider a wider range of problems and perspectives than those which have so far in this book occupied our time and attention.

3

From the Chinese Viewpoint

As we have noticed, there are varying views on what the Yellow Peril amounts to in our day, and how immediately and in what form it calls for countering action by those who see themselves and what they value threatened.

There is the prospect of a time when the Chinese will not just comprise nearly one-fourth but be a single nation constituting one-third of a world in which perhaps six thousand million people are trying to keep alive on this planet. There is the extreme prospect of a radically altered world political situation in which after China's nuclear bombardment of the rest of the world there will be Chinese governors in Washington, Canberra, Lima and Rome. There is the prospect too of the products of Chinese agriculture and industry flooding the markets of the world. There are other equally unpleasant prospects of what the Chinese might do. Certainly, judging by the picture drawn by the majority of news agencies, reporters, commentators and expert analysts of China's resurgence under Maoist leadership, China is now a threat and problem of much greater dimensions than was ever conceived by those who originally sounded the warning about her as a peril to the European races.

How is this phenomenon to be accounted for? Is there a racial explanation? The aggression, intransigence, cruelty, inhumanity, expansionism and love of war which is reported of China would seem to some observers to be a brash and defiant manifestation of characteristics which in her period of weakness were dormant and subdued, and in her period of Western tutelage were beginning to be transformed into, and overlaid by, more attractive and civilized ones. On the other hand, though some of the 'liberal' voices – newspapers, commentators and scholars – have taken a very 'hard' line on China, that is, made the most stringent and severe criticisms of her conduct, some of them have also tried to be just to the Chinese by looking for historical causes which would help account for the development of China into what those who follow Professor Fairbank would call a 'totalitarian monster'. They have pointed to the connection that exists between the reaction of the Chinese people to their treatment at the hands of Europeans, North Americans and Japanese and their present attitudes and actions. In other words they have seen the humiliation felt by the Chinese in the century before the second World War as a direct cause, or one of the direct causes, of the emergence of the China which we have been looking at in the last two chapters.

The Guardian, like *The New York Times*, is a liberal Western newspaper. In the editorial which we quoted earlier (p. 2), it also said:

Humiliation and ambition

Many people in the West seem still not to understand sufficiently what humiliations China – the State and the people – underwent at the hands of their forebears in the hundred years after the Opium War. The scramble for China was barbarous even by our definition, and still more by the definition of the Chinese. For they felt, from ancient tradition, that they alone had the secret of really civilized society, and the way in which most Westerners (and Japanese) behaved certainly did not shake that belief. Only in one important respect could they see that the barbarians were superior: they had the guns, and the machines and technology to make them. The Chinese yearned for the day when their empire would be reunited and strong and the foreigners chased from the land. It was the common ambition of all patriotic young men – traditionalists, nationalists, Communists – to bring it about.

The day came, and were the Chinese superhumanly virtuous we might have expected them to overlook the past humiliations and accept the Western governments as new-found friends. But they are human, and in any case the West seemed determined that this should not happen. For its leading government was so outraged by the way the resurgence had come about that it still does not recognize the first effective government that China has had for over a century and with the weight of its influence has managed to keep it out of the United Nations. If Chinese leaders talk about the desirability of World revolution, the United States leaders talk about the desirability of a revolution in China – something much more specific. And they arm the very faction dedicated to bring the revolution about. True, they also restrain General Chiang Kai Shek (for his own good) from an outright invasion of the mainland, but his Government frequently boasts of the commandos and saboteurs it puts ashore . . . China's crime is, of course, that it was reunified and revived by Communists.[1]

The Guardian cannot be included among those voices whose reports and observations are suspect on the ground that they contradict the portrayal of China as a problem and a menace; therefore what it says here is clearly very important. Even if we have never

[1] *The Guardian*, 8 February 1966.

doubted that China is a special and immediate 'problem' for the rest of the world, we may still like this appeal to our intelligence and historical understanding, rather than to our armoury of weapons, to seek a solution to it by way of a deeper and more complex diagnois of its origin and growth. A small hint has been given us that the problem might be a larger one in its dimensions than that which the Sinologists indicate; and one is tempted to follow up the hint by becoming more curious about what in fact happened to the Chinese from outside China, and what is being done to them by us, and about what the Chinese 'think' and 'feel' about it all.

In order to see if there is a solution to the China Problem which is more realistic, practical or effective than those proposed by President Johnson, Mr Wilson, Mr NcNamara, Mr Brown, Mr Harrison Salisbury or Lord Lindsay, we must take notice of a wider range of commentators on China than we have so far consulted. Otherwise we cannot find our way to getting to know what China thinks and feels, and what has gone on within her; we cannot even know and understand how the Chinese are taking and are responding to all the charges and accusations against them, and all that our own governments or other agencies are doing or are preparing to do to 'punish' Chinese aggression and expansionism.

1. The Well-Remembered Experience

Professor Owen Lattimore of Leeds University, in a lecture entitled *From China, Looking Outward,* wrote:

> The student of modern China, even when doing his research and teaching outside of China, should cultivate the intellectual method of seeing China from within, and looking from China outward at the world.[2]

He also pointed out that the Chinese are 'the most history conscious of all the great civilized peoples'.

The Chinese memory is indeed specific and historical. When, for example, one reads the translations of the talks and articles which early in his career Mao Tse Tung used in order to build up his revolutionary movement and instruct his followers, one notices the importance he attaches to *events,* historical happenings, which are within the memory of his audience or of the members of their families. Trying to discover what it is that Chinese think and feel one realizes how vividly and dramatically they remember their historical experience as a people. The very fact that all but a handful of Chinese have not lived abroad, and therefore do not have the

[2] Owen Lattimore, *From China, Looking Outward* (Leeds: Leeds University Press, 1964), p. 2.

Western or Russian views on China, makes this memory more important. *For the majority of Chinese, in the act of reliving in their minds and hearts their humiliating experience as a people, recall also what they have learnt by personal experience about those peoples of the world outside China who today condemn China as a peril, a problem and a monstrosity.*

Like most other Asian peoples the Chinese think of their *resurgence* in the middle of the twentieth century as a re-emerging after a period of submergence by alien rule and domination by alien interests – a kind of rebirth or resurrection after the old life had been drained away.

The last complete century when China was 'The Centre Country' for the Chinese was the eighteenth century. To recall the events in the middle of the eighteenth century, however, is not easy. That was a time when the United States was not even in existence. Eighteenth-century China was a China far from her earlier glories; the ruling dynasty and the court were Manchu, the semi-civilized people on the northern fringe of China. Even so there was then no other society comparable to China in size or advancement. Of the several civilized kingdoms and principalities on her periphery, with the possible exception of the remains of the Moghul Empire, none had yet reached the stage of not being better off for what China could teach them. Sun Yat Sen in 1924 in *San Min Chu I*, one of the classic texts in which the Chinese 'remembrance of pre-colonial things past' is expressed, wrote of the kind of empire the Chinese Empire used to be. He recalled it as an exercise of suzerainty over neighbouring peoples which did not involve exploitation. Sun was perhaps idealizing the past too much when he thought too exclusively of China in its great periods as a great nation which could give to other, smaller nations, what they needed. His successors were more critical of the values of 'feudal' China. But the feeling that something great and magnificent had disappeared was shared by nearly all modern Chinese.

The European imperial nations had penetrated considerably into Asia by the beginning of the nineteenth century – the sea-faring peoples of Britain and Holland across the seas to Asia, and Russia annexing vast areas of land in Northern Asia. (As early as in 1689 the Russians in their insatiable desire for more territory had come up against the Chinese, and been contained by The Treaty of Nerchinsk.) But China was then intact. She had relations with the Europeans to the extent of selling their merchants all that they wanted of silks, porcelain and tea. There was nothing that China felt she wanted from the West.

But British and American merchants found that they could cheat the Chinese government by smuggling opium into China. In 1808 the Emperor had issued an edict making it clear that opium smuggling was forbidden. Britain, however, saw no reason why the laws of China or the welfare of the Chinese need be respected when her superior force would enable her people to get what they desired in China. On the other hand the Chinese, from their viewpoint, encountered in the ensuing war with Britain a moral and political order which was very different from theirs, and which they had always regarded as barbarian. Arthur Waley, in his *The Opium War through Chinese Eyes*[3] relates how Commissioner Lin, the high official who had the duty of seeing that the law was respected in Canton, had come to the job after experience which had given him a rather low opinion of British honesty. In the subsequent negotiations the attitude of the British officials, traders and government seemed to Lin utterly cynical. They refused to accept the Chinese regulations, and fought their point out in 1839 in the first Opium War. (Not all Chinese were patriotic, however, for there were a few who collaborated with the foreigners.) By The Treaty of Nanking of 1841 and a later agreement in 1843 the British imposed on the Chinese, as fair conditions of trade, demands of the kind not normally made or allowed by Britain or the United States in trade with European nations. The British got Hong Kong, and the Chinese were forced to admit to Canton, Shanghai, Foochow, Amoy and Ningpo – all the important Chinese seaports – British traders and residents who were not to be subject to Chinese authority. A large sum of money was imposed as a 'fine'. Britain was also automatically entitled to any privileges that China would allow to other foreigners.

China now came to know and began her dealings with all the civilized nations of the Christian, Western world. The following year the United States (by The Treaty of Wanghia) and later France, aware now of China's weakness, forced China to sign 'treaties' on the same terms as Britain had exacted. In the next few years China was forced by Belgium, Sweden, Norway and in 1851 by Russia to allow them free access. The Sino-American Treaty of Wanghia, by which the Chinese had to allow the Americans access on the same terms as the British had to the five 'Treaty Ports', contained this provision:

> . . . if additional advantages or privileges, of whatever description be conceded hereafter by China to any other nation, the United States, and the citizens thereof, shall be entitled thereupon, to a complete, equal and impartial participation in the same.[4]

[3] Published by London: Allen & Unwin, 1958.
[4] Sino-American Treaty of Wanghia, 1844, article 11.

The United States thus had since 1844, from the Chinese viewpoint, a vested interest in aggressions committed by other imperialist powers; and exactions made by them gave her increasing commercial and financial opportunities in China at the expense of the Chinese themselves, as well as special rights and privileges for her citizens in their dealings with Chinese citizens.

China during the time of the Ching Dynasty, many Chinese nationalists in later years acknowledged, brought the disintegration and humiliation of the years following the first Opium War on herself by her own decay and the rottenness of her ruling class and social system. All the high notions held by feudal, pre-industrial China of what conduct between one nation and another should be excited only the contempt of the rising capitalist and industrial nations. Far from acknowledging her unrealistic claim to superiority, the militarily and technically superior Western nations would not acknowledge China even as an equal, with the right to administer her laws and protect her security which they claimed for themselves. The Chinese would say that they were being taught fast by the middle of the nineteenth century what the statesmen, writers, soldiers and missionaries of the West meant when they spoke of Chinese 'provocation' and 'aggression'. The seizure for piracy of an unregistered ship in Chinese waters illegally flying the Union Jack provoked the second Opium War. It was led by Britain and France, and after the Western capture of Canton in 1857 and the destruction of the Taku Forts outside Tientsin in 1858, the Chinese government, by treaties signed in Tientsin with the British, French, Americans and Russians, was compelled to yield a great deal more of her control of and sovereignty over China. Eleven additional ports, some in the interior of China, were 'opened up' to foreigners with extra-territorial rights for them; 'missionary activity' was to be allowed without restriction or regulation; Peking itself was to be opened up. The levying of customs duties on foreign trade was to be administered and controlled independently of the Chinese government by a foreign commissioner. China had to legalize the opium trade, which had done so much harm to the country economically, and to the Chinese physically and morally. A large 'indemnity' was also exacted as punishment for Chinese 'aggression'.

Such treatment was unprecedented, and the Chinese government's hesitation over taking the suicidal step of ratifying and implementing the terms of the Treaty led to the seizing of Peking and burning of the Emperor's Summer Palace by the British and French. The Emperor abjectly accepted what seemed to the Chinese as the still more exorbitant demands made in The Treaty of Peking.

Some Chinese writers recall these and the following years not just in terms of the difficulties of the government. They portray the people's experience in day-to-day dealings in their own towns and villages with the officials, religious men, soldiers, merchants and financiers from a number of foreign countries – dealings which affected their movements, their work, their personal security, their laws and customs, and much else. Han Suyin's evocation of this experience in *The Crippled Tree*[5] is most moving.

Before the period that opens with the Opium War a number of countries which were on the periphery of the Chinese Empire had a tributary relationship to her. This implied some obligation on China's part to protect them. But China, in her impotence and military backwardness, had to accept the humiliation of being unable to protect her neighbours. In 1852 the British annexed Lower Burma, and in 1862 France took Southern Annam. By 1885 the whole of 'Indo-China' had been taken by France and the next year Britain, having taken Nepal in 1881, seized the whole of Burma. Britain was later to begin to detach Tibet (part of China itself, and not a tributary state) from China. The government in Peking already had enough trouble on its hands, and the worst days of China proper were yet to come.

The Russians had made enormous territorial gains at China's expense, by what the Chinese called 'unequal treaties' – treaties, that is, not entered into by two free and civilized states, but signed under duress. In the course of her drive through China to the Pacific, Russia acquired hundreds of thousands of square miles of Chinese territory.

The scramble for China by other imperial nations had been so far mainly a scramble for concessions and opportunities for economic exploitation. Territorially and strategically China was a rich prize, Han Suyin quotes a Japanese doctrine: 'Who conquers China conquers the world.' Many of the countries from overseas, however, had too much at stake in having their way with a weak China for it to be politic for any one of them to annex her territory. But in 1894 Japan, with United States encouragement, fought and defeated China, and by the Treaty of Shimonoseki (1895) which was imposed on her, China had to submit to disastrous terms. She lost control of Korea to Japan; and also of parts of China itself, Taiwan, the Pescadores and the Liaotung Peninsula. Further concessions to Japanese authority in China were also included.

Even worse for her was the colossal 'indemnity' which, on the now

[5] Published by London: Cape, 1965.

established tradition, she was compelled to pay Japan. How do 'patriotic' Chinese remember these exactions?

Two hundred million ounces of silver was too much, more than the revenue available to (China) after having paid all she owed the Western powers for the previous wars they had waged against her. (A loan had therefore to be arranged, and) the French, the Germans and the Russians quarrelled over who would lend money to China. Britain won the largest portion of the loan. It was the five per cent loan of 1895, to pay the war indemnity of Japan, which really ruined the Empire.[6]

It might be said that the way the concessionaries loved China was different from the way the Chinese did, especially the Sun Yat Sens, the Mao Tse Tungs and the Han Suyins. In the latter's words:

In order to guarantee this loan the West asked for mortgages and concessions in the land, in mines, in natural resources, in factories, in import goods, and in railways.

Then started the terrible years, the years of accelerated, wholesale, headlong plunder. China's weakness exposed, the Powers rallied to dismember the foundering land. Britain took control of the whole of the Great River basin, from Shanghai to Szechuan. In the words of Archibald J. Little: 'A region to China, what the valley of the Mississippi is to North America, what the valley of the Amazon is to South America; the heart of a continent, comprising six hundred thousand square miles, one hundred and eighty million of the most industrious and peaceful people on the world's surface; a magnificent prospect.'

Russia took Manchuria and Mongolia as her dependencies, building railways there to move her troops into China. France again marshalled her forces for the invasion of Yunnan. America evolved the Open Door Policy, which meant that no goods from any one country were to be taxed more than any other country's goods, when imported into China. Japan began to prepare for another war. Not to be outdone, Kaiser Wilhelm II of Germany suddenly proclaimed China the Yellow Peril; when she was at her weakest, with a fine flourish of drums he announced himself leader of Christendom and the White race in a crusade against the coloured and the yellow, and seized the province of Shantung.[7]

Han Suyin expresses some of the horror that the Chinese, and Asians – all but a few Westernized ones – generally feel when they contemplate what appears to them as the 'peril' of white racialism, with its greed, rapacity, destructiveness and double standards. From the time of the first Opium War the press in Britain had been offensively racialist in its presentation of China and the Chinese. The whipping up of a hysteria about the peril in which the white races were placed by China seemed just a racialist justification for

[6] Han Suyin, *The Crippled Tree*, pp. 84-5.
[7] *Ibid.*, p. 85.

imperialist aggrandizement and expansionism. Public opinion in the West was persuaded to see the action of Western soldiers, businessmen and missionaries in China as a defence of Christian civilization against a mortal threat from savage yellow hordes. China was represented as a Peril; altruism demanded that she be contained, subjugated and broken up. It was the American interest in seeing that the vast market of China was not parcelled out into colonies that preserved China from partition.[8]

In 1898 Britain proposed to Germany that they divide up the unoccupied part of China. Germany was suspicious, and no action followed. Attempts to team up for common ends in the Far East resulted in the treaty of alliance between Britain and Japan in 1902 – an alliance which set Japan free to proceed on the course she had begun with American backing in 1894. A recent and highly significant reminder of Anglo-American support for the Kaiser's Yellow Peril campaign came under a newspaper heading 'EARLY WARNING BY CHURCHILL ON CHINA'. Winston Churchill, in an interview given in Michigan in 1901, had said:

> I think we shall have to take the Chinese in hand and regulate them . . . I believe that as civilized nations become more powerful they will get more ruthless, and the time will come when the world will impatiently bear the existence of great barbaric nations who may at any time arm themselves and menace civilized nations . . . I believe in the ultimate partition of China – I mean ultimate. I hope we shall not have to do it in our own day. The Aryan stock is bound to triumph.[9]

China had no friends at that time of grave danger. America in her pursuit of her 'Manifest Destiny' was at the beginning of this century still involved in expansions and annexations nearer home. It is true that she had in 1898 taken possession of the Philippines opposite China. But she did not have the same 'need' to annex Chinese territory as Russia, Japan and France felt they had. Any partition of China at that time would be untimely for her. The United States had a strong interest then in 'the territorial integrity of China', not in a partition of it among the Europeans and the Japanese which would close the doors to China on her, in the same way as she had been excluded from the rest of the colonial share-out. She was a rising power, on her way to outstripping her rivals, and it seemed logical for her to calculate that once she had got all that she wanted in Mexico and the Caribbean, she would find it easier to deal with a weak *Chinese* government than with European

[8] See Walter Le Faber, *The New Empire* (Ithaca, Cornell University Press, 1963), pp. 352ff.

[9] *The Times*, 9 April 1966.

and Japanese colonial regimes in what had once been China. As long as there was an 'Open Door' for all, the *whole* of China could one day become a prize for the imperialist country which could compete most successfully for domination. In the meantime, as Woodrow Wilson was to write in 1907,

> Since trade ignores national boundaries and the manufacturer insists on having the world as a market, the flag of his nation must follow him, and the doors of nations which are closed against him must be battered down. Concessions obtained by financiers must be safeguarded by ministers of state, even if the sovereignty of unwilling nations be outraged in the process. Colonies must be obtained or planted, in order that no useful corner of the world may be overlooked or left unused. Peace itself becomes a matter of conferences and international combinations.[10]

For the Americans there were two difficulties in the way of acquiring colonies involving American responsibilities for the order and security of other peoples. One was the isolationist policy – a reluctance to become involved in the tortuous diplomacy and conflicts which characterized big power relationships in the old world. The other was the American political tradition which, some Americans at least felt strongly, excluded rule by Washington over remote peoples who were not represented there. The Open Door policy, implicit for a long time in American actions in China and enunciated officially by Hays, was well chosen. It implied that in territories where American business interests were involved, the United States would refuse to allow monopolies by other imperial powers; but she would co-operate with them in keeping such territories under weak governments. The American Ambassador to China had written to the Secretary of State in 1889:

> There is no room for doubt that foreigners hold their place in China by force and force alone . . . The fear of interfering with international rights or offending China should not for a moment be allowed to stand in the way of ordering immediate, and armed protection to . . . all foreigners in China.[11]

China's nominal sovereignty was thus preserved by manifest destiny. She never became wholly or completely the colony or colonies of other powers. But Chinese writers note that from the middle of the nineteenth century onwards China had to suffer the worse humiliation, as well as the heavier economic, cultural and political costs, of a multiple occupation of her territory and exploita-

[10] Richard Van Alstyne, *The Rising American Empire* (Oxford: Oxford University Press, 1960), p. 141.

[11] *Ibid.*, p. 181.

tion of her natural resources and people by the major as well as the minor imperialist powers. In all a dozen foreign countries lorded it over China.

2. *Chinese Reactions*

Sun Yat Sen, writing in 1924, explained that China was worse than a colony, her position lower than that of Annam and Korea, which her enemies had seized.

> China is the colony of every nation that has made treaties with her, and the treaty-making nations are her masters. China is not the colony of one nation but of all, and we are not the slaves of one country but of all.[12]

In the course of the nineteenth century 'the culture of the coolie had replaced that of the Mandarin'[13] – to use Professor Peter Worsley's phrase. But it was from those, both in the Chinese diaspora and in the country, who were the 'coolies' that the foreigners thought all Chinese were, that the reaction came. It was in Canton, whose people had had the first experience of the superior firepower and cynical behaviour of the foreigners from the Far West, that an anti-Western nationalism had begun to manifest itself as early as 1841.

In the volume *China's Response to the West*, edited by Ssu-yu Teng and John K. Fairbank, one can read the translated text of part of the 'Placard of the Patriotic People of Kwantung denouncing the English Barbarians'. It said:

> You English barbarians have formed the habits and developed the nature of wolves, plundering and seizing things by force . . . In trade relations, you come to our country merely to covet profit. What knowledge do you have? Your seeking profit resembles the animal's greed for food.[14]

Mass feeling and determination to get rid of the foreigners and their collaborators was manifested in the years that followed, though the court in Peking was less interested in the Chinese people and their interests, livelihood and security than in preserving its own position.

[12] Sun Yat Sen, *Sun Min Chu I*, E.T. under the title *The Three Principles of the People* by Frank Price (Calcutta, 1942), p. 24.

[13] Peter Worsley, *The Third World* (London: Weidenfeld & Nicolson, 1964), p. 13.

[14] Ssu-yu Teng and John K. Fairbank, eds., *China's Response to the West* (Cambridge: Harvard University Press, 1954), p. 36.

The smouldering discontent among the proletariat of that time burst in 1851 into the Taiping Movement. The 'coolies' of the area round Canton, in alliance with the anti-Manchu underground ('the Secret Societies'), and others swept through Hunan province to make Nanking in 1853 the capital of a new 'Heavenly Kingdom of Great Peace'. The support for this strongly Christian mass movement to drive out the incompetent Manchus and to institute a programme of modernization, including land-reform, in China was tremendous; and with Peking, which had already submitted to the West, itself in danger, it was in the interests of the Imperial regime and the Western forces to make common cause in destroying the Taipings. British, French and Manchus, with American help (the Civil War in the United States did not allow much American interest in Chinese affairs at that time) finally crushed the Taipings in 1864, in all some twenty to thirty million Chinese were estimated to have been killed. Thus the gains which the traders and missionaries had made by the 1860s, and were clearly going to extend in China, were preserved. The Taiping Movement made it clear that in the middle of the nineteenth century the Chinese masses were ready for drastic social change, and were capable of fighting for it; but they did not have the kind of leadership which could prepare for a revolution. The systematic, realistic appraisal of the situation, and the patient work of creating a new China, were a long time in coming.

After the Taiping Movement came the 'Yi Ho Tuan Movement' in Northern China (described by the West as the 'Boxer Rebellion'). It was a genuine movement of protest against the marauders from abroad, but it was badly led and politically confused, and was put down with fierce savagery by a combination of seven of China's imperialist masters: the United States, Britain, Japan, Russia, France, Italy and Austria. The large-scale massacres, rapes and other atrocities against the Chinese, and the enormous 'indemnities' (almost double that imposed by Japan in 1895) exacted upon her, only hastened the growth of an indigenous revolutionary nationalism. The search for programmes of action 'to change a China that is politically oppressed and economically exploited' began to take China in directions which were neither those taken by the liberal democracies of the West who had given her a good lesson in what their values and civilization were worth in Asia, nor those taken by Japan. Han Suyin recalled what her uncle had told her in 1940:

For me 1895 is when the Revolution began. If you get to the point where you have nothing to lose, then you get up and make a revolution. But a revolution is not made only by the people who are exploited, it is also prepared by those who exploit them. That is the paradox of history.[15]

Mao Tse Tung, addressing a youth conference in Yenan in 1939 on the twentieth anniversary of the 'May 4 Movement', had spoken for all patriotic Chinese when he referred to a century of 'foreign capitalist aggression against China' and then noted the very different 'struggles' over the past hundred years whose 'common purpose was to repel foreign enemies or change existing conditions'.

During that century, there was first the Opium War against British aggression, then came the War of the Taiping Heavenly Kingdom, then the Sino-Japanese War of 1894, the Reform Movement of 1898, the Yi Ho Tuan Movement, the Revolution of 1911, the May 4 Movement, the Northern Expedition, (and) the War waged by the Red Army. . . .[16]

In his *On New Democracy*, written in the following year in the midst of a revolutionary, new and free China established in the northwest, Mao again referred to the series of struggles which together represented what he called the 'first step' taken by the Chinese revolution. These were:

the struggles waged by the Chinese people, on different occasions and in varying degrees, against imperialism and the feudal forces in order to build up an independent, democratic society . . . Not only do we want to change a China that is politically oppressed and economically exploited into a China that is politically free and economically prosperous, we also want to change the China which is being kept ignorant and backward under the sway of the old culture into an enlightened and progressive China under the sway of a new culture.[17]

China, which had long been unconcerned about the world outside the Centre Country, entered the twentieth century very much aware of it. The Chinese saw that their country, her resources, and her people were almost completely at the disposal of any of the foreign merchants, bankers, missionaries or officials who were threatened by 'the Yellow Peril'. China, for those who knew, like Sun Yat Sen, became a microcosm of the subject world of Asia and Africa. Only her amazing resilience and long political tradition survived the burden of multiple taxation, ruin of the indigenous

[15] Han Suyin, *The Crippled Tree*.
1895 was the year when the Treaty of Shimonoseki was signed; see p. 50 above.
[16] Mao Tse Tung, 'The Orientation of the Youth Movement', *Selected Works*, II (Peking: The Foreign Languages Press, 1965), p. 243.
[17] Mao, 'On New Democracy', *Selected Works*, II, p. 340.

economy by foreign industries and banks, and other obstruction of piecemeal attempts by Chinese to improve their conditions.

It was in the years when China was in peril of coming to the end of her long history that Sun Yat Sen began organizing a movement which would do more for China than the frequent plots to overthrow the corrupt and anti-national Manchu Dynasty. He came to believe that it was necessary not only to drive out the Manchus but also to change the national polity and the people's mode of livelihood. Sun's thinking and his career is an important clue to the revolutionary nationalism of the generation that followed him.

Sun, it might be observed, was not thinking in terms which made sense to people who were trying to teach the Chinese how they should conduct themselves in a Western-dominated world. He tried to persuade his countrymen to avoid an immature cosmopolitanism, and to seek in China's history and social structure the causes of her desperate condition, as well as in what was best in her traditions and people the hidden sources of her power of recovery. He conceived of a national revolution, leading to a modern, *people's* China which would develop and thrive on indigenous, non-Western lines; it would be a China with a higher social ethic and a more just political system than the Western countries had. He was later to spell out his views on the weakness of Chinese political thinking which paid too much attention to foreign views: namely, the extreme conservatism which 'resisted foreign influence, and was absolutely convinced that China excelled every other nation', as well as the liberal reaction which 'swung about to an absolute reverence for foreign nations and was convinced that every nation was better than China'.

Sun, whose loyalties were wholly given to the Chinese people, was not allowed by the foreign interests to remain long in control of China after the Revolution of 1911, when the Manchus were overthrown. When he became President of the new Republic he still had to fight for control over the whole of China. His hopes that there might be some welcome in the West for the creation of a democratic Republican regime in China seemed rather ridiculous in the light of what actually happened. The Chinese nationalists, who had believed in the appeal of justice and freedom, and had disregarded the power of money and guns, found that they had no power to withstand the general, Yuan Shih Kai, who was backed by the foreign legations, the foreign consortia, the missionaries and the foreign press. Ousted, and in some cases exiled, Chinese patriots took to heart the lesson they believed their experience in 1912 and the subsequent treatment of China by the United States and her allies at the Versailles Conference of 1919 had for them.

The process of re-appraising the nature of the world of which the multiple foreign domination of China had made it a part had been accelerated and given direction by an event in 1915: this was the dictator Yuan Shih Kai's decision to submit to twenty-one demands by Japan which would have made China, in spite of all the hopes raised by the 1911 Revolution, virtually a colony of Japan. An outburst of protest throughout the country made it clear that Japan as well as Yuan had made a miscalculation. China's nationalist leaders were becoming aware of the struggle of other Asian peoples against imperialism. They believed that the end of the era of unequal treaties, extra-territoriality, and of foreign invasion, of annexation of Chinese territory and of foreign contempt for China and things Chinese would not be ended because of the 'goodwill' or 'kindness' of leaders or public opinion in the imperialist countries. The appeal to faith in a democratic solution to world problems was discovered to be equally foolish and futile.

Chinese nationalism began to grow up at this period, and became more heedful of the hard realities of politics. The collective action and virtual unanimity of purpose against Chinese protest which the United States' 'Open Door' policy had achieved was ended by the first World War among the imperialist powers. In this War China's enemies were not only divided but out to destroy each other. They were obliged to concentrate on Europe and the oceans, and their military presence in China was less obtrusive. The spontaneous mass protests against Japan in 1915 and the May 4 Movement of 1919 (related to the Versailles share-out) pointed to a new possibility of action even in an imperialist-dominated China. Then, the news began to come through, a much more fundamental split had taken place among the capitalist powers who had for so long oppressed China: Russia, one of the most ruthless and rapacious of China's oppressors, had renounced the whole capitalist order, and the hitherto oppressed workers and peasants in Russia itself were reported to have been brought to power by the Bolsheviks. This disruption of the imperialist bloc, and the challenge from within it to the established ideology and social order, had a similar effect on Indian nationalism, too. Russia was a major power, better-known to China than the Europeans from across the seas. Lenin's new government renounced the unequal treaties forced on China by the Tsarist regime; further, the attempt made by the imperialist countries to overthrow the new Russian government had made China's enemies Russia's enemies. From being an oppressor, she seemed to have become a friend. What possibilities of changing the old order there seemed to be![18]

In the years that followed the reversal of the 1911 Revolution, Chinese nationalism had taken on an increasingly radical character. The years of the first World War especially coincided, as we remarked earlier, with an intense rethinking by the Chinese of the problems and possibilities of national renewal. In Sun Yat Sen's later political teaching, servility to foreigners, premature 'cosmopolitanism', day-dreaming and impotent romantic idealism all came under attack. China's revolutionaries needed to strengthen themselves for action. To many non-westernized Chinese it seemed that amidst the degradation of a once-great nation there was a revival of self-respect, self-reliance, and the courage to act against foreign impositions—economic, political, ideological and cultural.

The May 4 Movement (1919) against the arbitrary disposal by China's enemies of her territory gave China's young nationalists a clearer focus on the world in which they lived than what they had had before. (It was under its influence that an ardent young nationalist of peasant origin from Hunan, Mao Tse Tung, started a review, in the first issue of which he wrote an article on 'The Union of the Popular Masses'.)[19] The Movement began in a year when many other things were happening in the world. Sun Yat Sen was aware of Ataturk's Revolution in Turkey and Ghandi's anti-British movement. And he began to give shape to the principles which would guide China's foreign policy after her liberation. The place of a free, independent and great China would be with the then-oppressed peoples, rather than with the oppressing Great Powers. As he put it when he gave his lectures on his Three Principles:

> The road which the Great Powers are travelling today means the destruction of other states; if China, when she becomes strong, wants to crush other countries, copy the Powers' imperialism, and go their road, we will just be following in their tracks. Let us first of all decide on our policy. Only if we 'rescue the weak and lift up the fallen' will we be carrying out the divine obligation of our nation. We must aid the weaker and smaller peoples and oppose the great powers of the world . . . Let us today, before China's development begins, pledge ourselves to lift up the fallen and to aid the weak; then when we become strong and look back upon our own sufferings under the political and economical

[18] There is relevant material quoted in Huang Sung-Kang: *Li Ta Chao and the Impact of Marxism on Modern Chinese Thinking* (The Hague: Mouton, 1965). See also the same writer's *Lu Hsun and the New Culture Movement of Modern China* (Amsterdam: Djambatan, 1957).

[19] An excerpt from it is quoted in Stuart Schram, *The Political Thought of Mao Tse Tung* (New York: Praeger, 1963), pp. 170-71.

domination of the Powers and see weaker and smaller peoples undergoing similar treatment, we will rise and smite that imperialism. Then we will be truly governing the state and pacifying the world.[20]

Sun's Three Principles of Nationalism, Democracy and People's Livelihood had been given a more practical interpretation before he died in 1925. The policy of the Kuomintang, the Nationalist Organization he had founded, was defined in its Manifesto in order to keep in line with the new world situation and the Chinese revolutionary nationalist understanding of who her friends were. A Communist Party had already been formed in China in 1921 by Chinese nationalists who were inspired by the Russian Communist policies and principles. Sun's Kuomintang was to ally itself internationally with the anti-imperialist Soviet Union; and it was to admit members of the Chinese Communist Party who shared its aims. There was also, thirdly, to be a clear identification of the Kuomintang with the interests of the working class and peasant elements in China, rather than with those elements which collaborated with China's foreign oppressors, or the landlords and militarists. Sun had come to realize that China's salvation from chaos and disintegration needed a disciplined party with a clear political ideology and the power to control China.

At the first Congress of the Kuomintang, in January 1924, these new policies were adopted. Thus it was that among those elected to the Kuomintang's Central Committee was the young nationalist from Hunan Province, Mao Tse Tung, who had already become a member of the Central Committee of the Chinese Communist Party. The political head of the Kuomintang Training Academy at Whampoa was Chou En Lai. More prominent than either of them in the leadership was Chiang Kai Shek.

In 1925, the year that Sun died, a 'National Government' for China was set up in Canton. The government was the Central Executive Committee of the Kuomintang, with three Committees under it: The Government Committee, the Political Committee and the Military Commission. The leadership was collegiate. One of the first aims of the new government was to end warlordism and get its authority as the national government acknowledged throughout China. Since the Nationalist Revolutionary Army was to set out for the north the post of Commander-in-Chief was created in July 1926, and Chiang Kai Shek, hitherto head of the Whampoa Military Academy, was appointed to it.

Nationalists of the same persuasion as Sun, who was by no means

[20] Sun Yat Sen, *Sun Min Chu I*, pp. 91-2.

the most radically 'left-wing' of the nationalists, saw China's interests as directly opposed to those of the imperialist interests and those elements of Chinese society who collaborated with them. The unification of China and the creation of a new China – democratic, nationalist and socialist in Sun's sense – was a vast undertaking. The alliance with Russia (which, unbeknown to the Chinese, increasingly meant being used by Stalin and his narrow type of Communist henchmen); the Kuomintang collaboration between the right, which had many of the corrupt elements of the old China, and an inadequately organized left-wing, which had several factions and inadequate contact with the Chinese masses in the rural areas and in the urban industrial areas, made the undertaking of Sun's successors after 1924 very difficult.

The 'Northern Expedition' which set out from Canton in 1926 got tremendous mass support, and carried all before it to Nanking, and the Kuomintang established its capital in Wuhan. In Shanghai, the stronghold of all the rotten elements – the foreign authorities, the warlords, the gangsters and smugglers, the Chinese collaborators – in China, the trade unions and left-wing forces were ready for an uprising to coincide with the entry of the Northern Expedition on its way to Peking.

3. *1927-1949: The Two China's Contend for Power*

But by May 1927, the Kuomintang as Sun Yat Sen had set it up had ceased to exist. This is how it happened. The nationalists had seized power bloodlessly in the Chinese quarter of Shanghai, and were waiting for the arrival of the Kuomintang forces to take over. But Chiang Kai Shek, at the head of the army from Canton, was returning to a city where before he had joined Sun he had had other connections, and had planned a coup which was to win him the support of the foreign bankers, merchants, and related elements in his attempt to become dictator of China. The gangster, Tu Yueh Sheng, with arms and other assistance from the international settlement in Shanghai, massacred the pro-Kuomintang forces in Shanghai, and it was on his own behalf rather than the Canton Government's that Chiang took Shanghai. Chiang's coup, like Yuan Shih Kai's earlier, split the movement to achieve independence and unity and order in China, and rendered it ineffective. But Chiang was a shrewd, ruthless and able man, who, unlike Yuan, represented post-feudal indigenous forces, just as his now proscribed ex-colleagues in the Kuomintang represented other indigenous forces which, perhaps, could not be reconciled with Chiang's. The civil war which began in 1927 was to last twenty-two years, and entail suffering even on a greater scale than anything China had known as a result of the depredations of foreigners.

'Power,' as Chiang's main opponents learnt, 'grows out of the barrel of a gun.' It did in 1912 with Yuan Shih Kai. It did in 1927 when the American Sterling Fesseden and the French authorities in Shanghai offered Tu Yueh Sheng 5,000 rifles to slaughter the non-violent revolutionary nationalists in Shanghai. It did that same year when Chiang, army commander of the Kuomintang, seized power.

The outbreak of civil war in 1927 meant that two Chinas came into being, contending with each other to dominate the future of China. But those whom Chiang and his allies attacked were pitifully weak in military terms, confused about their aims and in no condition to fight for power. While Chiang was seen as going from strength to strength, getting the money, international recognition, the enthusiastic support of the missionaries and the power to pass laws and impose taxes, such a regime, as his rivals could set up, had, by its own inability to withstand a direct confrontation, to lead a fugitive existence. It had to live by its wits, amidst people whose allegiance and opinions did not then count in China.

The Chinese regime which was counter-posed to Chiang's new one was originally a small base in Chinkangshan, a mountain stronghold in East China. The supreme position of its leader, Mao Tse Tung, in the alternative China was not assured for some time. Mao seemed to have tried his best and as long as possible to make the broadbased nationalist organization work, and had tried to avoid a break or the provocation for a break. His reasons were clearly different from those of the emissaries of Stalin who had been exerting pressure on the Kuomintang left-wing faction to accept Chiang's leadership.

The base in Chingkangshan in 1927 was the beginning of a China unlike anything else in Chinese history. In March that year, writing a Report on his *Investigation of the Peasant Movement in Hunan*,[21] Mao, already a believer in the potentiality for national renewal of the China of the peasants, had been moved as never before by what he discovered of the qualities of the peasantry in his native province. He wrote:

> . . . the present upsurge of the peasant movement is a colossal event. In a very short time, in China's central, southern and northern provinces, several hundred million peasants will rise like a mighty storm, like a hurricane, a force so swift and violent that no power, however

[21] In his *Selected Works*, I, pp. 23-59, the following three quotations of Mao are all taken from this essay.

great, will be able to hold it back. They will smash all the trammels that bind them and rush forward along the road to liberation. They will sweep all the imperialists, warlords, corrupt officials, local tyrants and evil gentry into their graves. Every revolutionary party and every revolutionary comrade will be put to the test, to be accepted or rejected as they decide. There are three alternatives. To march at their head and lead them? To trail behind them, gesticulating and criticizing? Or to stand in their way and oppose them? Every Chinese is free to choose, but events will force you to make the choice quickly.

The great excitement which Mao felt when he observed in his native province the 'tempestuous' attack on the old order is well conveyed even in the translation of his report. He described the leadership and organization, the vast membership and following, and the programme of action. The reaction of various classes of people to this revolutionary upheaval was, Mao had reported, 'It's terrible.' Even 'quite progressive people' thought so.

In short, nobody could altogether deny the word 'terrible'. But, as already mentioned, the fact is that the great peasant masses have risen to fulfil their historic mission and that the forces of rural democracy have risen to overthrow the forces of rural feudalism. The patriarchal-feudal class of local tyrants, evil gentry and lawless landlords has formed the basis of autocratic government for thousands of years and is the cornerstone of imperialism, warlordism and corrupt officialdom. To overthrow these feudal forces is the real objective of the national revolution. In a few months the peasants have accomplished what Dr Sun Yat Sen wanted, but failed, to accomplish in the forty years he devoted to the national revolution. This is a marvellous feat never before achieved, not just in forty, but in thousands of years. It's fine. It's not 'terrible' at all . . .

Mao had gone on to point out to his colleagues in the as yet revolutionary-nationalist Kuomintang that 'the national revolution requires a great change in the countryside'. Turning, obviously, to his Communist Party colleagues he took up the charge that the peasants were going too far, and continued:

Such talk may seem plausible, but in fact it is wrong. First, the local tyrants, evil gentry and lawless landlords have themselves driven the peasants to this. For ages they have used their power to tyrannize over them and trample them underfoot; that is why the peasants have reacted so strongly. The most violent revolts and the most serious disorders have invariably occurred in places where the local tyrants, evil gentry and lawless landlords have perpetrated the worst outrages. The peasants are clear-sighted. Who is bad and who is not, who is the worst and who is not quite so vicious, who deserves severe punishment and who deserves to be let off lightly – the peasants keep clear accounts, and very seldom has the punishment exceeded the crime. Secondly, a revolution is not a dinner party, or writing an essay, or painting a picture, or doing embroidery; it cannot be so refined, so leisurely and gentle, so temperate, kind, courteous, restrained and magnanimous. A revolution is an insurrection, an act of violence by which one class overthrows another. A rural revolution is a revolution by which the peasantry overthrows the power of the feudal landlord class. Without using the greatest force, the peasantry cannot possibly overthrow the deep-rooted authority of the landlords for thousands of years.

With remarkable sociological and psychological acumen Mao goes on to a systematic analysis, in the course of which he describes how the three, and for women, 'the four thick ropes binding the Chinese people', particularly the peasants – that is, the various feudal 'systems of authority' – are being broken.

Something of Mao Tse Tung's state of mind in those crucial years may be gathered from his Report, which his colleagues, incidentally, did not approve of. Nowhere else in the nationalist movements in Asia was there then any thinking like this, or any mass revolutionary movement like the one described. If Mao's insights were accurate, there were enormous resources of human energy, organizing ability and democratic conviction which a united nationalist leadership could mobilize for China's freedom. As it turned out, however, it was going to be many years before the movement, which began after Chiang's coup and the massacres of left-wing Kuomintang leaders and followers, was to make its impact on the world. Unfortunately for the Chinese nationalists, neither the foreign capitalist empires nor the Soviet Union wanted to allow the success of this movement.

From the point of view of the aspirations and needs of the Chinese people – that is, from the point of view of those who wanted to end the humiliations of a multiple foreign occupation and exploitation, to recover national self-respect and dignity, to end warlordism and unite the country, to end economic chaos and develop the economy and to bring about the social and political reforms needed to modernize the country – the institution of Chiang's dictatorship over a large part of China was a disaster.

Foreign business interests, the missionaries, the landlords and others who had feared Chiang before 1927 as the military head of a revolutionary Kuomintang welcomed him after his coup. Chiang paid a visit to Japan in 1927. In the same year he was 'converted' to Christianity, becoming a devout Methodist. He also married into a highly-regarded, American-educated family; he married the sister of Sun Yat Sen's widow and, although Madame Sun regarded him as a traitor, claimed to be Sun's heir. His Nanking regime in 1927 was claimed to have begun, in the words of Professor Doak Barnett, 'a period of considerable progress and hope. The new regime started to modernize the country. It introduced some moderate social reforms. And it took initial steps towards fostering economic development.'[22] This view was widely publicized.

The Chinese saw it very differently. For whom was it a period of progress and hope? Which China did it modernize – the China symbolized by Shanghai or Chinese China; warlord, landlord China or the China of the people? Whose economic development did it foster? What social reforms did it introduce? Chiang concentrated from the start on massacring the modernizing elements in China. He had arranged with the rulers in Shanghai to kill off a good number of the Chinese industrial workers in the country. His political power was based a good deal on absolutely the most disreputable type of gangster. Tu Yueh Seng, for example, whose power and wealth were based on the gangster organization by which he monopolized opium smuggling, opium dens and prostitution, was a pillar of the new order. The rapidly increasing expenditure on maintaining a number of armies to suppress the mounting discontent among the Chinese people absorbed an increasing proportion of the Nanking government's budget. Far from instituting social reforms, Chiang built up a military and secret police apparatus to eliminate all who voiced the desire for reform.

In 1931 Japan occupied Manchuria, the richest of China's regions in industrial resources. While the nation waited for Chiang to act, Chiang ordered Chinese troops in Manchuria not to resist the Japanese, but to withdraw. Early in 1932 the Japanese invaded Shanghai, shooting and killing the undefended Chinese there; Chiang's reaction was to evacuate his capital from Nanking.[23]

Chiang, busy even at that time hunting out and killing 'Communists' with his large army, soon made it an offence for Chinese to condemn the Japanese outrage. In Shanghai in 1932 the Nineteenth Route Army, contrary to orders, fought back, but Chiang forced it to withdraw. The Chinese people, many of whom were too young to remember personally the treatment China had received some years previously, felt terribly humiliated. Japan followed up her annexation of Manchuria by taking steps to take over the rest of north China.

[22] Doak Barnett, *China on the Eve of Communist Takeover* (New York: Praeger, 1963).

[23] Chinese and foreign reactions are described in Gunther Stein: *The Challenge of Red China* (London: Pilot Press, 1945) pp. 7-10; also in Edgar Snow: *Journey to the Beginning* (London: Gollancz, 1959).

The contrast between Chiang's ruthlessness and arrogance in dealing with the Chinese, and his servile and cowardly attitude to the Japanese could not have been greater. Those who knew of his meeting in 1927 with the Japanese Prime Minister Tanaka in Tokyo had reason to suspect that Chiang had made a 'deal' with the Japanese – to let them have in northern China what the imperial nations called, in the then United States Secretary of State Lansing's words in 1917, Japan's 'special interests in China', while he got Japanese help in seizing power and holding it against those who did not want him. Chiang was clearly more afraid of the very Chinese forces – the Chinese nationalist pride, the tremendous revolutionary potential, the democratic aspirations of the masses – which were there to be mobilized if the imperialist threats were to be faced successfully. He was more afraid of them than of the Japanese or the Americans. Since the Japanese and the Americans were equally afraid of a Chinese resurgence, Chiang got more for himself out of being master of what would be allowed him by these nations than in letting loose a nationalism which would sweep him as well as them away.

Most of the European nations had ceased by the early thirties to count for much in China. They had problems at home and in other parts of Asia. A Chinese common front to throw out the Japanese would not have been met by the old type of combination of eight or ten nations. America was supplying a good part of the Japanese war machine, it was true, but her active support for her rival was unlikely. The chief obstacle to China's resurgence was the whole apparatus of the Chiang dictatorship. All the praise that was and is lavished on Chiang is in fact an appreciation of what he did for those who stood in the way of the new China – in the way of the creation by the Chinese, by their own courage, vision, co-operation and hard work, of a new China. It was not praise for what he did for China – although he was continually pressed to become the country's real leader. Chiang's hatred of democracy, the sadistic brutality of his regime, his extreme right-wing ideology and his personal ambition – all amply attested by anti-Communist observers – made him more akin to the Japanese than to his former colleagues in the Kuomintang.

The Japanese kept on moving into China, terrorizing the people, demanding the peaceful co-operation of Nanking. Chiang carried out his 'Extermination Campaigns' of anti-Japanese forces. But in the course of the sixth of these campaigns he was kidnapped and persuaded into calling off his campaigns to exterminate Mao's forces, and instead to combine his forces with them to resist the Japanese. Thus, when the Japanese attacked in force in 1937, there was, at least for another few years, a national resistance. And for the first time Chiang became a national leader.

China today can remember all that happened when Fascist Japan attacked her; using all the anti-Communist and imperialist cliches to justify her action, and to present herself in the role of defender of Chinese civilization and freedom against 'Communism'. The rape of Nanking in 1937 was the fitting opening to a World War in which the latest bearers of 'civilization' to the colonial peoples would perpetrate savageries hitherto unknown to man. The Japanese, who had already pioneered in the neo-colonialist technique of setting up puppet or quisling regimes when they took Manchuria in 1931, were able to set up their new nationalist China, devoted to 'peace, anti-Communism and national construction', under former Kuomintang politician Wang Ching Wei. It had its capital in Nanking and attempted to establish itself in the villages. Those who attacked this new regime and its officials were, according to current reports, said to be engaging in aggression against not only Japan but also 'China'. The Japanese then were the heroic defenders of China against 'Communism'. In the face of a popular resistance, the Nanking 'government' in July 1941 launched a Rural Pacification Movement, which established in the pacified areas 'Model Peace Zones'.

Left without any assistance in their critical hour, the Chinese learnt the importance of national unity and of self-reliance. But though, for the first time, Chiang became a national leader, it was the existence of the other China, *people's* China – which had grown hidden from but parallel with Chiang's corrupt and Fascist China – which enabled the Chinese to work out their own salvation; and to make sure that when they were delivered from the Japanese they did not fall under the domination of other foreign interests, either American or Russian.

The memory of the Chinese – what happened and what did not; what was glorious, what was shameful, who the heroes were and who the villains – is different from that of China's antagonists, of those who despised the Chinaman, of those whose interests in China took precedence over the interests of the Chinese. The period of Chiang's dictatorship from 1927 to 1949 in those parts of China which he could control was not one 'of considerable progress and hope', 'social reforms', or 'economic development' for more than a handful of Chinese – the landlords, the financiers, the generals and so on. More Chinese men, women and children were poor, miserable and frightened than ever before. The regime which was highly praised and supported by foreigners was almost incredibly corrupt and tyrannical. Even with the immense help it received—the vast amounts of money and materials poured in by the United States to strengthen it against its rivals, the advice, and the friendly propaganda – it was not even efficient.

Yet, by 1949 the Chinese people, in spite of first the Japanese, then the American and Russian attempts to prevent them, had a government of their own in Peking; they were a united, independent people with a government, stable, incorrupt and efficient by any standards. Foreign control had been decisively got rid of. Chinese were no more coolies, to be despised and kicked about. A truly indigenous revolution and renaissance had shown that the Chinese people could work out their own salvation, that their creativity had not come to an end. Child labour, torture, prostitution, mass starvation and chronic famine, gangsterism, crime and warlordism had been brought to an end. The Chinese people as a whole were enjoying as a right a higher material, cultural and moral standard of living than ever before in their history; and they could work for their own welfare.

That this dramatic and incredible change could take place was due, China's revolutionary nationalists would say, to one man above all others—Mao Tse Tung. He had already rooted the Chinese Revolution in the peasantry in the heart of China before the Chiang coup of 1927. He saved it from liquidation in the terror that followed. He saved it also, at some risk to himself, from the deadening influence, the doctrinaire sectarianism and anti-Chinese orientation of the Muscovite Communists. At a time when life was cheap, when the political struggle was savage beyond description, and when factionalist tendencies were strong, Mao had the capacity to inspire the revolutionaries with his humanism and tolerance, his patience and far-sightedness. For example, the virtual capture in 1934 of the new China's base in Kiangsi province in the southeast, was followed by the almost incredible exodus of the revolutionary leaders to found a new community in Shensi province in the northwest – the Long March of 10,000 miles.

At a time when no one had yet charted the path by which the victims of imperialism could find authentic deliverance, by which, at the same time, the once-great non-European peoples could renew and modernize themselves on genuinely democratic lines, Mao, working among one-third of the colonial world, was realistically thinking, learning, discovering a way; and using his genius as a teacher to reveal it to others.

The age-long determination of his fellow-countrymen, 80 per cent of them peasants, to throw off the oppression of landlords, officials and gentry captured him; and it was he who turned it into intelligent and purposeful mass action. The intense desire of Chinese nationalists of all classes to resist and expel the imperialists, whose presence was most immediate in the person of the conquering Japanese – this, too, was turned into successful action. Chiang was forced to remove the ban on opposition to Japan, end his collaboration with them, and allow his troops to fight the Japanese, at least for a time. When he slackened off his resistance to Japan, and instead turned his American-armed and equipped armies against the revolutionary areas and started attacking the badly-equipped revolutionary troops under his own command (the most notorious being the ambush and destruction on Chunking's orders of part of the Fourth Army, one of the most successful anti-Japanese forces, in East China in January 1941), the Chinese revolutionaries, with no assistance from China's allies, carried on a continuous struggle within the Japanese areas, putting the Japanese on the defensive, and foiling their savage 'pacification' programme. It was largely because of Mao that a common national and international front was maintained until the defeat of Japan.

But the war was no sooner over in August 1945, than China faced another crisis. The situation that Mao confronted showed that China's problems with regard to foreigners were not over.

Stalin had joined with the United States and Britain in deciding, over the heads of the Chinese people, that Chiang Kai Shek and his men were the sole and supreme government of all China. All these developments were highly satisfactory to the Chiang regime, which by 1945 was execrated in all China. In a 'Treaty of Friendship and Alliance' signed with the Chungking regime and blessed by the Americans in August, Moscow, while professing belief in 'non-interference in the internal affairs' of China, interfered considerably in China's affairs: she established a puppet Soviet regime in Outer Mongolia, got Dairen declared a 'free port' for Soviet use; and in exchange agreed in the midst of a civil war situation, to 'give support and aid . . . entirely to the National (i.e. Chiang's) Government as the central government of China'. The Russians also recognized that Manchuria was part of China, but this did not prevent them from looting Manchuria on a big scale.[24]

The Americans had already been in communication with the Russians asking for an assurance that the 'Open Door' policy would be revived; this they secured. They had also been assured that the United States could have a free hand in China. All this did not

[24] See, Text of Sino-Soviet 'Treaty of Friendship and Alliance', *United States Relations with China* (Washington: United States State Department, 1949), p. 95.

accord with what the revolutionary Chinese had expected. They had assumed that the war was to end with the defeat and punishment of the Axis Powers, the freeing of India and the other colonial territories from foreign rule, and the total restoration to China of all that had been exacted from her, all her national territory and resources under foreign control.

In the event, the sequel to the second World War turned out to be not very different from that of the first World War. For example, Japanese troops, in the north of China, which were supposed to surrender to Chinese forces were told not to. The Vietnamese nationalist movement had already taken control of their country and proclaimed their independence; but Western imperialist troops had, before the end of 1945, begun the attempt to reconquer Vietnam using Japanese imperialist forces. In Indonesia the same thing happened. In India the humiliating colonial rule remained. The Koreans were not allowed to run their own affairs. What the nationalists called the neo-colonial era had begun for Asia.

In China itself the utterly discredited and hated Chiang's apparatus was trying to impose itself by military force and diplomatic manoeuvre on a China it had done little to liberate. The vast mass of the people wanted peace, national unity and an end to the fighting. The negotiations between Mao and Chiang dragged on, while the situation got worse. Even though the Americans, who succeeded in maintaining a special position in China, considered Chiang, in General Marshall's words, as China's, their China's, 'most valuable asset', for the Chinese who had fought to create a new China a return to the corruption, tyranny, terror, inefficiency and neo-colonialism of Chiang's dictatorship was unthinkable.

Chiang's belief that he could get his way by military force made civil war inevitable. Thus it was that under Mao's leadership the Chinese people, completely on their own resources, fought and put to flight Chiang, with all the American and other international support he was getting. The last phase of the civil war (1946-9) was not just a military victory. For it was largely on the confidence of the masses and the intellectuals that the tremendous forces arrayed against the Chinese revolution could be overcome. The battles were won not only by the genius of the leaders and the courage of the People's Liberation Army, but also by the massive transfer of allegiance by Chiang's troops to the revolutionary forces.

The heavy backing of the Americans in training and equipping Chiang's troops, in economic aid and in advising on counter-revolutionary strategies, had come to naught. Chiang's regime was to be the last foothold of anti-Chinese forces in the Chinese mainland.

4

From the New China, Looking Outward

1. The New Era of China's Liberation and Unification

ON 1 October 1949, at the end of a ten-day session of the Chinese People's Political Consultative Conference in Peking, the new Chinese People's Republic was formally proclaimed, with Mao Tse Tung as Chairman of a democratic coalition government. Represented at the Conference were, 'all the democratic parties, people's organizations, democratic personages in all walks of life, minority nationalities and overseas Chinese'.

In addressing his fellow-delegates on the preparatory committee some months earlier Mao had said that the defeat by the People's Liberation Army of the foreign-aided Kuomintang attempt to impose Chiang's dictatorship was 'a victory for the people of all China, and also a victory for the peoples of the whole world'. But, he warned, they must never relax their vigilance against 'frenzied plots for revenge' by the imperialists and their clients.

> (They would) smuggle their agents into China to sow dissension and make trouble; (they would) incite the Chinese reactionaries, and even throw in their own forces, to blockade China's ports . . . Furthermore, if they still hanker after adventure, they will send some of their troops to invade and harass China's frontiers . . . (The Chinese people would have to be united and vigilant) to smash resolutely, thoroughly, wholly and completely every plot against (them) by the imperialists and their running dogs, the Chinese reactionaries. *China must be independent, China must be liberated, China's affairs must be decided and run by the Chinese people themselves, and no further interference, not even the slightest, will be tolerated from any imperialist country.*[1] (italics mine)

This kind of talk had been heard before from Chinese nationalist leaders. But for the first time it carried, and was clearly intended to be heard to carry, a note of realism – the promise of tough action. Mao continued:

[1] This and the following two quotations from Mao were taken from his 'Address to the Preparatory Committee of the New Political Consultative Conference', *Selected Works*, IV, pp. 405-9.

> The Chinese revolution is a revolution of the broad masses of the whole nation. Everybody is our friend, except the imperialists, the feudalists and bureaucrat capitalists, the Kuomintang reactionaries and their accomplices. We have a broad and solid revolutionary united front. This united front is so broad that it includes the working class, the peasantry, the urban petty bourgeoisie and the national bourgeoisie. This united front is so solid that it possesses the resolute will and the inexhaustible capacity to defeat every enemy and overcome every difficulty. The epoch we are living in is an epoch in which the imperialist system is heading for total collapse, the imperialists have fallen inextricably into crisis and, no matter how they continue to oppose the Chinese people, the Chinese people will always have a way to win final victory.

But though Mao challenged the imperialist governments which at the time were still clinging to, trying to reconquer or seeking to control colonial or ex-colonial territories, he went on,

> We are willing to discuss with any foreign government the establishment of diplomatic relations on the basis of the principles of equality, mutual benefit and mutual respect for territorial integrity and sovereignty, provided it is willing to sever relations with the Chinese reactionaries, stops conspiring with them or helping them and adopts an attitude of genuine, and not hypocritical, friendship towards People's China. The Chinese people wish to have friendly co-operation with the people of all countries and to resume and expand international trade in order to develop production and promote economic prosperity.

According to this kind of nationalism, the proof of the end of the imperialist era in the world would be seen when racial arrogance, the insult and abuse of Asian and African peoples, and the looting of their resources and violation of their territory, ceased to be facts of life. The first requirement for the Chinese people was that they should be able to look after themselves in the face of imperialist designs on China of the kind the newly independent Vietnamese were then experiencing. This the Chinese were prepared to do. But their liberation from imperialism did not mean that they 'minded their own business'. In so far as there was a struggle between imperialist and anti-imperialist forces, capitalist and socialist forces, China took sides.

But China, as the civil war neared its end, was willing to be on friendly terms with any country which left China's domestic problems absolutely alone. The state to which Japanese occupation in Northern China and Kuomintang exploitation of Southern China – coming on top of the previous hundred years of foreign and warlord activities – had brought the country was incredible. China was a country of mass starvation, unemployment, child labour and prostitution, coolies and dope-pedlars, bandits and assassins, and even money had almost ceased to have any meaning. The usurped powers of Chiang's regime had been used to the very end – arbitrarily arresting, torturing and murdering people, embezzling public funds and ruining the economy. The brilliant and decisive victories of the People's Liberation Army in northern and central China had led to a rapid collapse of Chiang's rule in areas where the popular experience of self-government, the discipline, the restraints, of the Yenan regime were not known. As in all revolutions where a long-hated apparatus of tyranny collapses, it happened that as the big tyrants fled, the local tyrants and their instruments of terror and oppression were left exposed and unprotected. As the Chinese People's Republic came into being, Mao and his band of colleagues and associates – the surviving Chinese Communist-Party members, the People's Liberation Army, and the other parties, organizations and unattached individuals who fought beside them or welcomed liberation by them – had the enormous and unprecedented task of preventing China from losing herself in 1949 in an orgy of destructiveness. The Chinese had at last gained control over their country. Mao, the national leader, was clear that they had to use that new power and authority for constructive and peaceful purposes. Hope had to replace despair. The waverers had to be won over. The passions of narrow partisanship and sectarianism had to be transformed into a passion for national unity. Above all, the hundreds of millions of newly liberated peasants had to learn to think of the future, not of the past; they had also to learn to take political responsibility. The pent-up hatreds and resentments of the peasant masses – and all others who had suffered under the abuse of the old authority – had quickly to be civilized, and transmuted into humane and creative forms. China in 1949 had a much bigger task of reconstruction than the whole European continent had in 1945.

Life under the old order had been cheap in China, and people the most expendable. In 1949 China's government was headed by a Chinese who had tried to convince his compatriots that 'Of all the things in the world, people are the most precious'.[2] 1949 was a great year for the people of one of the world's great civilizations, it was a great year for a quarter of mankind. It was in many ways and from the non-Western viewpoint a great year for the world.

2. *How China's War-time Allies Welcomed Her Liberation*

But, the Chinese ask, how was this inauguration of a new China

[2] *Ibid.*, p. 454.

regarded? Speaking for the West, Churchill, in Boston in 1949, called it 'the worst disaster suffered by the West since the war'. China's war-time allies acted as if this was their official view. Britain, which that year had in sending warships up the Yangtze had her last shot at gunboat diplomacy in China, dallied over having relations with the new Chinese government. To be told by a formerly subject people (or non-people) that diplomatic relations henceforth would have to be on the basis of 'equality, mutual benefit and mutual respect' was a novel experience. The British, and the Americans, and the French, debated among themselves about China as though it were in London or Washington or Paris, and not in China, that the legitimacy of China's government were decided. Had 'Eur-american' attitudes of overlordship towards non-white peoples changed? The Chinese and other Asians wondered as the first half of the twentieth century came to an end. Why was it a disaster *for the West* that the Chinese people were again able to stand on their own feet? Why was it a problem for them to treat completely independent Asian nations as equals, and on the basis of mutual respect and reciprocity?

The Chinese were learning a great deal. Their fathers and grand-fathers had learnt from experience what people from the world beyond the seas were like, how they behaved, what their values were, what principles they lived by. Now they realized that they were getting lessons in what the rest of the world was like in the middle of the twentieth century. Their assumptions during the second World War were that the victory of the anti-Fascist forces would lead to changes which would end imperialism, exploitation and oppression. But these assumptions were shown to be rather romantic. A post-War world in which Asian and other hitherto subject or subservient peoples would take over the running of their countries – be self-reliant, independent in their political decisions, and able to protect their own national interests – was proving intolerable to the new imperialism which had arisen.

The success of the long revolution was an occasion for celebration in China. But the hope, the great sense of release from oppression and the sense of the possibilities for good in humanity which was felt in China found no echo in the world (i.e. official positions of various governments) outside. Instead, from the beginning the new China found herself confronted with a tremendous and complex campaign to undermine the loyalty of the Chinese people, to interfere with China's foreign relations and trade, to obstruct her economic reconstruction, to subvert or overthrow her government and to attack her people. A campaign of systematic denigration of the

Chinese People's Republic was carried on by classes of people who claimed special knowledge of China – many of the missionaries, the 'scholars', the soldiers, the diplomats and the journalists who were 'Old China Hands'.[3]

During the war-time alliance the people of Yenan-ruled China had met and got to know American officers, journalists, escaped airmen and diplomats; and reports of that period indicate that out of the mutual respect and understanding of their common democratic aspirations the hope of continued friendship between the two nations had been born. Visiting journalists had, sometimes with surprise, noted the portraits of Churchill, Roosevelt and Stalin and of Chiang Kai Shek placed together, which had expressed revolutionary China's solidarity with the rest of the anti-Fascist alliance and their concern for a unified national resistance to Japanese imperialism. Disunity, as Mao said in 1945 in his article 'On Coalition Government', would obstruct the creation of 'the new world order led by the united Britain, the United States, the Soviet Union, France and China'.[4]

Some of the visitors to North China were obviously beginning to understand that China's internal politics was far more complex than Chiang's foreign mentors and apologists made them out to be, and the leaders of revolutionary China, Madame Sun Yat Sen, Mao Tse Tung and others, assumed that after the war the Chinese people alone would be left to decide domestic political issues which had not been settled since Chiang's coup in 1927. The question whether China wanted the dictatorship of Chiang's Kuomintang, or Mao's 'New Democracy', or a Chunking-Yenan-led coalition effectively guaranteeing the liberties and well-being of China's masses had to be answered by the Chinese people alone. And China's allies would respect that answer.

The Westerners whom the non-westernized, rural Chinese met in Yenan during the war seemed to them very unlike the (to them) unsavoury characters whom they had known at other times, or heard about. The attitude of Mao and his colleagues at this time was one of warm friendship for nations the Chinese had had no cause in the past to love. Mao even believed that the Americans, being aware

[3] There were first-hand accounts by observers who took a different line from those who were influential. Their work has rarely been publicized since the McCarthy Purges. See Gunther Stein, *The Challenge of Red China* (esp. Chapter 11, 'Yenan's Political ABC'; Chapter 12, 'The Credo of Mao Tse Tung'; Chapter 36, 'What American Officers Saw at the Front'. It quotes passages from a report by (then) Representative (now Senator) Mike Mansfield.)

[4] Stuart Gelder, *The Chinese Communists* (London: Gollancz, 1946), p. 2.

of their own tradition given by Washington and Lincoln, would welcome what the Chinese revolutionaries were trying to achieve. When Chiang Kai Shek's book, *China's Destiny*,[5] was published, it was severely criticized for its chauvinism, its anti-foreign and anti-liberal ideas and its expression in the middle of the anti-Fascist war of Chiang's Fascist ideology. It began to look as though revolutionary China might forget the kind of Western world it had once encountered.

But official Western policies brought about a great disillusionment about American interest in Chinese democracy. American diplomats who urged allied assistance in arms and equipment for the Chinese forces fighting the Japanese in the north were disregarded, later even penalized. Massive aid and assistance was given to Chiang, who Western observers discovered to their surprise was using this Western aid to obstruct and attack the Chinese armies and guerrillas in the north who were pinning down large Japanese and quisling forces. And after the surrender of Japan the Americans did all they could, short of direct massive intervention, to bring about the defeat of the Chinese revolutionaries. 'The United States,' wrote Mao in June 1949 after his own illusions were lost, 'wanted to enslave the whole world; it supplied arms to help Chiang Kai Shek slaughter several million Chinese.'

The Chinese people were reminded of all this and were told a great deal of what had gone on behind the scenes in Washington and Chunking, when in August 1949 the State Department published its thousand-page White Paper on *United States Relations with China*. The White Paper had been published by the United States government for internal political reasons, in order to exonerate it from blame for the 'loss of China'. It revealed the extent to which Washington had committed itself to ensuring the subjugation or defeat of the anti-Chiang parties and groups, especially the revolutionary organizations Mao had created – the Chinese Communist Party and the People's Liberation Army. It also made it clear that the United States government had not accepted as final her loss of China. Her policy was still, it declared, 'the Open Door' policy. And she was committed to an overthrow of the revolutionary order using the enormous resources at her disposal. The subsequent establishment of an American protectorate over China's island province of Taiwan, after professions of regard for 'China's territorial integrity' had been made, made American intentions clear.

[5] The original edition was suppressed because of foreign criticism. But a lengthy review from Yenan is included in Gelder's collection of documents in *The Chinese Communists*.

3. *China's Assessment of the World Situation*

It was clear to the Chinese government that all that they had suspected about the United States government's post-war aims in China were justified. Now that it was American policy to support the overthrow of the new order and to re-establish the 'Open Door', it followed that China would have to do without Western help or co-operation in the task of cleansing the Augean stables in the former Kuomintang-controlled areas, and in reorganizing and reconstructing China. In Mao's words,

> Thus Western bourgeois civilization, bourgeois democracy and the plan for a bourgeois republic (had) all gone bankrupt in the eyes of the Chinese people. Bourgeois democracy (had) given way to people's democracy under the leadership of the working class.[6]

The Soviet Union alone among China's major war-time allies was openly hostile after the Kuomintang, which she had supported to the very end, had been defeated. The Chinese were not happy about, and they were to get more and more distressed by, Soviet attitudes to China and post-War Soviet actions elsewhere. But if they were to be realistic they had no choice but to lean to the Soviet side. Since Sun Yat Sen's time, as Mao had pointed out in his 'On New Democracy' there had been a tradition of friendship between China and Russia, and it was in Russia's interest to be friendly to China. The Sino-Soviet Pact of 1950 gave devastated China the assurance of getting at least some of the material she needed for development. But the imperial Russia of Stalin was rather unlike the revolutionary, idealistic Russia of Lenin's days, and the Chinese revolutionaries and their supporters were not entirely happy.

Mao's 'On the People's Democratic Dictatorship' reflects the debate that went on in China in 1949.

> 'You are leaning to one side.' Exactly. The forty years' experience of Sun Yat Sen and the twenty-eight years' experience of the Communist Party have taught us to lean to one side, and we are firmly convinced that in order to win victory and consolidate it we must lean to one side. In the light of the experiences accumulated in these forty years and these twenty-eight years, all Chinese without exception must lean either to the side of imperialism or to the side of socialism. Sitting on the fence will not do, nor is there a third road . . .
>
> 'We want to do business.' Quite right, business will be done. We are against no one except the domestic and foreign reactionaries who hinder us from doing business . . . When we have beaten the internal and

[6] This and the following two quotations from Mao were taken from his 'On the People's Democratic Dictatorship', *Selected Works*, IV, pp. 411-24.

external reactionaries by uniting all domestic and international forces, we shall be able to do business and establish diplomatic relations with all foreign countries on the basis of equality, mutual benefit and mutual respect for territorial integrity and sovereignty.

'Victory is possible even without international help.' This is a mistaken idea. In the epoch in which imperialism exists, it is impossible for a genuine people's revolution to win victory in any country without various forms of help from the international revolutionary forces, and even if victory were won, it could not be consolidated . . .

'We need help from the British and U.S. governments.' This, too, is a naïve idea in these times. Would the present rulers of Britain and the United States, who are imperialists, help a people's state? . . . Throughout his life Sun Yat Sen appealed countless times to the capitalist countries for help and got nothing but heartless rebuffs. Only once in his whole life did Sun Yat Sen receive foreign help, and that was Soviet help. Let readers refer to Dr Sun Yat Sen's testament; his earnest advice was not to look for help from the imperialist countries but to 'unite with those nations of the west which treat us as equals'. Dr Sun had experience; he had suffered, he had been deceived. We should remember his words and not allow ourselves to be deceived again . . .

This assessment of the unwillingness of Britain and the United States to regard China as an equal was a realistic one. The main threat to the security of the countries which had asserted their independence from the West seemed to come from the West.

Mao, on his first journey out of China, went in December 1949 to meet Stalin in Moscow. He persuaded Stalin to agree that Russia's special privileges in Manchuria would be completely withdrawn by 1952. The Treaty of Friendship, Alliance and Mutual Assistance signed by the Chinese and Soviet leaders did not do much to help China, but the very modest annual credits promised China for its development were not negligible. And at least on her 7,000-mile border with the Soviet Union China did not have to worry about her security. It was clear, however, that China would have to rely on herself for her reconstruction.

In 1949, even while remaining pockets of Kuomintang activity were being eliminated, something had to be done urgently for the Chinese masses, who had hailed the new government as their deliverer. Civilized life had broken down in many parts of the country. The enormous amounts of money, materials and advice given by the United States in order to keep Chiang in control of China had not prevented economic collapse. The inflation had reached an unimaginable condition. This inflation, and the banditry, anarchy, gangsterism and oppression of the people, which had characterized the old regime in the South, had to be eradicated, not just driven underground. Work had to be organized, food and other vital needs procured and distributed fairly.

As Mao had reminded those who worked and suffered for a whole generation to create a new China, they were setting out to enter the realm of (what the Chinese called) Great Harmony, but its path was a difficult one.

We still have much work to do; to use the analogy of a journey, our past work is only the first step in a long march of ten thousand li. Remnants of the enemy have yet to be wiped out. The serious task of economic reconstruction lies before us. We shall soon put aside some of the things we know well and be compelled to do things we don't know well. This means difficulties. The imperialists reckon that we will not be able to manage our economy; they are standing by and looking on, awaiting our failure.

We must overcome difficulties, we must learn what we do not know. We must learn to do economic work from all who know how, no matter who they are. We must esteem them as teachers, learning from them respectfully and conscientiously. We must not pretend to know when we do not know. We must not put on bureaucratic airs. If we dig into a subject for several months, for a year or two, for three or five years, we shall eventually master it . . .

(China was to be a) 'People's Democratic Dictatorship'. Who are the people? At the present stage in China, they are the working class, the peasantry, the urban petty buorgeoisie and the national bourgeoisie. These classes, led by the working class and the Communist Party, unite to form their own state and elect their own government . . . Democracy is practised within the ranks of the people, who enjoy the rights of freedom of speech, assembly, association and so on. The right to vote belongs only to the people, not to the reactionaries. The combination of these two aspects, democracy for the people and dictatorship over the reactionaries, is the people's democratic dictatorship.

Why must things be done in this way? The reason is quite clear to everybody. If things were not done this way, the revolution would fail, the people would suffer, the country would be conquered.

Don't you want to abolish state power? Yes, we do, but not right now; we cannot do it yet. Why? Because imperialism still exists, because domestic reaction still exists, because classes still exist in our country. Our present task is to strengthen the people's state apparatus – mainly the people's army, the people's police and the people's courts – in order to consolidate national defence and protect the people's interests. Given this condition, China can develop steadily, under the leadership of the working class and the Communist Party, from an agricultural into an industrial country and from a new-democratic into a socialist and communist society, can abolish classes and realize the Great Harmony . . .

The people's state protects the people. Only when the people have such a state can they educate and remould themselves on a country-wide scale by democratic methods and, with everyone taking part, shake off the influence of domestic and foreign reactionaries (which is still very strong, will survive for a long time and cannot be quickly destroyed), rid themselves of the bad habits and ideas acquired in the old society, not allow themselves to be led astray by the reactionaries, and continue to advance – to advance towards a socialist and communist society.

Here the method we employ is democratic, the method of persuasion, not of compulsion . . .

China's new leaders believed that she could not begin a new chapter in her history, as a self-respecting, independent and progressive country, simply by assuming that the degradation, oppression, corruption and violence of feudal China, of the unChinese urban centres, of the foreign enclaves and of the civil war could as a matter of course be obliterated. But, in spite of the United States government's clearly-expressed and clearly-demonstrated interest in a counter-revolution, it was expected that the work of creating new structures, institutions and organizations, forming a new culture, and discovering new ways of doing things could be done humanely as well as firmly and resolutely.

For those who had nursed the new people's China from the days when with Sun Yat Sen they founded the revolutionary Kuomintang and, in spite of all the set-backs, led it to its victory in 1949, the Chinese Revolution seemed to have a profound and complex meaning which few non-Chinese could even understand. Now the leading cadres were dispersed throughout China, very much on their own in a country where communications were poor. In many places cadres who had not had much training or experience were in office. They were all exercising new political, administrative and judicial powers in a great country which once again could 'stand up', and were defending a revolution which had cost China, and them personally (in terms of families and friends slaughtered) a great deal. In the cities, where the level of personal, political and business morality had been abysmally low, heroes of the anti-Japanese resistance faced hitherto unknown temptations, when they had to deal with shrewd and wily businessmen.

As Mao was aware, the question of leadership at all levels was crucial. It was the Chinese Communist Party which alone could provide the far-sightedness, selflessness and revolutionary thoroughness which were needed to carry forward the work of creating harmony and peace in a new China. The People's Liberation Army had been trained from the beginning to be a model of schooling in constructive leadership in new China, 'equivalent', in Mao's words, 'to several thousand universities and secondary schools'. Even as the civil war was going on Mao, early in 1949, had thought of demobilization, or rather, re-mobilization of the People's Liberation Army, a body without a counterpart in any other country. He had instructed the Revolutionary Military Commission then:

> The army is not only a fighting force, it is mainly a working force. All army cadres should learn how to take over and administer cities. In urban work they should learn how to be good at dealing with the imperialists and Kuomintang reactionaries, good at dealing with the bourgeoisie, good at leading the workers and organizing trade unions, good at mobilizing and organizing the youth, good at uniting with and training cadres in the new Liberated Areas, good at managing industry and commerce, good at running schools, newspapers, news agencies and broadcasting stations, good at handling foreign affairs, good at handling problems relating to the democratic parties and people's organizations, good at adjusting the relations between the cities and the rural areas and solving the problems of food, coal and other daily necessities and good at handling monetary and financial problems. In short, all urban problems with which in the past our army cadres and fighters were unfamiliar, should from now on be shouldered by them . . .[7]

The tasks of keeping the affairs of five hundred million people in working order were most urgent, and they were new ones. Rapid demobilization of the People's Liberation Army alone could not cope with them. The Chinese leaders would, if they had not been reminded, have been completely oblivious of the preoccupation of the British, American and other imperialist countries with such matters as the retention of their old privileges, the preservation of the 'Open Door' and the restoration of capitalist 'freedom' in China. The problems and interests of their people, and their own tasks, absorbed their attention. After all, Britain and America were remote foreign countries, thousands of miles away, and *their* people were not in desperate need of Chinese help. And whereas, it seemed to the Chinese, the British and Americans were, with rare exceptions, completely indifferent to or contemptuous of the mass of the Chinese people (and interested only in exploiting them) their own leaders had the totally opposite viewpoint. The new leaders assumed that China and her resources had to be used for the welfare of the people of China, and that their first loyalty as a government was to the Chinese people, not to remote foreign countries which had already helped to ruin China in the course of exploiting and invading her.

China, even if she had to rely almost exclusively on her own efforts, needed to be left alone. The land reform, which began in the newly liberated areas in 1950, was not popular with the big land-

[7] *Ibid.*, p. 337.

lords and their families, whose number was in the millions. A large section of the urban intelligentsia had been well orientated to Western interests and ideology, and their loyalty to a China which was implacably opposed by the West was shaky. The campaign against corruption, bribery and tax-evasion by businessmen also created disaffection. Reforms such as the marriage law which ended the subjection of women would have displeased many men. Moderation in the handling of opposition or disaffection would be possible only if China was left alone. The Kuomintang agents left behind by Chiang were enough of a problem for China's security. There were also 'bandits' (mostly remnants of Chiang's troops), secret societies and other 'underworld' elements which would not be easy to get integrated into a peaceful society. There were natural disasters in 1949 which added to the other problems of breakdown. But China's leaders, like other Asian nationalist leaders who did not believe that they needed foreign tutelage, were confident that they could handle China's problems humanely and efficiently. They had had many years of experience and success in reconstructing on new-democratic lines and governing a large part of China. By 1949 the threat to China's security posed by the presence of Western imperial domains on China's borders had largely been neutralized. The Vietnamese people, it is true, were defending their newly-independent state against an attempt at reconquest, but European neo-colonialism was in serious difficulties. China could afford to turn in on herself, and concentrate on minding her own business. Indeed, for the Chinese China was the centre of attention. Millions of her own people had to learn to absorb themselves in the urgent problems of their country and in meeting her needs. Their way of life had to be 'remoulded' so that they could become responsible citizens – accepting the high ethical norms, the sense of community, the overturning of vicious and false standards and values.

4. The New Face of Imperialism

But from the start the new China faced a powerful and vicious campaign mounted from abroad, which was aimed at undermining the loyalty of Chinese citizens, interfering with China's foreign relations and trade, subverting and overthrowing her government, and attacking her people. Ironically, some of this was financed by Chinese public funds illegally banked in private accounts abroad by Kuomintang dignitaries. American politicians, missionaries and businessmen who hoped to win back the China they had lost formed or supported the activities of the China lobby which prevented the people of the West from learning the truth about China. All but a few of those who had been in China as 'friends' of China appeared to find her recovery of her sovereignty and independence intolerable; missionaries, 'scholars', journalists, and others who had patronized the Chinese now turned quite vicious. There was born a new school of 'China experts', whose function was to distort and misrepresent what People's China was doing, to invent 'facts', and to prevent genuine scholars and reporters from having an influence in normalizing relations. Some of these people, in the frenzy of hatred and resentment, became much more openly racialist in their talk than they had dared to be. Hence there is the revival of the Yellow Peril scare. This anti-Chinese campaign gulled the public into believing that China's former coolies could stand on their own feet, demand the end of the pretended white supremacy and superiority, and take the management of their affairs out of the hands of foreigners only because they are 'brainwashed' and terrorized.

To prevent the American public (which had no reason to hate China) from learning how false the picture drawn by the anti-Chinese lobby was, and how much was hearsay, the United States government banned visits by American journalists to China. Indeed, in the United States during the dreadful McCarthyist purges any truthful account of contemporary Chinese history would have invited disaster for the author. Most China 'experts' who were approved used the McCarthyist style: they made wild, fantastic accusations against China, but did not allow the facts to be known. Thus the myths of the totalitarian monster, the snarling dragon, the Yellow Peril, were born. The virulent anti-Chinese propaganda can only be interpreted as the result of deliberate policy, to cover the hostile designs of the new imperialism.

Much of the foreign-sponsored education of Chinese in China and abroad seemed to have been designed to alienate the modern Chinese 'educated class' from their nation, and to create an elite disloyal to the national interest but loyal to imperialist interests. Foreign control had been eliminated by 1949. But intense psychological warfare of the kind conducted against China from then on, while being of no consequence to the new leaders, was designed to appeal to the westernized intelligentsia on the wavelength to which they had been tuned. This factor, combined with the fact that increasing signs of an imperialist attempt at a come-back to the Asian continent raised the hopes of a section of the formerly imperialist-supported businessmen and landlords, made the revolutionary process increasingly harsher for the beneficiaries of the old order. The increasingly serious threat to China's security made for a correspondingly increasing intolerance of and impatience with counter-revolutionary elements in China.

In the White Paper of 1949, then Secretary of State Acheson, referring to the Chinese revolutionary government, had recommended that the United States government 'should encourage all developments in China which now and in the future work towards (the) end' of an overthrow of 'the foreign (sic) yoke'. United States policy would be based on 'our traditional support for the Open Door and for China's independence and administrative and territorial integrity'. Apparently, imperialist domination was so acceptable to its Chinese collaborators that an uncompromisingly Chinese regime was 'a foreign yoke'. But to China it became clear that the United States was hoping to revive nineteenth-century practices (as the French were doing in Indo-China) when, as General MacArthur had proposed in 1949, an American protectorate was established over her province of Taiwan, and a massive American fleet was in Chinese territorial waters. Apparently it was necessary to have a foot in the 'door' in order to keep it from closing.

The Kuomintang remnants, who had retreated to Taiwan, (after a massacre of the Taiwanese) were set up by their American sponsors there as 'the government of Nationalist China', just as the French had tried to set up ex-Emperor Bao Dai in Saigon as their puppet 'government of Vietnam'. Taiwan thus became an American base on Chinese territory for the reconquest of China. So much, it seemed, for respect for China's 'administrative and territorial integrity'! The American plan became clear when through the United Nations (of which they had taken control) they took further action against China.

When fighting broke out in Korea in June 1950, the Chinese, absorbed in their own problems, were taken by surprise. In common with other revolutionary nationalists in Asia they had seen Syngman Rhee's South Korea as an American colony, which gave the United States a foothold on the Asian mainland. In 1945 the leaders of the anti-Japanese Korean resistance had held a national assembly in Seoul, and formed the People's Republic Government for the whole country. But the Koreans, who had a long tradition of struggle for national independence, found, like the Vietnamese, that they had acted out of turn. Korean independence under a democratic, indigenous government was not on the agenda of the big powers. Their country, without any reference to them, was virtually partitioned at the thirty-eighth Parallel between Russia and the United States. The Korean People's Republic was suppressed, and an U.S.-sponsored 'government' formed by Syngman Rhee outside Korea was imposed on South Korea. Then it began to look as if policies and events were taking a certain direction. A well-equipped and large army was built up by the Americans in South Korea, and by 1950 there was much talk of 'unifying Korea by force'. In spite of the suppression of anti-Rhee elements, it was impossible to get support for Rhee; in the elections of May 1950, there were only forty-seven Rhee supporters in an Assembly of two-hundred and ten. It was clear that even non-Communist South Korea did not want Rhee. Conferences between Chiang Kai Shek, Rhee and the very pro-American President Quirino of the Philippines, then took place. Chiang, as ruler of Taiwan, and Rhee, in South Korea, were both totalitarian rulers hated by the people they ruled over, and desperately in need of an irreversible American commitment to support them against the tide of revolutionary nationalism. Quirino was anxious about the increasingly radical and Asian Asia which was replacing the Asia of the colonial period. But his attempt at a conference in Baguio to enlist other Asian support for a pro-American counter-revolutionary front failed completely. General MacArthur, however, who carried great authority and prestige, openly and aggressively backed the Chiang-Rhee line, and he spoke for many Americans. John Foster Dulles went in June 1950 to South Korea (visiting the Front at the thirty-eighth Parallel), and then to Tokyo, with then United States Defence Secretary Louis Johnson and Chairman of Joint Chiefs of Staff General Bradley. He was reported on 21 June to have promised 'positive action by the United States to preserve the peace in the Far East'. There was frequent talk in America of 'holding the line' – to include Taiwan within the United States sphere.

When the fighting broke out in Korea a few days later, the United States persuaded the United Nations Security Council, without even inquiring into the details, to invoke sanctions against North Korea and to assist Rhee's forces. The United States herself had entered the war. MacArthur ordered the bombing of North Korea and visited Chiang in Taiwan. Chiang then proclaimed 'Sino-American (sic) military co-operation' and a joint 'struggle against Communist aggression'. MacArthur on his part made it clear that the retention of Taiwan and an American crusade in Asia were necessary.

The American-led invasion of North Korea followed. The United Nations, whose American-controlled majority was from China's viewpoint the *façade* behind which the United States and other imperialist governments had been operating, passed a resolution in October 1950 authorizing MacArthur to 'unify' North and South Korea. This would have meant that Syngman Rhee (and through him the Americans) would get control of North Korea, including the great dams in the Far North which supplied some of the much needed power for the industries of North-eastern China. It could have meant even more.

An invasion by imperialist forces of an Asian neighbour and one in which the ruling party was Communist, was difficult for the Chinese to ignore. When American troops, under a supreme commander whose views on attacking China were notorious, drove along the path which the Japanese had once taken, and would not heed repeated Chinese warnings, their ultimate goal could be suspected of being an invasion of China. And Rhee's forces were already carrying out their reign of terror in the areas of North Korea from which the so-called United Nations forces had pushed back the North Korean troops. For China, which in 1949 had thought that, after over a century, an era of peace had begun, the decision to fight would be a costly one. But it looked as if the American imperialists were set on conquering the world. North Korea had been annexed. So, in October and November Chinese troops, at the invitation of the North Korean government, crossed over the Chinese border into Korea to meet the advancing American forces, and drive them back. Just a year after the end of the civil war, China was fighting to defend the new order, with men she needed so much for reconstruction.

But MacArthur refused to negotiate. Even while the Chinese delegation was on its way for talks with the United Nations he decided instead to 'end the war' by a massive victory. In the ensuing battle the Chinese forces inflicted a major defeat on MacArthur's troops. The Chinese asked for a comprehensive peace settlement. President Truman spoke of the United States using the atom bomb on China. The United States wanted to be 'tough' and refused to negotiate with the Chinese the disputes at issue – the invasion of North Korea, the restoration of Taiwan to China, the barring of China from her seat in the United Nations, and others. The American leaders were hysterically anti-Chinese, and determined to fight it out. Why was it so difficult for the West to meet an Asian nation peacefully on equal ground? Was it that the image of Asian coolies submitting to white masters was still persisting? A Western scholar quoted an American general as saying that the atom bomb ought to be used at once on the Chinese; 'they'll understand the lash when it is put to them'. China's proposal in 1951 of a seven-nation conference on outstanding East Asian questions was rejected out of hand in Washington. Having at will outlawed China earlier, the United States in January 1951 had persuaded the United

Nations to brand China, one of the four founders of the United Nations, as an 'aggressor'.

MacArthur, addressing a joint session of the United States Congress and Senate in April 1951, spoke of 'China's lust for expansion', and called for an all out land, sea and air attack on China. The invasion of China from Taiwan and a blockade continued to be discussed in the following years.

The United States, in the course of the discussions on the Korean peace conference, made it quite clear that on a question concerning peace in Asia she would not tolerate participation by India or any other independent Asian state. She had her way, though it was clear that the American threat to China was the chief threat to peace in East Asia.

The pressure of the imperialist threat on Asia, and in particular on China, was never relaxed. As reported on 24 and 25 February 1954 in *The Guardian* and *The New York Times*, the notoriously anti-Chinese, then United States Assistant Secretary of State for Far Eastern Affairs, Walter S. Robertson, had in that January testified to this effect at a congressional inquiry. He admitted,

> (the) heart of the present policy towards China and Formosa is that there is to be kept alive a constant threat of military action *vis-à-vis* Red China in the hope that at some point there will be an internal breakdown . . . a cold war waged under the leadership of the United States with constant threat of attack against Red China led by Formosa and other Far Eastern groups and militarily supported by the United States . . . *The United States is undertaking to maintain for an indefinite period of years American dominance in the Far East* . . .[8] (italics mine)

It seemed generally accepted in the West that the United States government had the licence to act in this way.

The discovery of Ngo Dinh Diem in Japan, his grooming in the United States and installation as Prime Minister of the French puppet regime in Saigon, American behaviour over the Geneva Peace Conference, the special invitation to Syngman Rhee in July to address a joint session of Congress in Washington, and call for a war against China by the United States and United States-sponsored Far Eastern groups, the coming together of the five new-imperial states (the United States, Britain, France, Australia, New Zealand) together with three pro-Western regimes to form the South-East Asia Treaty Organization military alliance – all these developments in the same year, 1954, could not have been regarded by China with equanimity. In January of the following year the

[8] Mr Harold Wilson, referring to these reports in the House of Commons at that time, protested against the policy implied.

United States Congress gave President Eisenhower advance authority to go to war with China if she tried to attack or take possession of various Chinese islands off the east coast. Some of these islands were only a few miles away from important Chinese ports, and they were occupied by United States puppet troops. Their function in America's vital 'line of defence' seven thousand miles away from its west coast was as bases from which the mainland was bombarded, and from which the use of the major Chinese ports of Amoy and Foochow was made virtually impossible. So hysterical was the reaction of some very influential Americans to their possible liberation that in April 1955 the President's military advisers actually recommended a nuclear attack on China. It was the fear that this would lead to a third World War that moderated the influence of Dulles, Admiral Radford, Admiral Carney and others. The 'lesson' that the Chinese were to be 'taught' about American power was not given. As Mr Denis Warner would have known, when he wrote his *Out of the Gun*, it was because the Chinese had the power to prevent a take-over of China that there was no war at that time.

All the aggressive talk and bomb-brandishing of the American government did not make China's reconstruction any easier. At the Asian-African Conference at Bandung in April 1955, Prime Minister Chou En Lai expressed China's continued interest in a sane and civilized approach to American-Chinese disputes. He stated:

> The Chinese people are friendly to the American people, the Chinese people do not want to have a war with the United States of America. The Chinese government is willing to sit down and enter into negotiations with the United States government to discuss the question of relaxing tension in the Far East, especially in the Taiwan area.[9]

This initiative, like other similar ones, was rudely and patronizingly rebuffed by Washington. Efforts to start negotiations for an American withdrawal from Chinese territory failed. American aggressiveness and threats of war over Quemoy were later to be revived in 1958, and the line of anti-Chinese bases and 'alliances' extended.

5. *Who is Menacing Whom? The Chinese Argument Continued*

If one looks at the facts (whether they are reported or not) and does not go by the fantasies of the public relations men, the 'image

[9] This statement made officially at Bandung, was elaborated in 1961 in one of the most important public interviews ever given by the Prime Minister, an interview with Edgar Snow. See *Look*, 31 January 1961. It is reproduced in Snow's *Journey to the Beginning*, (London: Gollancz, 1963), pp. 86-92.

makers' and the propagandists and pseudo-scholars, one discovers that China's independence and security have been and are gravely endangered by the policies of the new imperialist alliances. The propaganda-talk about China's 'xenophobia', 'paranoia' and 'collective mental instability' does not alter the facts. What has made China's enemies so frantic as to concoct every possible allegation about the viciousness and intolerable aggression of the yellow peril is, the Chinese would explain, the steadfast refusal of the Chinese people and government to be intimidated. China stands solid as a rock on her convictions: the policies for social change adopted and carried out in China are the business of the Chinese people, and no foreign government or agency, however much they may delude themselves about the divine right of 'world policemen' or 'super-powers' or defenders of a world of free-enterprise, are going to be allowed to exercise authority over China's affairs.

In fact the fulminations of Dulles and his associates, and the massive display of armed force on China's borders, only served to accelerate the revolutionary process. The same thing had happened when mild reforms during the anti-Japanese Yenan-Chungking coalition of 1937-45 gave way, as Chiang insisted on destroying 'Communism' in north China, to very radical and immediate land reform, in the Yenan-ruled areas of China. The increasing threat of foreign-backed counter-revolution forced very sharp distinctions to be drawn between those who were loyal to the People's Republic and all those who were not. There was less readiness on the part of the masses to give their old exploiters time for amending their ways. The pressures of war from 1950 onwards made the treatment of reactionaries harsher – less humane.

Charges of xenophobia conflict with the facts. The Chinese People's Republic has been absorbed in her vast internal problems, but she has been friendly with and very conscious of her obligations to neighbours in Asia and in other areas of the Third World. The *de facto* expulsion of China from the United Nations and from all international bodies is, as the record will show, the work of the United States and her satellites. Having tried, unsuccessfully, to obliterate the existence of any Third World nation which is completely independent of the imperialists and super-powers, the United States government has resorted to pretending that independent China (or independent Vietnam) does not exist. It is the United States which has done a massive public relations job about projecting its 'image' as a peaceful and peace-loving nation, while being the most aggressive and ruthless of military aggressors. China has her loyalties to the victims of the new imperialism. She can no more 'co-operate' by ceasing from publicizing this fact than she can by surrendering her independence. When the facts are different – when the exploitation, aggression and misrepresentations actually stop – then China can begin saying complimentary things about those who are now giving cause for criticism.

The fact is that China has *never* attacked the United States, or wanted to do so. The off-shore islands are not part of the United States. As Prime Minister Chou En Lai stated to the American journalist Edgar Snow in 1960, there is no clash of interests between the peoples of the United States and of China, and as Foreign Minister Chen Yi said the following year, 'particularly in view of the fact that the traditional friendship between the peoples of China and the United States has had a long history . . . and their relations and friendship have always been good . . .'[10] China has seriously tried to establish friendly relations with the United States. She has appealed for 'cool-headed consideration' of the obstacles to better relations between the governments. In spite of this, the United States government has extended her system of military 'alliances' and military bases to form a ring of massive armaments round China. She has created, at terrible cost to Asian peoples, satellite regimes which will give her land bases on or just opposite the Asian mainland. Submarines with nuclear missiles at the ready are waiting off the coast and sometimes in Chinese territorial waters. An elaborate programme of espionage and subversion is being carried on, with agents of Central Intelligence Agency being dropped in the country. Chinese air-space has been violated hundreds of times by American military aircraft. Coastal shipping has been attacked, and Chinese fishermen on numerous occasions have been killed while at work either simply because they are Chinese or in order to destroy China's fishing industry. Wherever possible imperialists and their agents have tried to stir up violent attacks, on racialist grounds, on Chinese people. Sweet words on either side mean nothing when these are the facts of the situation.

A sentimental 'niceness' to the United States will be highly dangerous for the Chinese, in view of the fanatical nature of anti-Chinese pronouncements of the United States leaders and their supporters. But it is not the mere hatred of a few influential westerners which is the problem for China. The public in other countries looks as though it is being conditioned to accept as normal the mass destruction of Chinese (and Vietnamese) by nuclear and chemical and biological warfare; nuclear attacks on China, for which the United States has been making ready, are given an excuse

[10] *Peking Review*, 14 April 1961.

in advance by the fictitious account of how Chairman Mao loved war, and was quite ready to sacrifice hundreds of millions of Chinese lives in order that China might rule the world after the destruction of the other big powers. So it is possible for United States Defence Secretary McNamara to calculate cold-bloodedly that a single American nuclear attack on China could dispose of fifty million Chinese. Never before in history has a major country whose security is so gravely threatened on all sides, refrained from going to war, as China has all these years.

China maintains that she is not the only victim of a rampaging imperialism. Others are much worse off. Ironically, the very revolutionary and libertarian tradition which China's revolutionary masses believe they share with the American people is now being vilified, attacked and crushed where possible by United States imperialism and its allies in various parts of the Third World. This is the most significant fact about the world situation: the oppressed peoples of the exploited 'countryside', the underdeveloped areas, are rising up in revolt against old and new oppression; to quote Lin Piao's words,

> the courage and spirit of sacrifice possessed by the revolutionary people . . . is a spiritual atom bomb . . . far more powerful and useful . . . than the physical atom bomb . . .[11]

Indeed, all the world is involved in this situation, which is such that China is united with the other revolutionary peoples. United States imperialism is active outside the United States, 'bullying and enslaving various peoples, plundering their wealth, encroaching upon their countries' sovereignty and interfering in their internal affairs';[12] it is this exploitation, rapacity and lawlessness which is the cause of war, unrest and instability. To criticize people who protest against oppression and injustice is to ask that the true nature of the world's ills and miseries should not even be mentioned or discussed. 'Should (the oppressed nations and oppressed peoples) submit and remain slaves in perpetuity? Or should they rise in resistance and fight for their liberation?'[13]

What the Chinese have in mind when they speak of the intolerable oppression of imperialism which causes revolution are specific historical features of our time. Just beyond their own border Vietnam is being ruthlessly destroyed, because the brave Vietnamese do not want anything less for their country than complete independence. The Chinese *know* that United States imperialism's 'new

[11] Lin Piao, *Long Live the Victory of People's War* (Peking: The Foreign Languages Press, 1965), p. 57.

[12] *Ibid.*, p. 53.

[13] *Ibid.*, pp. 44-5.

order' in Asia is much more cruel than Japan's. The very same techniques of 'strategic' hamlets' and 'pacification programmes' are there. The same pious jargon is used to prevent the victims of United States policy in Vietnam from getting even the sympathy of the world. Vietnamese villages and towns have been destroyed in a manner which the German Nazis would have found horrifying; new weapons of mass torture are being tried out. Enraged by the repeated offers of the Vietnamese to negotiate peace only on terms which will preserve their national independence, the Americans have deliberately directed their attack against civilians, including women and children. The Chinese can see for themselves, and can appreciate the suffering of fellow-Asians. They also point to the United States intervention in the Dominican Republic to prevent the restoration of democratic rule, to the invasion of Cuba, and to the organizing of subversive movements and *coups* in defence of the 'right' to foreign economic exploitation. The officially admitted activities of United States corporations, agencies, and 'missions' in such places as Brazil, Peru, South Africa, the Congo, Indonesia and Thailand are the *modus operandi* of a world-wide imperialism which, to use Lin Piao's words, 'sets itself against the people of the whole world, including the people of the United States'. The Chinese believe that oppressed peoples can benefit by studying the way in which Mao achieved China's liberation.

This world-wide oppression, which knows no restraint of law or conscience or respect for humanity, is something which the Chinese believe will one day be overthrown by the revulsion and rebellion it creates among the victims all over the world. It is not for the Chinese to take any initiative or play any active role outside China.

China's leaders feel that they need not respond to insults and injuries done to China which other countries, especially big powers, would have considered sufficient provocation to war. Mature and responsible nations do not resort to force or the threat of force, to settle disputes. Even if they are rebuffed and misrepresented they are willing to be patient as long as the essentials of the new China are not compromised. Their contribution to the liberation of the oppressed peoples of the world depends on the resolute carrying through of China's own revolution. Imperialism, in the long term, was a 'paper tiger'. History is not on the side of reaction. It was important in the short run to be careful, to avoid playing into the hands of imperialism and not to be over-hasty, over-adventurous. The United States, for example, needed a foothold *in* China, to carry out the kind of policies attempted through the Seoul, Saigon and Vientane regimes. Having failed to use Taiwan as a springboard for an attack on China in 1950 and the years following, she tried through an attempt at a two-Chinas' policy to achieve the same purpose. China believes that true democracy will begin to be achieved, and oppression and imperialism defeated, when the world's peoples are ready and able to rely on their own courage, intelligence and leadership to take possession of their own lands, and secure the power to defend them against take-over by the oppressors. Hence her people – over 200 million able-bodied adults – are ready to defend their country if attacked. Of course China's militia is a threat, but only to those who invade or attack China, and to the bases from which they launch their attacks.

Apart from the United States, it is those Asian governments who have been allowing the United States to use their territory for her aggression against their neighbours who are to blame for disturbing the peace. Some of them, China points out, have expansionist ambitions of their own.

Perhaps United States imperialism and its beneficiaries see China as a 'problem' because China not only points to and fearlessly criticizes the world that the new imperialism is creating, but also has frustrated those who are foolish enough to believe in the United States' 'Manifest Destiny', and has shown other victims that imperialism can be resisted. China certainly stands for another world order other than the one which now exists. But it is one in which there is an end to the oppression of peoples by their own or by other governments; it is a more just world, a more civilized world than that which lives by the mighty dollar and the nuclear threat; a world of peaceful co-operation of peoples; a United Nations Organization not controlled by one power or group of powers.

But there is no advantage in dreaming about the millennium. The present is a time for struggle against all that stands in the way of a more civilized world order. That struggle must go on resolutely with the enemy outside and with the enemies within one's consciousness and outlook. The revolutionary commitment, and the revolutionary agencies, must be continually renewed. This is what China's leaders are concentrating on. And they are hoping that all the world's people, because it is their common interest, will join together to break the trammels of the tyrannies, the authoritarianism and the cruelty which characterize the present unjust order.

5

Re-defining the 'Problem' of China

1. Can the Yellow Peril be Taken for Granted?

WE HAVE tried in the last two chapters to capture, with some of the cogency with which it is apprehended by revolutionary nationalists in the non-Western world and particularly China the sense of a continuing 'peril' to China, and to the social order of which it is a part. The attempt we have made, however imperfect it may be, to look over the shoulders of China's revolutionary nationalists at the events of recent and contemporary history – largely at the society which is now preparing to take action against the Yellow Peril – has inevitably made us traverse much more ground than seemed necessary at the beginning. Some, perhaps much, of this ground is unfamiliar to us. Therefore, our attempt to understand, firstly, why a resurgent China has continually been presented by our media of information about current history as fearsome, monstrous, and insufferable and, secondly, our own commitment to thought and action in the face of the movement both in the West and Russia to 'deal with' China, involve us in a considerably more complex effort to define the 'problem' than most of us have cared to make yet. We have to be cautious about the way in which we set about getting to grip with the task we now have to undertake of looking, independently of those who would like to conscript us on one side or the other, at what the protagonists are saying and doing, and of trying to probe their reasons and motives for their actions. It would be useful for us at this point, therefore, to consider these questions: what assumptions we may or may not validly make; how we can reach the viewpoints which reveal in their true perspective what is going on around us; and how we can identify the truly relevant issues.

The two sides – those whom China indicts as imperialists and war-mongers on the one hand, and the China which they on their part denounce and seek to 'contain' as the Yellow Peril on the other – are not themselves engaged in debate about specific facts and issues. The Chinese have ridiculed the stand of their antagonists. Early in 1966 the Chinese newspaper *Renmin Ribao* (People's Daily) carried an article entitled 'Refuting Bundy' by an editorial writer, Observer. It discussed an indictment of China,[1] which appears to have provided much of the material for anti-Chinese books like Mr Hevi's. It said:

William Bundy, U.S. Assistant Secretary of State for Far Eastern Affairs, delivered a lengthy speech on February 12th called 'The United States and Communist China'! It is invaluable material and warrants careful study as it testifies to U.S. imperialism's resolve to remain the enemy of the Chinese people to the very end and reveals its intentions to step up aggression and widen the war in Asia.

Bundy plainly declared in his speech that China is America's 'great enemy' and is 'the most serious and perplexing problem that confronts (U.S.) foreign policy', and that the objectives of the United States and China are 'totally antithetic' in Asia and throughout the world, and that the United States has 'little alternative but to stand up to China' and 'meet [China] with firmness'. He blustered that United States power 'is fundamental' in dealing with China and that 'what we (U.S.) are trying to do' in Asia is the 'containment' of China.

U.S. imperialism sees in China the biggest obstacle in the way of its world domination. Its inveterate hatred for and implacable enmity towards the Chinese people is itself evidence that the Chinese people are among the most revolutionary and most progressive. Otherwise U.S. imperialism would not be opposing us as it is doing now. To be opposed by our enemy is not a bad thing; it adds to our honour . . .

Nevertheless, every thinking person wants to know why the United States has 'little alternative' but to fight it out with China, since the two countries, separated by the Pacific, are thousands of miles apart and since China does not have a single soldier in the United States nor a single military base in its vicinity.

But Bundy tries to pin the charges of 'aggression' and 'expansion' on China to justify the U.S. policy of 'containing China' . . .[2]

The issue of *Peking Review* in which the translation of the article was published contained a cartoon of a huge United States soldier holding up two bombs and rushing over Japan, South Korea, the Philippines, Thailand and South Vietnam shouting: 'The Chinese are coming!'

We must return later to consider the arguments in this article more fully. It represents what answer the Chinese give to the Yellow Peril charges. On the other hands, the appeal for a discussion of issues implicit in the Chinese view finds little or no response in the

[1] United States Department of State Publication 8049, March 1966.
[2] *Peking Review*, 1966.

Western world. Were we right then to ignore the China Problem as it is eloquently defined for us by the majority of experts, and to have started on a more fundamental discussion?

A 'China in Agony', wracked by 'intolerance' and 'terror'; a problem nation on the rampage, expanding into neighbouring territory, subverting and overthrowing governments of distant countries, arming for a nuclear attack on the very centres of the free world! How – in the face of the impressive testimony and the solemn accusations, of both of which we provided examples in the first two chapters – can we withhold our assent to this verdict? Should we not have taken for granted the 'problem of China' as leading Western statesmen, reporters and scholars define it, and discussed only how this problem can be solved as intelligently and as humanely as possible? Was it not presumptuous for us – who, as newspaper readers, members of radio and television audiences, students and loyal citizens, have to trust and accept what expert reporters and analysts, scholars and teachers, and government ministers tell us – to question the correctness, competence or motives of our mentors and our rulers?

Questions like these will have troubled many people who have been aware that even outside China, and among well-informed people who do not represent Chinese opinion, the 'Yellow Peril' arguments are not infrequently received with total disbelief. But most people of goodwill will find it easier to join in thinking about ways in which a nuclear showdown with China can be prevented or put off, in which forbearance and patience in the face of alleged Chinese provocations can be commended to the leaders of the West, and in which a change of heart among the Chinese can be encouraged. One of these ways is to expose what a television programme introduced by the American writer Theodore White recently called 'The Roots of Madness' in China, and to acknowledge that the madness took root at all partly because of seeds planted in the remote past by careless or unduly tactless handling of the errant Chinese by the imperial powers. Our task, these people believe, is to find out how the world can, with a policy of firmness and vigilance on the one hand, and kindness and friendly persuasion on the other, achieve the taming of China's wildness. China, they would perhaps argue, is not the Yellow Peril – not because she is not guilty but because the Chinese are redeemable. The *rapprochement* between the two super-powers, the United States and the Soviet Union, in the last few years makes it comparatively easier for the world's policemen to keep order and prevent China's expansionism and aggressions. In so far as people like these believe that the seriousness of the China Problem has been exaggerated, they would tend to think that its solution is easier than the governments of the United States and Britain believe it to be: they would argue that China can be brought peacefully to stop its attacks on other countries, its planning of further aggression, its sending of regular or clandestine forces to other countries, its threats to attack the United States and Russia, and so on; and that thus all the countries in the world will be won over to support the present international order.

What a number of liberally-inclined people (Senator Fulbright of the United States, for example) would agree with is that there is the need for criticism of the *China policy* of those governments and other groups who are trying to deal with the problems posed by China's intransigence and love of violence by military preparedness, contingency planning for war with China, and hostile criticism of China's behaviour. They would also say that a policy which makes anti-Chinese bases necessary leads to the acquiring of bases in countries on China's periphery, and hence involves the United States in tiresome alliances and conflicts with people in Asia. They would rather see the task of preserving the existing peace given to people who have more pacific solutions to the China Problem. A policy of taking the edge off the discontent of the world's have-nots would perhaps be a more intelligent way of using resources now wasted on military budgets. And China might be made to behave in a less unlawful manner if the West allowed her into the United Nations Organization than if she were outside.

All this criticism of what the United States and Britain do and say to China and her friends is quite consistent with the loyal acceptance as truth of what, in the prevalent view, China is reported to be doing and saying, namely, her expansionism, aggression, xenophobia and totalitarian monstrosity. It is in the proposing of what are believed to be more realistic policies for dealing with the Yellow Peril that they are different.

But we must consider very carefully if we can take for granted either that this large nation is a peril or that its point of view is not justified. Are those who think that it would be presumptuous and even partisan to doubt the highly impressive and authoritative testimony to China's viciousness correct? Do we not have reason to believe that there *is* an urgent 'China problem', but that it is rather different from the one which is described in our first two chapters? Even if the charges against China were made in good faith and on the basis of facts as they are reported to us, do we not tend to ignore other pertinent facts and other opinions which are relevant to the issues between China and her opponents?

Let us recognize this. On the face of things it does seem that, if China's enormous guilt *can* be taken for granted, then the 'practical' approach we have outlined in the last two pages is not relevant. For it gives the creators of what *The New York Times* once described as 'hell' the benefit of too many idealistic suppositions about their good faith and capacity for redemption. Further, what we have been told about China's behaviour by her antagonists is not just about China only but amounts to a comprehensive picture of the contemporary world as a whole, and an explanation of what is happening in a number of countries which are neither Western nor Chinese. And, furthermore, it is no part of intelligence and good sense for any of us to take for granted a comprehensive picture of the world in which we live which ignores those very aspects of recent and current history – what we have called the Chinese view – which, non-Western nations like China are convinced, make up *the* significant pattern of contemporary history. The implications of what we have been doing by our investigation so far needs therefore to be examined thoroughly by all people who wish to have soundly-based opinions.

We began by surveying the grounds on which China is regarded in the West as the Yellow Peril. We have also been taking note of some aspects of recent and contemporary history which predominate in the non-Western and particularly the revolutionary Chinese view. This initial investigation has probably taken some readers much further into world problems involving modern China and Asia than some of them had bargained for. In so far as we are people who want to think and decide for ourselves this is inevitable.

It certainly does not seem likely now that the 'China Problem' is as simple as we are continually informed it is. It looks as if all those who would like all non-Chinese people to approve of, or join in, the condemnation of China as an aggressive, expansionist, war-loving and totalitarian tyranny have yet to make a convincing case if they are to be believed. For they have so far addressed themselves to people who have no background knowledge of East Asian affairs, and may have no independent access to genuine information about them. We need as responsible people to remedy that situation. It is still possible that China deserves to be condemned, even to be 'contained' and 'isolated', as her antagonists want her to be. But this is 'possible' only in the sense that anything, including the American or Russo-American peril, is 'possible'. China has to be indicted, if at all, on grounds other than those which have been sought to justify the Yellow Peril charge. So far this charge has been made on the 'evidence' of assertions which are considerably less and considerably more than the whole truth. It is by no means obvious, for example, that China is an exceptionally criminal element in an otherwise well-behaved and law-abiding world. There is no reason why any curious and intelligent person should accept assertions which are obviously doubtful. It is also not self-evident that the misdemeanours attributed to China, *even if they are facts*, are acts committed without due provocation. Even the argument of *The Guardian*, that the Chinese are behaving so badly today because of their resentment at what their ancestors suffered in the nineteenth century, appears to be invalid and irrelevant as a sufficient explanation when we look at what is happening in our own day in and around China. Before we can decide whether or not others are in touch with 'reality' we had better make sure that we are in touch.

It is of course possible that the facts of the case may appear to those who try to 'look outwards' from China as they do in the preceding two chapters simply because they are deluded or have misinterpreted what has actually happened. But the clarification which is called for is then not the task of 'international applied psychiatry', as Michael Lindsay or U Thant would have it, but the task of research into, and analysis and discussion of, specific contemporary historical events. The exercise of our 'right' to know the truth about matters which affect our hatreds and loyalties, our relationships and commitments, cannot do us harm.

2. *Allegations and Facts*

The issue here is not one whether or not we trust those who keep us informed about current events: those who are calling for a commitment 'to deal with' the Yellow Peril are making demands on us which are quite out of the ordinary. If Professor Fairbank, the doyen of American China scholars, wants us to believe that the resurgence of Asia's, and Afro-Asia's, major nation in the form of the Chinese People's Republic has resulted in the emergence of a 'totalitarian monster', we are being asked to accept something quite remarkable, something which, if it is a secular phenomenon and not a figment of the imagination, is difficult to get hold of historically and sociologically. There are no past precedents for the revolutionary nationalist modernization of a now underdeveloped once-great Asian civilization. In every sense the implications of this phenomenon – the emergence of a totalitarian monster of a nation – for a world in which non-Westerners and non-Western social systems are in an overwhelming majority are immense. The properly intelligent stance in the face of the incredible is not either credulity or incredulity, but an alert scepticism, and in this case a determination to get to the bottom of the whole matter of the miracles of evil which are attributed to China by her enemies, or the miracles of human achievement which, as we shall see, are claimed for her by her admirers. To open the door to doubt about what we are told a thousand times a year is then to open ourselves to fresh knowledge of the nature of the world of which we are a part, and which influences our personal destinies.

To be kept all the time in the world of allegation cannot satisfy us. Allegations must be validated or invalidated by facts. Is 'totalitarianism' a *description* of Maoist China or is it an expression of emotion? Let us take the case of China's 'expansionism'. Specifically what territories has China 'expanded into', and when? Since this question calls for information about the historical-geographical realities with which we are familiar and not for speculation about or diagnosis of intangible experience, states of mind and perceptions, it demands fairly simple answers. For China to expand Chinese troops or other forces will have to have invaded or attacked or otherwise annexed at least a square foot of non-Chinese territory. Where have the Chinese attacked, when, and whom? In what numbers have they attacked? What happened when they did? We need specific answers to these questions. China's intention of attacking or destroying the United States also cannot be discussed as a state of mind, especially when this allegation contradicts important statements of policy and actions. Have the Chinese ever stated that they are enemies of the Americans or British or Australians? If they have, what have they said? On what occasions have they threatened to attack or destroy the United States or other North Atlantic countries? What preparations, public or secret, are they making for this? What is the evidence for the allegations that the Chinese are making ready to launch attacks with missiles, bombs, etc. on foreign territory? The evidence for one set of allegations cannot be just another set of allegations however socially or politically eminent the sources are. One cannot go to party headquarters, propaganda agencies or government or semi-government functionaries for the truth.

We have to press questions which seek to elicit facts from both sides; and these have to be facts which are relevant to the main issues. And in this case we need to have it clearly established that attacks by one country against another, or the occupation of foreign territory, are to be condemned. It is also on the principle that for the troops of any country to move outside their own territorial boundaries except temporarily in the course of driving out an invader is for them to change a legitimate defensive role to an illegitimate aggressive one that we must seek these facts in support of the charges against China. If the facts are not available, or point to different conclusions, then we must make an assessment of our assumptions about Chinese expansionism and aggression.

The charges against China refer to areas of the world in which there have been or are mass uprisings or insurrections, sometimes directed against the presence of the United States or one or more of the other imperial powers. Is China responsible for insurgency and mass opposition of this kind? Would there have been peace if it were not for the work of Chinese agents? In what countries have Chinese agents or military missions been identified? Why does Lin Piao's pamphlet on People's War make clear that self-reliance is essential? Going into more fundamental issues, we must ask if revolts and insurgencies occur only when the rebellions and revolutions are stirred up or organized by others. If not, why have they occurred?

We need to know very specifically if revolts and wars of national liberation from imperialism or despotic regimes are organized by the Chinese or their agents before we accuse the Chinese or make war on them for this crime. We know the allegations of Mr McNamara, Denis Warner and the press in general. The facts in support of them are of the kind which should be easily and clearly established, if they are available. They must be sought, for example, in the historical details of the Vietnamese assertion of independent nationhood in 1945 and their subsequent defence against the French under Vietminh leadership in the years following, in the Indonesian national revolution of 1945, in the Cuban revolution, in the April 24 (1965) uprising in the Dominican Republic, in the South Vietnamese struggle against Diem and the United States, in the Zanzibari overthrow of the Sultan, in the insurgent movements led by Hugo Blanco and Luis de la Puente in Peru, in the rebellion in Portuguese Guinea. The nature of the indictment of China is such that in seeking for the facts on the ground we must get to the truth about situations geographically remote from China. We must get to know something about the world, but we must do so independently of those who see the Yellow Peril everywhere.

In other words, the *truth* or falsity of what China's accusers say (and what the Chinese reply) about the world in which we live is relevant, and that the very fact of our *knowing* whether they are true or false is also relevant and important; till then we can only treat the charges on which the Chinese have been condemned as war-loving, vicious, expansionist, subversive and so on only as accusations which have yet to be proved, and as allegations the truth of which still needs to be established by facts.

If one is asked to say why this hard-headed scepticism, this rationality, is valued so much in a discussion of the subject, one can only say that without it any attempt at objective analysis will be quite impossible. A mere indictment, however impressive the list of accusers, is not reason enough for us to be committed personally. The China Problem is so much taken for granted, and there is so little discussion of the truthfulness or competence of those who tell us that China is evil, that prejudice can easily be taken for judgments. We need rational grounds for believing the amazing things which we have been asked to accept about China and the Chinese people. We need to be sure that we do not have jaundiced views about the non-Western world.

The making of intelligent judgments requires much more thought than the retailing of stock opinions. It depends not only on the ability to get at the facts, and to distinguish relevant or significant fact from that which is of trivial import. It requires also skill in analysis of the interaction of the different parts of the world society which make sociological sense.

Let us try to establish the authenticity, or dispose of, some of the more important charges. For example, there is the allegation that China's revolutionary nationalists are moved by an unmotivated hatred of the American people, and for no objective reason treat a well-disposed United States as a deadly enemy, and educate their children accordingly. There is much in the third and fourth chapters that bears directly on what the Chinese have experienced at the hands of the United States after the end of the second World War. But let us look freshly at some of the 'evidence'.

Mao Tse Tung, in the first of his reviews of the 1949 State Department White Paper, wrote that the various imperialist aggressions against China since 1840 were followed by that of the United States:

(they) were followed . . . finally, by the latest war of aggression against the Chinese people, which has gone on for three years, waged to all appearances by Chiang Kai-Shek but in reality by the United States. As stated in Acheson's Letter, the United States in this last war has given the Kuomintang government material aid to the value of 'more than 50 per cent' of the latter's 'monetary expenditures' and 'furnished the Chinese armies' (meaning the Kuomintang armies) with 'military supplies'. It is a war in which the United States supplies the money and the guns and Chiang Kai-shek supplies the men to fight for the United States and slaughter the Chinese people. All these wars of aggression, together with political, economic and cultural aggression and oppression, have caused the Chinese people to hate imperialism, made them stop and think, 'What is all this about?' and compelled them to bring their revolutionary spirit into full play and become united through struggle. They fought, failed, fought again, failed again, and fought again and accumulated 109 years of experience, accumulated the experience of hundreds of struggles, great and small, military and political, economic and cultural, with bloodshed and without bloodshed – and then won today's basic victory. These are the moral conditions without which the revolution could not be victorious.[3]

In his second article, 'Farewell, Leighton Stuart', Mao wrote,

U.S. naval, ground and air forces did participate in the war in China. There were U.S. naval bases in Tsingtao, Shanghai and Taiwan. U.S. troops were stationed in Peiping, Tientsin, Tangshan, Chinwangtao, Tsingtao, Shanghai and Nanking. The U.S. air force controlled all of China's air space and took aerial photographs of all China's strategic areas for military maps . . . Chennault's air fleet took an extensive part in the civil war . . .[4]

This belief in the slaughter of several million Chinese from 1946-1949 'with United States carbines, machine-guns, bazookas, howitzers and bombs dropped from aeroplanes' made a profound impression on post-war China. For the Chinese revolutionary leaders felt very strongly about the sufferings of their people and the destruction of their land which followed the devastation of the anti-Japanese war.

But is China's sense of outrage justified? Though the killing of a few million Chinese is naturally a matter of little concern in Washington or London, one can understand the offence it might cause in China. But is it true that the American government gave offence by interfering in China's internal affairs and actively helping to slaughter Chinese? The general Western assumption is that United States policies and actions have been only altruistic, and that the Chinese charges are false.

The United States government's White Paper of 1949 does not deny that as a matter of high policy she sought to promote her own interests in China by playing a part in post-war Chinese affairs, particularly in the civil war between Yenan and Chungking. Senior American officers assisted 'the Chinese Government', that is, Chiang's regime. The White Paper, *United States Relations with China*, says:

Any assessment of military aid provided to the Chinese government

[3] Quoted from his 'Cast away Illusions, Prepare for Struggle', *Selected Works*, IV, pp. 425-32.

[4] *Ibid.*, p. 434.

by the United States since V-J Day must take into account the fact that no dollar value can be put on three of the most vital forms of aid – that rendered by Headquarters, United States Forces China Theater, in planning the redeployment of the Chinese army and the repatriation of the Japanese, aid rendered by the Marines in North China in occupying key areas and maintaining control for the Government of essential lines of communication, and aid provided by the advisory groups.

Apart from these forms of aid, the American Government since V-J Day has authorized military aid for the Chinese Government in the form of grants and credits totaling approximately 1 billion dollars. During this same period an additional 1 billion dollars of economic aid has been authorized. It was, of course, inevitable, that economic assistance had indirect military value.

After reviewing the details, it goes on,

It is evident from a review of these transfers of military equipment that American aid to the Chinese Government since V-J Day in the form of materials and services has been extensive . . .'

In November 1948 President Truman had written to Chiang Kai Shek (whose regime was on 22 January 1949 to be described in a public statement by fifty-five representatives of China's democratic parties and groups as 'the reactionary KMT [Kuomintang] Nanking bloc under the wing of American imperialism'):

As stated in my letter of October 16 1948, everything possible is being done to expedite the procurement and shipment to China of the weapons and ammunition being obtained in this country under the China Aid Program.

Various attempts by Mao Tse Tung, Chou En Lai and leaders of other non-Kuomintang parties to stop the civil war and create a coalition government came to naught. But on 10 August 1948 Ambassador Leighton Stuart, then the United States Ambassador to China, from Chiang's capital wrote to then Secretary of State George Marshall,

Even though at present some form of coalition seems most likely we believe that from the standpoint of the United States it would be most undesirable . . . We question whether a Communist government can in the foreseeable future come to full power in all China by means other than coalition. We would recommend therefore that American efforts be designed to prevent the formation of a coalition government and our best means to that end is continued, or, if possible, increased support to the present government.

The appearance of bafflement on the part of people like Michael Lindsay (and even an intelligent and liberal writer like Robert

Guillain) at Chinese hostility to American 'imperialism' is surprising. Chinese anger with America's rulers, and suspicion of their motives, could be the most rational and understandable consequence of their post-war experience. It may be unfortunate, but it certainly is not unmotivated, pathological or excessive; on the contrary, it appears to be healthy and sensible. There are grounds for discussion of the precise extent of American responsibility for what the Chinese suffered between 1946 and 1949, however, there is no doubt about the facts in general. But no evidence is available at all of Chinese hatred for the American *people.* (Hostility to enemies of one's country is a normal attitude, however much we may deprecate it on religious grounds.)

Another common charge against China is the infiltration of other countries by her agents, and their use for the subversion or overthrow of independent governments. But it is not the incredible allegations about illegitimate Chinese activity in Vietnam, Laos, Thailand, Indonesia, Nepal, Malawi, the Congo, Kenya, Ghana, Cuba, Brazil, Belgium and others which we need, but some Chinese 'bodies' and facts. Let us take the case of Brazil since there is believed to be a Yellow Peril in Latin America.

In April 1964 the elected and legitimate government of President Joao Goulart was overthrown by a Western-backed military *coup d'etat* under Marshal Castelo Branco. Nine Chinese citizens in Brazil at that time were seized and imprisoned. They were later accused of trying to change the Brazilian regime and to start a mass revolution. The Chinese were in fact reporters, translators, members of a trade delegation, and men preparing to set up an exhibition in Brazil. It turned out that all of them were in Brazil with government permission, and on perfectly normal business. It was the overthrow of the Brazilian government by people with whom they had nothing whatever to do which exposed them to arrest and maltreatment. President Goulart's government was in fact at the time of its overthrow asserting its independence of the United States, and moving towards deciding its own foreign policy, and the possibility of entering into diplomatic relations with China. It was difficult to believe that nine Chinese civilians, most of whom did not know Portuguese, could have been trying to start a revolution in a vast country like Brazil. There was absolutely no factual support for the allegation of Chinese attempts at subversion in this Latin American country.

It does seem as if it is not at all safe to assume that because indictments of China are backed by statesmen, scholars, church dignitaries and leading journalists they have any basis in fact.

We are not all required to be expert analysts of what is happening in the world. But we can make ourselves alert to 'expertise' which substitutes more or less elaborate rationalization of prejudices, wishful thinking and political aims for close and scientific analysis, that is, analysis that gives facts their true weight and sets them in their proper context of relationships. One of the general prejudices which can prevent us getting at the relevant facts and thus interferes most with our description and analysis of a situation is the identification of our aims as scholars or reporters with what we believe to be the national interest. Another inconvenient prejudice is the general assumption that the status quo has got to be justified against developments or values which challenge it and thus make for social change. Scholars and analysts can also indulge in wishful thinking about the world around them, and try therefore to convince themselves and others that the world is in fact as they wish it to be; they can also be sentimental.

These are general difficulties. The difficulties we have in trying to understand why the resurgence of China is a problem are not ordinary ones. There is something 'special' about China, which makes it a problem for almost a whole generation of reporters and analysts. That something has happened among a quarter of mankind to challenge and, perhaps, affront or threaten the accepted ways of the Euramerican world we can suspect. We have to learn more. But it is not easy to approach what is to be known with minds open to knowledge. For we are thinking about major historical events, and about decisions and achievements of non-Westerners which have changed the destinies of hundreds of millions of men, women and children. Institutions and practices which we may have been taught to regard as sacrosanct have been swept away. We must not ignore the danger of discussing historical events and actions as if goodness and badness, success and failure, could be absolute. To face the fact that they can be only temporal, limited, and relative is not necessarily to be relativistic or opportunistic in our own evaluations. Even those who approve of revolutionary change may demand that action should not be taken unless it is perfectly good. But aims and ideals are distinct from performance in individual human action. They are much more so when human collectivities, especially whole nations, are in action. The final self-caution in our present list is against mistaking evasiveness for moderation. Especially when profound issues are at stake, it is easy, for the sake of being moderate and objective, to take a position mid-way between two so-called extremes – to regard the mediocre and the irrelevant as the standard of good. As most readers will realize for themselves, nothing can be as nonsensical as the result of this tactic. Not only is the midway position probably the status quo, but it may well be the least intelligent, the least realistic and the least aware. Moderation consists, surely, in being collected and honest, in not making hasty judgments or condemnations. It does not rule out the appreciation of enthusiasm, the passion to create or to serve, the dedication to visions or dreams which are not the stuff of everyday life, and the demand for equity and justice.

3. A Proper Sense of Context

The Yellow Peril is the name for something that is deeply feared in what has been called Euramerica – Europe and North America – and among those outside Euramerica whose interests are bound up with the preservation of the West's power and prestige in the world. Some readers of this book may be among those who believe that there should be no slackening of the resolve of the major powers, of the United Nations and of what they call the Free World, to keep the Chinese in their place. They may therefore have wondered why – and perhaps even if it is proper that – there has been in the preceding two chapters an attempt at a forceful presentation of activities and events of the kind on which the attention of revolutionary nationalists in the Third World and especially in China, is often focused. This is not the way detached Western scholars normally write the recent and contemporary history of mankind, especially of the relations between the great powers of the nineteenth and twentieth centuries and China. Non-Western views of the contemporary world, especially when they are formed outside the centres of learning or the international community of scholars, are not normally accepted as scholarship.

This objection must be taken seriously. There have been a few examples of non-Western viewpoints which have been admitted into the literature of acceptable scholarship; the Indian historian, K. S. Panikkar, wrote his *Asia and Western Dominance*,[5] which has been regarded as an eccentric, sometimes biased, but still brilliant work of history. The sociological and economic contributions of the Argentinian, Raul Prebisch, have been admitted. But generally the research and writing done within the Third World (that is, by people who do not take the Western viewpoints) has not been considered of the 'standard' which merits equal consideration with Western scholarship. If therefore the Chinese view is to be taken as more than just polemic, we need to test it more closely by detailed exami-

[5] Revised edition published by London: Allen and Unwin, 1959.

nation of the sources of information, the historical record, the authority of the documents and the thoroughness of the analysis. Quite obviously we cannot do this exhaustively here, since this is not a book of contemporary Chinese history. We shall discuss it later in this chapter, but it is left to readers to do their own research, and to decide how authentic the non-Western view on China may be.

But even if we come to the conclusion that what the Chinese think and feel about American and European actions and policies is reasonably factual, does the Yellow Peril fear, and the policies that follow from it, become invalid? We have yet to go deeply into the nature of the Chinese revolution – the way in which it has affected the Chinese, and the way it has affected the world society in which it has occurred. Further, in the world of harsh realities would it not be sentimental to deny that in order to keep China weak it may be necessary to get the Chinese to fight each other, and necessary even to attack China? The Chinese view is, it might be said, insensitive to, often unaware of, what 'China' signifies to people and governments in the United States, Britain, Italy, Australia, etc. For the latter, that aspect of 'China' that can serve *their* own lives and prestige and influence and activities is naturally of primary importance; what happens in or to the China of the Chinese is naturally a matter of trivial importance. It may be that the Chinese are being spied upon, harassed and threatened by Western forces in the area, and are irritated by all this. But why should people in the West share the Chinese sense of the importance of their own happiness and security and comfort and dignity when these stand in the way of what the American and Australian governments see as their interests? Anyway, what is being done to a 'totalitarian monster' is by definition a good thing. It is also good to do it *out there* if worse things were not to happen *in here*. Is it not the sensible thing for us to look after ourselves by keeping the world the way we want it? From what direction then should we approach the facts?

At the risk of being tediously elementary we need to recollect that 'facts' in human affairs cannot be grasped unless we know what shape they are, what weight they have, at what speed they are being transformed and what their interconnections with other facts mean.

In the determination to be straightforward we may seize on a bare detail of a fact in the record, that is, the historical detail in abstraction from the actual context. But we have then only as good a clue to the realities it originally captured and conveyed as the isolated detail of a photograph gives us to the whole reality of its original subject to which we do not have independent access. Trick photography can give us much fun. If trick history was written only to give us fun it would be harmless. But facts about the actions and sufferings of other peoples are in fact a means of our establishing a relationship with them as people.

As we shall see later, our relationships with the rest of the world of our time (and the way in which these relationships are decided by the understanding we are given of the world in which we live and of the way it regards us) are among the issues raised at a profound level by the China Problem. But for the immediate present we must ask if a proper sense of context makes a difference to the way in which we understand the facts about China. If historical truth is available to us only if events and actions are placed in their proper context, to what sequence or sequences of events, in what series of human interactions, do the present happenings belong? Where in the sequence do they occur? What are their interconnections? There are hardly any historical or sociological facts which are complete in themselves. Even the most skilful attempt to grasp them and convey them intact to those whose experience has been outside the context leaves them incomplete, and drained of some of the life which in their true habitat they pulse with.

For the non-Chinese, even if there had not been the problem of the Yellow Peril arguments to contend with, it would have been very difficult to understand China. But the attempt is necessary all the more now.

It is significant that to many Westerners the Asian countries are 'new nations'; they are 'emergent', and it is their 'rise' which we are aware of. Independence is spoken of as being 'promised' or 'given'. But most Asians do not see themselves as new peoples, or an emergent, nor do they think of their independence as a gift. They think instead of the resurgence of once-great peoples with long histories of civilized achievements, of a new phase in a long and glorious history. There is a world of difference in the outlooks of the imperial nations and of the once subject peoples. Especially for Americans, to whom history in the national, *felt*, sense, is only a few hundred years old, the experience of thinking nationally in a time-scale of millennia must be quite foreign; so must the outlook of Asian peoples who in spite of their non-history in the eighteenth, nineteenth and early twentieth centuries think of a distinctive past and of valuable traditions.

Except for the majority of those who were westernized by Western educational institutions, Asians did not think of themselves as primitive peoples needing civilization. Nor did they think that whatever was achieved in their countries presupposed the tutelage or initiative or leadership of outside forces and organizations. Non-industrial civilization was perhaps non-knowledge to their American visitors, but the Chinese, even before they knew modern industry, knew what civilized living was, what science was, what advanced forms of social organization were. With the rest of Asia they regarded their period of subjection to the Western empires, with their humiliations and sufferings, as an interruption of their own history. That is why the much-publicized mission of the British, the French and the Americans to teach the coloured peoples civilization and how to govern themselves was not very convincing to peoples who remembered traditional civilizations whose origins were contemporary with or much earlier than those of ancient Greece and Rome. In China, for example, the civilization of the 'coolie' replaced that of the 'mandarin', as a British sociologist put it. But the coolie could remember what he once was, and knew what he could be if he made good use of his own resources. In his consciousness he was still being carried on by his own stream of history, not by the alien Western one.

It is not easy for people in Euramerica to get outside their own experience of the world, or to imagine that extra-Western experience is even possible at a post-primitive and post-European stage of human advancement. But an effort of imagination may lead one to understand that the compulsions to Western expansion – the lure of easy profit, the gain in national and racial prestige, the extension of power and all the other communal and individual satisfactions that drove Europeans to world domination – could not be shared except by a very small westernized group in the colonial sector; whose education, as the sociologist would say, initiated them into European (or Euramerican) society. History is made by people, and it is natural that the impetus, the influences, the traditions, the ambitions and the prospects of gain, which have driven Westerners to make their impact on the non-Western world, are not felt intimately or shared by people whose traditions, needs, aspirations and fears have driven them along the contradictory streams of their own, non-European, history.

All this discussion may seem a tiresome digression from the main theme of this book. But we have not till now tried to indicate where one must, from outside, break into, enter, the sequence of events, that is, the resurgence of China under the leadership of Mao Tse Tung and the revolutionary organizations he created, which we are seeking to evaluate. We also mentioned earlier the inescapable task we have of assessing the weight and disposition of the various facts and people we are talking about. In the analogy we made earlier with the photographic detail, we noted that a picture may not give us a clue to information about what is happening to its original: if it is an object we are shown, we do not know whose it has been and is, what uses it has been put to, whether it is moving, and, if it is moving, who propelled it, why, at what speed, in what direction and so on. A verbal record of an event may not have meaning until we know of what act this scene is a part, and what the drama as a whole and who the *dramatis personae* are.

The widely held assumption that Asian societies were static and inert, and waiting to be awoken to progress and freedom by imperialist domination and tutelage is considerably misleading. It induces us to look at China from a direction which exposes to our view few of the events and human and social factors that account for what is happening. Asian societies in the eighteenth and nineteenth centuries were generally passing through a 'low' period in their long history, but there is no evidence to show that they welcomed Western and Japanese rule as their liberation. In any case, from the point of view of the people of Europe and America, the hearts and minds of Asian peoples were in the wrong place. In the preface to his book on Asian nationalism the Dutch historian, Jan Romein, quotes a French Deputy on a point which is now highly topical. It was from a speech made by Jules Delafosse in 1885, when official Annamese (Vietnamese) resistance to the French had finally been broken.

> He who seeks to colonize Asia is dreaming of a utopia. He creates a dangerous situation. He has not considered fully that the peoples of Asia are like ourselves, that they have known a culture that is older than ours, that they have retained the memory of it and take pride in it. They have been in turn conquerors and conquered, and now demand to resume their fight for freedom. It is not hard to prophesy that once they come under the influence of our culture, they will, thanks to the urge towards liberty which is everywhere affecting the world, quickly find awakening in themselves that desire for independence which is at once the predominant aim and the honour of a people. They will be roused to anger and their anger cannot but carry the day, for it is the eternal prerogative of freedom to be everywhere victorious. I am convinced that before fifty years have passed there will not be a single European colony in Asia.[6]

In fact the urge to liberty was shown to be much stronger in the traditions and make-up of the Vietnamese themselves, who bided

[6] Jan Romein, *The Asian Century*, E.T. (London: Allen & Unwin, 1962),

their time and opportunity to reassert their 'eternal prerogative of freedom'. The rejection of subject status was virtually a reflex action of the community, and it turned out that it was French (and later Western) society which found unpalatable and offensive the libertarian and nationalist ideals of the Vietnamese. The Vietnamese example is the clearest example of Asian nationalism, partly because it pioneered the creation of independent Asia and partly because it has been so totally dedicated to national independence. Whatever we may think of them (and some readers will certainly be committed to Western aims in Vietnam) it is important to recognize in them the mentality which has been a vital factor in the creation of what Romein calls 'the Asian Century'. We can understand now that this fanatical devotion to national independence and militant refusal to tolerate what is regarded as tyranny could describe life under French and Japanese rule as a hell: 'the situation between boiling water and burning heat', as the declaration of the revolutionary nationalists in 1941 put it. 'National salvation is the common cause to the whole of our people', as the same document put it. And after setting up the first of the post-colonial governments in 1945 on the basis that 'Vietnam has the right to be a free and independent country', they declared

> The whole Vietnamese people, animated by a common purpose, are determined to fight to the bitter end against any attempt by the French colonialists to reconquer their country.[7]

The point now is not to discuss the merits and evils of this kind of intolerance of the West in Asia, but to understand the thoughts and feelings of non-westernized subject peoples in Asia which led to the resurgence of contemporary Asia. In much of Asia it was less single-minded and less radical, but it is the militants who were responsible for the conflicts which arose between independent Asia and the West. It is with great passion that the colonized peoples feel that subjection, subordination or a less than equal status reduces them to something less than human stature.

It was in terms of their own interests that Asia's revolutionary nationalists looked at the world. Unlike Vietnam there were countries, China among them, which could not act to recover their sovereignty until national unity and social revolution had first been achieved. Then, people were judged to be friends and enemies according to whether they helped or hindered the movement for national survival.

[7] *Declaration of Independence of the Democratic Republic of Vietnam*, 2 September 1945.

The concern of subject peoples was very remote from that of the West or Russia: it was not the promotion of trade or profit for Europe, America and Japan, but rather their own self-preservation and survival. Sun Yat Sen in his opening lecture in *San Min Chu I* asked: 'Is not our China of today, I ask you, in need of salvation?' He said later:

> What is the standing of our nation in the world? In comparison with other nations we have the greatest population and the oldest culture, of four thousand years duration. We ought to be advancing in line with the nations of Europe and America. But the Chinese people have only family and clan groups; there is no national spirit. Consequently, in spite of four hundred million people gathered together in one China, we are in fact but a loose sheet of sand. We are the poorest and weakest state in the world, occupying the lowest position in international affairs; the rest of mankind is the carving knife and the serving dish, while we are the fish and the meat. Our position now is extremely perilous; if we do not earnestly promote nationalism and weld together our four hundred million into a strong nation, we face a tragedy – the loss of our country and the destruction of our race.[8]

The sequence of, the flow of, the road taken by (call it what we will) Chinese history is different from that of European or American history. To recognize this fact is to be sensitive to two things. Firstly, there are certain directions taken, a build up of certain events over generations. The recurrence of peasant revolts is part of Chinese history, and becomes more frequent as China begins to disintegrate, and population pressure on the neglected land becomes unendurable. The Chinese revolutionaries follow a line which leads from these revolts and the Taiping Rebellion to the great revolution of 1924-49. Secondly, the form that nationalism takes is a resolve that China's long history should not come to an end. China must survive and continue her history as China in the modern world. This is the basis of the modernization programme of nationalism.

The passion of the Chinese or the Vietnamese or the Indians who wanted to save their nation from disaster is a motivation for action which others cannot share. The events which are significant in the Chinese perspective, for example, may not even exist as events in the consciousness of those who saw the Western encounter with China as just part of the course of Western, or Euramerican, history. The European or American attitude to China has not been un-

[8] Sun Yat Sen, *San Min Chu I*, pp. 8-9.

changing, but it certainly depended a great deal on information provided by the few people who had visited China for their own purposes.

Before the second World War few people in Euramerica had had much intercourse with Chinese people, very few could claim to have mixed with and known at first-hand the Chinese people in their homeland. There were the Western-educated and the converts to Christianity of whom much was expected. Soong Mei Ling, the influential Christian, American-educated wife of Chiang Kai Shek, was the supreme example of a 'good' Chinese. But the majority of Chinamen had appeared vaguely as sinister and hateful inhabitants of the world of Fu Manchu. A well-known British rhyme expressed what some Europeans thought of the Chinaman:

John Chinaman a rogue is born,
The laws of truth he holds in scorn;
About as great a brute as can
Encumber the earth is John Chinaman.
  Sing Yeh, my cruel John Chinaman,
  Sing Yeo, my stubborn John Chinaman;
  Not Cobden himself can take off the ban
  By humanity laid on John Chinaman.

With their little pig-eyes and their large pig-tails,
And their diet of rats, dogs, slugs and snails,
All seems to be game in the frying pan
Of that nasty feeder, John Chinaman.
  Sing lie-tea, my sly John Chinaman,
  No lightee, my coward John Chinaman,
  John Bull has a chance – let him, if he can,
  Somewhat open the eyes of John Chinaman.[9]

(Though most Westerners would find the rhyme crude, their contemporary notions about China are still influenced by their racial attitudes.) What a Chinese thought it meant to be Chinese and what a European thought a Chinaman was did not exactly agree.

[9] This, and other representative notions are quoted and discussed by Raymond Dawson in *The Chinese Chameleon: An Analysis of European Conceptions of Chinese Civilization* (London: Oxford University Press, 1967). The popular consciousness as well as the basic attitude of many statesmen and journalists, appears to have been formed in more recent times by the role played by 'chinks' in films, crime stories and cartoons. The racialist aspects of the China Problem need to be studied. Mr Stucki, whose book (from which we quote in Chapter Two) has in fact been republished in an American edition, gives an eye-witness account of the Yellow Peril: 'a rather mysterious, half-smiling, half-snarling face, behind which our imaginations can conceive all kinds of demons, a dragon . . .'

4. Getting to Know the China Reality

The fact that China is so momentous an issue suggests that we have a problem or at least a riddle. Why is China being made to appear so vile and vicious? Is it because she is in fact so, or is it for some complicated reason we have yet to discover?

Urged to take action against China, we must take action first to see what is happening in China, what the revolution has meant for its people, what it means for the rest of the poor and once subject peoples of the world. As we saw, what is important for most of the world is not the remote China we see distantly and abstractly and feel so little about in the context of our own Western history, but rather the China of the Chinese. Once we have seen in their intimate context the changes and policies which have been cited as reason for China's condemnation as the Yellow Peril, we shall be in a better position than we are now to understand why there is a China Problem. We need therefore to know about developments in China by reading not just the charges against her, but by reading more basic reports and other studies which are not written from either an anti-Chinese or anti-Western point of view.

How do people in the West get their information about China? Each of us has to reflect carefully on this, as we are often not aware of how we have come to form our opinions and attitudes about the state of the world, and particularly about what the Chinese people are like today. But, generally speaking, Western approaches to information about China are as much influenced and decided by pre-war notions about that country as Chinese opinions of Western actions and motives are coloured by the memories of the same period. What people in Europe and America read and hear about China is about a coloured race, about an Asian people, whose ways are strange and alien. We must, then, seriously examine the traditional consensus about China and the Chinese in which our more recent attitudes are rooted. For the way we interpret what they say and do, the emotional charge we receive when China and the Chinese are mentioned, the assumptions we make about whether they can be lived with as part of the same community, about how honest, trustworthy and intelligent they are, and about their status racially in a world in which Euramericans are the top strata, are all important. How have our basic impressions of China been formed? Firstly, as we noted earlier, the missionaries, businessmen, diplomats and soldiers did much of the reporting about China before 1949. And it is their China which we learned about at school. They naturally presented the Chinese as good or bad according to their own purposes. Secondly, a good deal has been written about China since 1949 by people who either have been expelled by the Chinese government for allegedly anti-Chinese activities or are not allowed to visit China for the same reason. A good deal of material derived from what these old-China hands and Chinese exiles have to say is processed and published by various organizations in the British colony of Hong Kong – the American Consulate General with its large research staff, anti-communist research institutes and others – as well as in U.S.-protected Taiwan, both Chinese-speaking territories. Tokyo is also a centre from which information about China is propagated. But much of the 'research' is done by people who are politically committed. A journal like *The Far Eastern Economic Review*, though by no means in favour of the revolutionary changes in China, is a more detached observer. And, thirdly, there are the Western reporters who report from outside China proper for newspapers, journals, and television and radio programmes which engage, overtly or covertly, in anti-Chinese polemic.

All agencies of contemporary information from outside China share some common sources: Chinese newspapers and broadcasts, the wall posters (which have been plentiful since the Proletarian Cultural Revolution began), and actual reports from foreign correspondents and diplomats stationed in China. Wall posters or *dazibao* are the colourful equivalent of broadsheets or pamphlets through which a vigorous political debate is carried on among those who are basically loyal to the revolution, but disagree with one another about policy. The few wall posters whose contents have in 1966 and 1967 been retailed by the British and American news agencies are the odd ones which have often been copied hastily by Japanese correspondents in Peking, published in a not always accurately-translated Japanese version, and then transmitted via Tokyo to the rest of the 'Western' world; or they are selected ones interpreted by East Europeans for retailing outside China. (One can judge if random selections from the *Daily Express* and the *Morning Star* were offered as a picture of political debate in Britain.) The contents of Chinese press and radio news and comment are available without the middleman in two ways: directly in what can be heard abroad in English, French, Spanish, etc.; the selections published in *Peking Review* and other journals; and in translation in the transcriptions of monitored broadcasts. Much of the documentation on contemporary China becomes available in this way, though it is true that the careful scrutiny of less public material by Western 'intelligence' agencies occasionally makes available documentary material which has more restricted circulation in China.

Another source of information about China includes books, serious articles and films on China and her problems. One highly-important kind of published material is the book which is based on written reports, photographs and analysis by trained observers. But for the ordinary reader who wants to know how he can get trustworthy information about China, and also how the more specialized scholar dealing with China gets his information, the greatest difficulty is not the scarcity of material but the sorting out of the more honest and *bona fide* book or article from that which is primarily polemical or propagandist. The expert reports and discussions we quoted from earlier (cf. pp. 36-37) about desperate famine conditions in China in 1962 would have led people to believe things about China which have been shown to be untrue.

In discussing books about China in the first two chapters we excluded from consideration the books which contradicted the picture given of China as the Yellow Peril. We did that because books which make a matter-of-fact or sympathetic approach to China are not in the West generally treated as dependable sources of information. Those who deal professionally with the publication or broadcasting of reports and analyses of current affairs know that labels which are meant to deny or cast doubt on the authenticity of such accounts are applied. This is logical: if China is the Yellow Peril to Europe and North America, is behaving in a vicious manner, and is subverting law and order internationally, then it follows that any picture of the Chinese as normal people, or as wise and humane and efficient and pacific, is against the policy of the governments, newspapers, and editors who want China to be 'dealt with'.

But this attitude is not logical if we are *not* assuming that China is evil, and in fact want to discover for ourselves what is going on in China, what the Chinese think and say and do, and what China's achievements are. Newspapers and broadcasting systems may exclude those who are not anti-Chinese; but why should we, as those who want to be open to what is happening in the world of which we are a part, do so?

Let us look at the kind of people and books we would otherwise have to treat as suspect, partisan, seditious or 'Chinese propaganda'. There is the American Edgar Snow. From 1928 he was in China as a journalist. Few foreigners in the China of those years saw as much as he did, or got as close a view of much that went on in Shanghai, Peking, Yenan, Chungking and elsewhere. His first-hand report on the revolutionary China which grew round Mao Tse Tung and his colleagues in Yenan was published first in Western journals and then as a book in 1937, *Red Star Over China.*[10] In *Journey to the Beginning*[11] he published more about what he had seen of China. Snow left China in 1941. In 1960 he returned to China for an extensive visit, and wrote a lengthy and well-documented report and analysis of the way in which the revolution had affected all of China, *The Other Side of the River.*[12] In 1964-5 he went back to China and had an interview with Chairman Mao Tse Tung which was published later.

Mr Snow must by the most exacting standards be judged a skilful, scrupulously honest and painstaking reporter in the tradition of the greatest American reporting. He has apparently worked on the assumption that it is quite consistent with his being a loyal American for him to write freely and objectively about a very un-American country, China; he has presented the picture of a China which is as unlike the 'totalitarian monster' of Professor Fairbank (who has never set foot, literally or metaphorically, in post-1949 China) as anything can be. Another source of information is the work of Felix Greene, an American by adoption who went to China in 1957 for the first time to check for himself if all the bàd things he had been told about China were true. Out of this visit and a second one in 1960 there issued the book *The Wall Has Two Sides* (published as *Awakened China* in the United States).[13] Mr. Greene, who clearly went with no more or less ideological commitment or prejudice than any other radically-inclined American liberal, was surprised by what he saw, and impressed. He reported not only what was being done in China, but what he had come to understand of the assumptions and values of the Chinese. On the basis of subsequent visits to China he produced a documentary film, *China,* and also an excellent study of the nature and value of American reporting on China, called *A Curtain of Ignorance.*[14]

Another foreign observer who does not contribute to the Yellow Peril view of the Chinese, but who is at the same time very little inclined to give the Chinese the benefit of any doubt, is Dick Wilson, formerly editor of *The Far Eastern Economic Review.* His visit to China in 1964 was preceded by six years of observation from Hong Kong. His book, *A Quarter of Mankind,*[15] reflects some of the diffi-

[10] Published by London: Gollancz, 1937.
[11] Published by London: Gollancz, 1949.
[12] Published by London: Gollancz, 1963.
[13] Published by London: Cape, 1962.
[14] Published by London: Cape, 1965. New York: Doubleday, 1964. The book is indispensable reading. Chapter 18 demonstrates how reports on China are often written.
[15] Published by London: Wedenfeld & Nicolson, 1966.

culties which any honest Western student of the Chinese revolution has to grapple with. Alexander Eckstein's *Communist China's Economic Growth and Foreign Trade*[16] is an example of a critical but scholarly discussion.

One can also learn a great deal from the kind of 'existential' view of how past and present looks to westernized Asian nationalists, to be found in Han Suyin's excellent *The Crippled Tree* and *The Mortal Flower*.[17] The author, a novelist who lives in Hong Kong and frequently visits China, was formerly married to one of Chiang Kai Shek's generals.

But personal travel to China is even more important than books by other visitors. A good example of what an intelligent non-specialist can learn by visiting China is the informative and amusing *Love and Hate in China*[18] by Hans Koningsberger. One would think that to travel around China, to see and be among her men, women and children, is the best way of getting to know for oneself. One does not need for this purpose knowledge of Chinese, or a vast store of statistical information; what one needs most of all is knowledge and experience of how to live among other human beings, perceiving and responding to the life that is in them, reading what is to be read in their eyes, faces and bodies, taking in the man-made environment with our senses; one needs also an openness to unfamiliar types of experience, the absence of prejudices about Asians which cripple one's faculties of perception and appreciation.

To say that observers who see reason, good sense and virtue in what the Chinese are trying to do are not to be trusted, and then to say that among those whom we can trust there are few people who give a favourable account of China is to be, at best, rather confused. The best reporter is neither the hostile, carping reporter, nor the dreamy-eyed seeker after heaven on earth, but the mature, cautious, sceptical observer, who is honest and candid. There is unfortunately not much of a tradition of Western reporting with respect and perception on what Asian peoples once believed to be helpless and inferior can do for themselves without Western tuition or help. This is partly because of the unfortunate past in attitudes of racial aggrandizement; partly because there was so little to report in the hundred years before the second World War began in 1937. We cannot complain if visitors, like Edgar Snow, to a resurgent China report things which in the tradition pioneered by the missionaries and the businessmen should have been impossibilities.

[16] Published by New York: McGraw-Hill, 1966.
[17] Published by London: Cape, 1965, 1966.
[18] Published by London: Cape, 1966.

What we are told about China we must take with caution, but also with minds open to conviction and ready to understand phenomena foreign to our experience. It is not only the general description of China which gives us the kind of information we need. Accounts in greater depth of what has happened in China, especially the strange events of the revolution, are important. Isabel and David Crook have stayed on in China and have published the results of their intensive study of the Chinese commune.[19]

One of the most outstanding books of this kind, an epic of sociological narrative, is William Hinton's detailed account of how the revolution took place in the lives of the members of a village in the North-western province of Shansi in 1948. Hinton had been sent to China as a tractor technician working for the United National Relief and Rehabilitation Agency. The Agency closed down, but Hinton remained in rural Shansi to teach, and then studied the land reform process. His book, *Fanshen, A Documentary of Revolution in a Chinese Village*,[20] is an unromantic but deeply moving account of what the peasants, whose circumstances had made them mean, cowardly, vindictive, untrustful, learned how to make a revolution. On a smaller scale than Hinton's book is Jan Myrdal's *Report from a Chinese Village*.[21]

There are other kinds of sociological and economic studies. But an essential key to contemporary China is what has come to be called, sometimes derisively by China's antagonists, as 'the thoughts of Mao Tse Tung'.

While honest reports on China by foreigners are valuable sources of information (and thus clues to why there is a China Problem), the best guides to what is happening in China are the Chinese themselves. Outsiders cannot for any intelligent purpose arbitrarily give whatever meanings they please to what the Chinese are saying and doing in China. We do not, let us hope, want to live in the world of delusion and fantasy. It would be better to know what things really mean rather than to give fancy meanings to things and thus cut ourselves off from knowledge.

The best single guide to contemporary China is the writings of Mao Tse Tung. We may not like him or his work, but we cannot ignore that he is by far the most important single personal factor in the creation of the 'new' China. Thought and action were continuous with each other for Mao, and Mao's own life epitomizes China's

[19] Isabel and David Crook, *The First Years of Yangyi Commune*, London: Routledge & Kegan Paul, 1966.

[20] Published by New York: Monthly Review Press, 1966.

[21] Published by London: Heinemann, 1965 (also by Penguin Books, 1967).

development. The Boxer Movement took place when he was a boy. He was a youth when the 1911 Revolution took place and also when Yuan Shih Kai, with imperialist support, supplanted Sun Yat Sen. He was involved in the May 4 Movement, the formation of the Chinese Communist Party, the formation of the Kuomintang Government of 1925 and the Chiang *coup* of 1927; he led the formation of the Kiangsi Soviet and the Long March to Yenan. He is certainly the heir of Sun Yat Sen.

Leading people, teaching others to lead China into a new era, as he saw it, Mao used his speeches and writings to teach, to argue, to demonstrate what was happening. The four volumes of his *Selected Works* up to the end of 1949 contain many items which get their fullest meaning when seen in the context in which they were first written or spoken. Many of Mao's teachings, which have both a Marxist and a classical Taoist-Buddhist style, are very simple. The slogan *Serve the People* was at first the title of a sort of homily for the funeral of a revolutionary worker. It is now one of the themes of the ideal which people at all levels of leadership are continually exhorted by Mao and his followers to realize.

It is in Mao's writings more than anywhere else that the rationale of revolutionary China's programmes and policies, goals and methods is spelled out. For that reason the only label which adequately describes the kind of China which is now coming into being is *Maoist*. It applies to the Marxian way in which the categories of Chinese and world society are defined and distinguished, to the mode of analysing contemporary society-in-change, the evaluation of social purposes, and much else. Before we can talk sense about China we need to understand the inheritance, the problems, the goals, the motivations and the achievements of Maoist China. Undoubtedly there have been and are within the ranks of China's revolutionary nationalists differences of opinion, divergencies of aim on certain matters; there is controversy; and on occasion, as we shall notice, Mao has not been able to carry his colleagues with him, and has deferred to them. But basically it is Mao who since the 1930s has been the most important single person among China's nationalists – both Communist and non-Communist. And though other policies have at times been followed, it is in the long run those following Mao's line who have given shape to contemporary China.

The term 'Communist' has so many connotations which are mutually contradictory, and which are irrelevant to the Chinese revolution, that we would do well to use it only when it is the only and correct term to use. Our main concern here is about China, the nature of her resurgence, and why she is a 'problem' and a 'peril' for some people. The focus now is on China. There are less essential questions which are interesting but which are irrelevant here. Among the parties which call themselves Communists the Communist Party of China is one. What does Communist mean? Among Asian nationalist leaders one of those most influenced by Marxist ideas is Mao; this is of interest to students of Marxism. Among writers on war and strategy, Mao is one; Mao is therefore also of interest to students of war and strategy. But these questions are not of fundamental interest to China's hundreds of millions, nor do they touch very much on the destinies of the twenty-five hundred million non-Chinese in the world.

We will gain more if we left it to be discovered what the essential nature and importance of China is. Among the least reliable guides to China are the professional 'Kremlinologists', who have as little of a clue to the meaning of the peculiar political jargon of the Chinese revolutionaries as the Russians have. What the Chinese say is rich in Chinese allusions and most of us can at least keep that fact in mind if we are not to make fools of ourselves.

6

The Chinese Revolution: Some Human Implications for China

THE LARGE and general issues we have just now been touching on may have made the reader impatient to get back to our subject. But what is our subject?

It is sometimes necessary for us to force ourselves to focus our minds on what has been and is happening in China, and to take in the realities before we begin to denounce or admire, march or counter-march, mobilize for attack or for defence. China is not merely, as this book has so far persisted in trying to say, a cause or an anti-cause, a set of slogans or anti-slogans for non-Chinese who have had no normal and civilized relations with the Chinese; it is a reality of flesh and blood, which can stand up and speak for itself. If any one wants to denounce or march or attack it is his own business. But all of us non-Chinese must address ourselves to the men, women and children whose land China has traditionally been, and try to listen with imagination and discernment.

1. Four Preliminary Points

What is the China reality? Can we, who have not experienced it, understand it?

Most of us, even scholars, have enough difficulty in getting an unbiased, coherent and accurate picture of what is happening in our own country, with whose background, history, language and social system we are familiar, and to every part of which we have personal access. We know as a matter of fact that what is solemnly declared or reported by politicians, journalists or scholars is often not true, and may even be intended to deceive or mislead us about the situation in which we live. Usually what even the most expert reporters publish is treated as controversial. Most intelligent people know so much of the background that it is only for short periods that they can be fooled. On the affairs of most North Atlantic societies a vast deal of carefully checked published material exists. But the stage which sociological and political studies of Third World countries has reached in Euramerica is still primitive. Wishful thinking and writing which are intended to deceive, incompetent scholarship and sheer ignorance about the Third World are not subject within our societies to the kind of close, well-informed scrutiny that good scholarship thrives on. We are always ready to believe strange things about strangers. Crude pseudo-sociology of the kind which can lead the author of the much-quoted *Oriental Despotism*, the Marxist Karl Wittfogel, to make the patently false prediction that China was moving towards a state of 'general slavery' is still too common in Western studies of the Third World.

The sociology and history of this society with this enormous membership which has persisted continuously and taken its peculiar course for three thousand five hundred years is still in its infancy. Various ideological interpretations of 'China' have been made, but they are not necessarily the same as the actuality. Our answers to questions such as how much and how fundamentally China changed over her long history, what China and being Chinese means can only be tentative.

Secondly, China has been and is predominantly a country of peasants, not of just peasants but Chinese peasants. In most Asian societies it is the village and not the town that is the unit of society. Even the large cities are sometimes clusters of villages. In China, there is reason to believe, it is the structure and activity of village life which has been the economic and political mainstay of China for thousands of years. The dynasties came and went, the capital cities were often in chaos, there were invasions and revolts, manufacture and trade was on occasions seriously disrupted, and yet 'China' persisted. This was due partly to the scholar gentry who continued to perform administrative functions, partly to the power of Chinese culture to 'absorb' invaders; but most of all to the fact that it was the Chinese peasants who were repositories of the Chinese tradition.

The villages were in significant ways self-sufficient, and important contributors in taxes and other services to the maintenance of government and the more conspicuous aspects of Chinese 'culture'. In other ways, too, their historical role and contribution to the Chinese tradition of political change is important. Peasant revolts were frequent in China, and time and again they played a vital role in the overthrow of kingdoms and imperial dynasties. Though China has been, like most of Asia, a predominantly rural society remaining virtually unchanged over many centuries, Chinese peasant society has features which are absent from the traditions of the Indian subcontinent, for example. The peasants' key role in the revolution which brought them to power over all China in 1949 was not due to any eccentric notions of revolutionary leaders like Mao.

The lushness of the vegetation and the easy climatic conditions in some parts of tropical Asia makes life comparatively easy where social conditions permit. But China's peasants have always been extremely hard-working, intelligent, frugal and ingenious. Periodic droughts and floods, hunger, poverty and starvation have been their perennial enemies. China has not been a nation of Confucian philosophers. In proportion to her size and population China's animal population, apart from pigs, was very small. This was probably because a larger number of draught animals, for example, would have added to the strain on the food resources – except in the thinly populated grasslands of Mongolia. Consequently in many parts of agricultural China the animals available for ploughing and transport were not adequate. The peasants who laboured included in their tasks many of the economic functions of animals in agriculture. They were the beasts of burden, and the suppliers of manure, and the draught animals. But even such hard tasks did not make labour undignified or mean. The fruits of work were treasured, and used frugally; wasteful and 'conspicuous consumption' by the rich does not seem to have been a feature of ancient or mediaeval Chinese life.

Traditional China also does not seem to have provided metaphysical and other-worldly palliatives for social and political injustices or discontents; a practical approach to life helped people to see that they had human causes. There was no economically parasitical Brahmin class which held power; society was not elaborately graded; and recruitment to and membership of the important scholar-bureaucracy was not restricted according to birth or wealth, though wealth was a significant factor. It was a society in which learning in the practical arts as well as the classics was highly valued. The comparison of mediaeval China with mediaeval Japan, Europe and India is by no means to China's disadvantage.

Cities in the modern sense, when they developed, were a non-Chinese type of development, and those who lived and worked in them appeared in terms of traditional China to be a lower order of being. Merchants had never been held in high regard for a variety of reasons. The contempt in which the so-called 'compradors' of the period after the Opium War were held derived as much from traditional attitudes to people (including soldiers and bandits) who did not make an honest living either as farmers or scholars as it did from nationalist resentment at those who were associated with the 'foreign devils'.

Thirdly, much of the reason why Chinese society has certain features which have persisted is her geography. (This is a truism, but it is often ignored.) Roughly of the same size in area as the United States, Brazil and Canada, China is virtually a continent of peoples or nationalities. It is dominated by four historic areas of concentrated population – centred, respectively, on the fertile plain of North China, the middle and lower reaches of the Yangtze river, the river deltas and coastal plains of the south, and the Red Basin of Szechuan province. The climate and the type of crops cultivated vary tremendously in these regions, but all of them make cultivation and communication easy. The traditional method of intensive cultivation has appeared to be impossible in the rest of the country. There is, therefore, good reason why nine out of every ten Chinese live in much less than a third of the country's area, to the south and east.

In the grasslands of the north, and the mountains and deserts of the west, have lived for centuries considerably more backward sections of the Chinese population, nomad-style on the grasslands, at a comparatively primitive level in the areas of poor soil. These parts of China were neglected in the past. Everyone knows that several of the world's highest mountain ranges are in China, though few associate the problems of life in China with those of how to live in these areas. The image people may have of bamboos, rice-fields and tea fits mostly South China. Further, most of us cannot enter into the way Chinese from Szechuan or Hunan may regard those from Chekiang or Kwangtung or Heilungkiang. Canton, for example, is not just a provincial city.

For all the industry of the Chinese in the past, the standard of living was very low. Before the second World War the annual income per head of population was estimated at only twenty-seven dollars. By the end of the nineteenth century the traditional crafts had been destroyed. The imperial administration's discouragement of independent commercial activities and of modern technological education had prevented the growth of an indigenous mercantile sector, as in Japan, and industrialization. China, like the rest of the Third World, had, apart from the food-producing activity of the peasants, a colonial economy; but it was not even engaged in primary production for export. It supplied cheap labour for foreign enterprises in China and other parts of the world.

Fourthly, the Chinese Revolution cannot be dated simply as having 'happened' in 1949. It is a legitimate controversy how far back it began before 1927 – the year when Chiang's *coup d'etat* broke up the revolutionary Kuomintang of 1924-5, and turned it into a rather anti-revolutionary body. We need to discuss this later on. But the Maoist revolution was certainly already active in 1927. For Mao Tse Tung's early revolutionary ideas had already created the basis of a Chinese government with a clear territorial base by the time the Japanese attacked it in 1937; and by 1945 had won the allegiance throughout North China of most Chinese who had not co-operated with the Japanese.

The Revolution did not end in 1949. It was clear that it was going to be a long process. This was a continuous revolutionary process, as more and more people followed the lead given by the thinking, teaching and actions of Mao Tse Tung, and joined the leading revolutionary organizations, the People's Liberation Army and the Communist Party of China.

From the revolutionary nationalists' viewpoint the 'gun' out of which grew their power to 'liberate' their country came first into their hands when China's 'Red Army' was created in 1928. China had known countless armies which were perfectly useless for national security, but which preyed on and terrorized the people, recruited by press-gang methods, and with a few exceptions were the lowest form of Chinese society. (It was not unimportant that Chiang, a military leader, a generalissimo, using military methods, was more respectable and impressive in foreign eyes than in Chinese eyes.) Conceived by Mao Tse Tung, Lin Piao and Chu Teh, the People's Liberation Army was a fighting corps of model citizens of the new revolutionary China-to-be. It was not an 'army' in the professional sense. Its members did not live off other people like bandits, but lived alongside them and worked with and sometimes for them. Since 1949 it has, in spite of conflicting opinions within China's leadership, continued to be an organized, political elite highly trained for broadly revolutionary, pioneering functions. In ending the civilian-military dichotomy China's leaders have attempted the 'civilizing' of the military role and the disciplining of the role of ordinary citizens. The role of the People's Liberation Army in the launching of the Proletarian Cultural Revolution in 1966, and in leading the 'triple revolutionary alliance', which ensures continued mass leadership in China, has been crucial. Lin Piao's nomination as vice-chairman is a safeguard against military rule in China.

The break-up of the Kuomintang after Chiang's bloody purge of its revolutionary elements in 1927 left China without a revolutionary nationalist party for a while. The Communist Party of China under pressure from Stalin was tending to go the way of other Communist Parties – with their dogmatism and Comintern control. In 1934 Mao and his colleagues were able to get control over its thinking, policy and organization, and thus turn it into a political party which could work in a systematic and disciplined manner for the task of building up a new China. Whether it is mostly owing to the genius and quality of Mao and his associates, or to the accuracy and appeal of its political analysis and programme, or to accident, the Communist Party of China played the leading role in bringing about China's resurgence. The strategy which brought China's revolutionary nationalism to success, and the goals and methods in new China's reconstruction, have, as a result (or cause) of the role played by the Communist Party of China, been considerably influenced by the assumptions, insights and methods of Marx and Lenin.

Since the early fifties, however, the attempt to create other types of revolutionary leading organizations to supplement or supersede its apparatus appears to have been very much in Mao's mind. As a disciplined, clear-sighted, honest revolutionary organization dedicated to serving the Chinese people, the Communist Party has been found to be wanting. Some of the people in the top rank as well as the lower echelons of 'cadres' have manifested too much of the love of rule, the personal exploitation of office, the dogmatism and the contempt for people which it is the aim of the revolution to eradicate. The revolution-making process has been continuous, and more and more people have been mobilized to 'make revolution'. This does not mean that any comparable organization has been found yet to replace the Party, which still has large numbers of people of the type Mao seeks to serve China. The need to defend the revolutionary order against the danger of foreign-based attempts to overthrow it has created also the problem of ensuring security while the revolution continues, that is, to ensure that the freedom necessary for political initiative to come from the masses is not used by counter-revolutionary forces to build themselves a base within the country.

2. *The Impact of the Revolution*

(*a*) *On Traditional China*

In so far as there was anything left of traditional China a hundred years after the first Opium War, the Maoist revolutionary transformation of the country has had a profound effect on it. As we noticed, the revolutionary process had for years been developing as it encountered, was resisted by and sought to change the existing order. Precisely because Mao was not a dogmatist with programmes ready-made elsewhere, specific conditions – psychological, structural and others – were intimately studied, and thus deeply affected.

China, as it was pointed out earlier, had never been a nation of Confucian philosophers. Her traditional culture had been much more complex, especially at the village level. But Confucian ideas of order, authority, obligation and decency had virtually been perpetuated in the seemingly indestructible Chinese villages. Some of these notions were not peculiarly Chinese. The notions that justice is what is meted out by the authorities, that the good citizen is, above all, law-abiding, that the luxury and power of the rich have nothing to do with the poverty and helplessness of the poor, that truths are embodied in tradition, and others, are fairly widespread. The notions that the lives of the kings and gentry, the agonies of lords and ladies in love, the dreams and aspirations of those in power, are far more 'important' than anything the ignorant poor can think or feel were also widespread.

A China in which the 'revolutionary rebel' is the model of the good citizen has come a long way from traditional China; from the viewpoint of which there appears to be no sense of order or decorum in China today. Nothing seems to be sacrosanct any more. Anything or anybody can be questioned, doubted, put to the test, criticized, ridiculed, challenged to account for itself or himself. All decency has been stood on its head. During the Cultural Revolution, there was great indignation expressed about the inconsiderate way in which workers under contract labour in some construction-projects had been treated, while at the same time the head of state, a most distinguished man, and his wife were subject to humiliating treatment. Popular drama is insensitive to the terrors experienced by landlords and their families during land-reform, while it weeps over the emotions of peasants who have been given a fraction of an acre of land. In many respects, therefore, the whole ethos has changed.

But in other respects China is much more deeply Chinese than it has been since the Opium Wars. Can one not say that there is a true sense in which 'the mandate of Heaven' is felt to have returned to the rulers in Peking? The return to the peasantry, the emphasis on the dignity and application of the peasant-farmer as the model of hard work, co-operative enterprise, and the sense of dignity of and honour for things Chinese seem to prevail.

(*b*) *Conditions of Life*

A veteran journalist who had travelled in China and written a book in which he recalled seeing abandoned, dead, infants and hearing of cannibalism in the old days was taken to task by a China expert for making it out that the Chinese in pre-revolutionary days were 'eating each other's thin babies'. Undoubtedly, there were lots of fat babies in the parts of China ruled by Chiang, and few of them were eaten. But not only was infanticide practised in China, but thousands of people died prematurely every day because of the desperate conditions of life. That in the oldest of the surviving major civilizations people were driven to cannibalism was no myth or creation of political propaganda, but a simple fact. Millions of Chinese had been through the experience of feeding, in times of peace, on leaves, barks of trees and straw. In normal times, many of them had only one meal a day in winter. In some parts of China people were fortunate if throughout the year they could continue to have the unvaried and monotonous diet, of which vegetables, fruit, meat or fish hardly ever were a part. Any notions we may have formed that the vast majority of China's people would have seen or sniffed the delicacies we associate with Chinese cuisine we must discard. Those who find it difficult to imagine how short of the expectations of a sensitive and civilized people life fell would do well to read some of the life histories recounted to William Hinton, and recorded in his *Fanshen.*

What may seem to us absolutely incredible was endemic to China when famine struck a whole region, as it frequently did. The scene has often been described. One of the most easily accessible is the account in *Journey to the Beginning* of what the young Edgar Snow saw on his first visit to the interior of China in 1928. For many Chinese still living these are available not as literary accounts but as painful memories of things seen and done.[1]

Life was also precarious for the majority of Chinese, in the same way as it was for most other Asians, because the general breakdown of society just before and during the colonial period had contributed to the growth of diseases like plague, cholera, small-pox, malaria and typhus. China had far fewer doctors than India. In addition to disease there was the insecurity of life in places where crime and banditry were unchecked. All this added up to a situation where, except for a small minority, life was not worth much. Even as a child one could not count on having the care and protection of one's parents: a child could be sold into servitude or slavery, not because it was not loved but because it could not be fed. At the end of the civil war the salary earners in the Kuomintang area experienced the

[1] R. H. Tawney, *Land and Labour in China* (London, Allen & Unwin, 1932). Among works on China by non-Chinese this book is distinguished by the quality of its scholarship as well as by its tone and its insights. The suffering of poor peasants in at least some parts of China in the past is vividly described in the case-histories given in William Hinton's *Fanshen.*

insecurity of not knowing from hour to hour if the money they had earned was worth anything at all; the fantastic personal tragedies to which the inflation created by the corrupt Kuomintang gave rise have often been described.[2]

What has the revolution done for people who craved for the end of insecurities of these kinds? This is not easy to answer. There is a great deal of evidence to show what life was like up to 1949. But precise and full details about the effect of the revolution are not always available. The reported elimination or control of the diseases mentioned, as well as other scourges like venereal disease, have been an achievement which, for anyone with knowledge of similar situations, is difficult to believe; but there is no reason for disbelieving the reports. The strict sense of hygiene in revolutionary China has often been noticed, and one can only assume that if flies, rats, mosquitos and other sources of infection are still around they cannot easily be hidden from people who see China at first hand. Food is rationed, and the basic necessities are sold at controlled prices well within the purchasing power of even the least paid worker. China since the revolution has had natural disasters as bad as any in her history, with the consequent loss or disruption of production. In the unprecedented disaster years of 1959-61, typhoons, floods and droughts hit different parts of the country at the same time, setting her back considerably. But even hostile reporting has made it clear that the austerity, which was only temporary, was shared equally by all. Chinese people in the more remote areas seem now to be secure against the kind of death or great suffering that comes from starvation or extreme forms of malnutrition, even if China were to undergo foreign attack. In normal times rations of vegetables, meat and fish are available to all of her vast population; most people are getting more in a year than they could have hoped to get in a lifetime. The government also, in spite of the obstacles it has had to overcome abroad, has bought grain from abroad to ensure a reserve. Quite definitely the uncertainty that millions of Chinese used to feel about whether they would survive from one year to another has disappeared. That freedom from hunger, and from the fear of hunger, has been achieved is a fact that became very clear during the vigorous political activity of 1966 and 1967.

Inflation was wiped out virtually at one stroke at 'liberation'. The feat was a product of currency reform, honest administration, a new marketing system and remarkable economic sophistication. And in spite of the fluctuations in the economic situation, inflationary

[2] A recently published account is one by a missionary: William Sewell, *I Stayed in China* (New York: International Publications Service, 1966).

tendencies have been kept strictly in control. Varying pricing systems for staple commodities and for luxuries during the time of food shortages prevented prices of necessities from rising and a sizeable black-market from developing. It will be some time before the Chinese produce or secure by trade all that they need, but they are on the way towards this goal; in the meantime, what is earned by hard work is guaranteed to command everything that is needed for an equally frugal and healthy life for all Chinese.

Banditry and crime appears to have been eliminated throughout China – though there are some areas on China's frontiers and coast where, for special reasons, life is still a little insecure. This is related to the old experience people in China had of not being secure against foreign attack. How far the Revolution has been able to protect China in this regard we must consider later on.

(c) *The Rural Economy*

Though they were very important for China's economy and political stability, the peasantry of China as a whole in modern times had a low status, and little attention was paid to their needs and problems. Among them, however, were a number of lardlords and rich peasants, who enjoyed a relatively higher standard of living, a wider range of educational and economic opportunity for their children, and political power in the locality or province.

Landlords and rich peasants belonged to the two highest of the strata into which the peasantry, by their landholdings and status, were divided. Broadly speaking, they were the 'gentry'. Landlords owned a good proportion of the best land, the farm animals and the implements needed for cultivation; they not only rented out their land but also made money or acquired land through usury. They may have lived in the nearby town or provincial capital, or they may have lived in the village without working in the fields. Landlords were not a class, since it was possible within the same family to have landlords and poor peasants or hired labourers. 'Rich peasants' worked on the fair-sized plots of land which they owned, along with the necessary animals and implements, and could afford to engage hired labour. 'Middle peasants' were those who were independent small farmers who worked on their own land, using their own equipment and animals for ploughing. 'Poor peasants' had small plots insufficient for their subsistence, and had to make part of their living working for hire for landlords or rich peasants. In a purely agricultural community, those, apart from the artisans, who owned none of the means of production had to work as hired labourers. Those who toiled in the fields toiled for long hours, and it was their skill and persistence in working in primitive conditions which sustained the community. The rates of hire were low, rents and taxes were exceedingly high, and rates of usury were also high. Industriousness did not save peasants from starvation and death.

Feudalism in the European sense of the term did not exist in China; nor do there seem to have been communal forms of landholding as there were in other major Asian societies such as the Indian and the Javanese. But though the land was individually owned, the landlord-tenant relationship determined the social order which had persisted throughout Chinese history. It was, in practice, the landlords and rich peasants who had the opportunity to undertake political and other leadership functions, and thus exercise authority over those whom they were in a position to exploit economically. The difference of position became important in mediaeval China where the provision of labour for public works, conscription and such services was concerned. During the Chiang Kai Shek period the rising discontent of the middle and lower peasants and hired labourers on the one hand, and the policy of Chiang's clique of controlling and suppressing this through the gentry on the other, developed the long-standing antagonism between the gentry and the mass of peasants into mutual hatred.

The final stages of the civil war, when those whom Chiang represented threw all the resources at their disposal into the effort to crush the forces represented by Mao, ended with the overthrow of the former and the establishment of the Chinese People's Republic. Many of the most unscrupulous and ruthless elements in the Kuomintang had not expected the revolutionaries to win, and had therefore not been cautious about what they did to the men, women and children in their power. In so far as the old order (comprising the landlord-gentry on the one hand and the proletarian peasants on the other) was one of oppression and exploitation; these were built into the fabric of twentieth-century peasant society. Chiang Kai Shek, the Chen brothers, the Soongs, and their associates had fled when they saw entire divisions and armies go over to the victorious People's Liberation Army in 1949. But in almost every village the local tyrants who had taxed, fined, evicted, raped, imprisoned and executed at will were still there dominating the villages and exercising their cultural and psychological hold over those who had feared them; and the landlord-tenant basis of economy and society was still intact outside the areas which had been administered by Yenan before 1949.

The revolutionaries who had succeeded in seizing power were predominantly peasants, and were well aware of the fact that the revolution which had brought a peasant 'dynasty' to Peking had not automatically brought power to peasants in the villages of central, east and south China. In 1949 it could still have been, in spite of the existence of the People's Liberation Army, like the other revolutions in which peasants temporarily overthrew dynasties, only to find that their own living conditions had not changed. Mao Tse Tung, who in 1927 had learnt a great deal by watching the peasant uprisings in his native province, knew what a local revolution was like. Now the land reform, which was carried out in the whole country apart from Tibet, was going to be the revolution at village level. And it certainly was, as Mao had said, no 'tea-party'.

Though the landownership system had been sanctified by the practice of over three thousand years the landlords' and rich peasants' 'excess' holdings were expropriated on the assumption that the wealth and power of the gentry was based on the expropriation of the fruits of the labour of others. The landless were given land to cultivate; peasants who had lost their land to landlords or usurers, or who had never had land, had as a result of land reform land of their own. But land had been cultivated so intensively for so long that there was in any case not much land to go round. William Hinton in his *Fanshen* describes in fascinating detail how in the land reform in Long Bow village in 1948 the poor peasants had been disappointed by the amount of land and implements which were turned in by the landlords and rich peasants and thus became available for redistribution.

Was all that the peasant wanted a plot of land which he could call his own, however poor in quality it was? It is difficult to say. What people 'want' is not easy to determine; what they can conceive in terms of the society they have known, and what they can conceive when they can imagine practicable alternatives which could be more deeply 'satisfying' are matters for discussion.

As a result of the revolution agriculture was the key economic sector in a badly underdeveloped country which had very rapidly to build up a greatly expanded and diversified economic base with negligible foreign assistance. China was poor enough before the Japanese attacked it. And irrigation and other services to agriculture had been so badly neglected at least for a century that production was very inefficient. By 1949 the economy was in a sorry condition. How, out of an agriculture which had failed to keep the population even at subsistence level, and the nascent industries, was the country going to find the capital to construct the basis for a new economy which would prosper enough to raise the living conditions of the people on whose behalf the government was acting? This complex question was intimately bound up with the problems of agricultural production and distribution. It pointed to implications of land reform which went beyond the revolution in the village community – that is, the emancipation of the poorer peasants and labourers, and the equalizing of land-ownership. The peasant could 'make revolution' in the larger sense only by attaining a political consciousness which made him look beyond the 'settling of accounts' with local tyrants, and the release from the obligation to pay rent, taxes and high rates of interest. The sharing of implements and farm animals, the planning and construction of means to improve flood control, irrigation, soil improvement, grain storage, fertilizer manufacture and so on, and the long-term view of the returns on the sacrifices which saving and capital investment in industry involved, also required a new outlook, so did technical improvements in cultivation even before mechanization. 'Making revolution' and 'increasing production' had to be done together.

Looked at it nationally, *each* of the several problems involving agricultural policy in a developing country like China was truly of vast proportions. They all had to be worked out simultaneously at the local level and provincial level all over the country. And conditions differed considerably from place to place. Broadly speaking, the reorganization of agriculture was seen by China's experts as calling for, at various stages, land redistribution, the formation of what were called 'mutual aid teams', the creation of producers' co-operatives, and, at the stage when practically and industrially it became practicable, fully modernized agricultural production on a collective basis. The policy-makers had carefully considered the 'whys' and the 'wherefores', and assumed that because this long-term policy was rational the process would be voluntary, intelligent, and proceed with a steady increase in production and in the peasants' standard of living and political consciousness. The introduction of democratic procedures at the basic level where people lived and worked was made quite early in order to convince the peasants of the need for far-reaching modernization. In the event, the cadres (or officials) in charge of overseeing these changes were not all competent. There was much confusion and disorganization; policies laid down were not always followed, and were sometimes contradicted; and instead of increased social justice, real injustices sometimes resulted. Peasants who did not understand or approve of proposals were coerced by various means. The distinction between revolutionaries and counter-revolutionaries was blurred. Production actually declined in some places because of the high-handed methods of some government officials.

When the peasants had been given the opportunity of overthrowing the system under which they had been oppressed, and 'settled accounts' with landlords and rich peasants, they naturally tended to reflect in the use of power and authority the meanness, cruelty, violence and greed of the old order. The corrupt and oppressive system of the Kuomintang having been abolished, it was the hope of Mao and his colleagues that the new revolutionary tribunals would be firm but fair. But the now unprotected tyrants whom the liberated 'people' confronted with accusations, and whose activities they investigated, were so deeply hated by those who were trying them that they were sometimes beaten to death. This was not the only sense in which the poison of the old order continued to work in the new. In some villages the very people who overthrew the landlords adopted their style and attitudes when they took office in the new set-up. Given the ordinary peasants' habits of caution and fear, these 'cadres' were in a position to commit serious injustices before they were exposed or punished. They, after all, seemed to have the authority and protection of the government just as the former landlord-magistrates had had in Kuomintang territory; and the peasants were neither used to the new democratic liberties nor familiar with the thoughts and values of Mao and his associates. (In the Kuomintang areas whatever was permitted to be said about them before 1949 was far from the truth.) The peasants learned the hard way that opposition to the high-handed methods of the cadres, 'commandism' as it was called, was not the same as counter-revolutionary activity. Indeed, there were times when criticism of cadres by 'the proletariat' would not have been kindly received even by higher officials in the Communist Party.

Revolution in the villages sometimes clearly involved much suffering and injustice. But it seems to have been the means by which people learned to manage their affairs, acquired courage, learned what was right and wrong action. A profound analysis of the moral, spiritual and political aspects of revolution in a single village is given to us in William Hinton's *Fanshen.* One of the most remarkable episodes in the story of this village is the confrontation by the village of the hard core cadres of whom they have been most afraid. It is only when they have been persuaded, that anyone dares to accuse the worst of these men, a father and son, who have with impunity been acting as a law unto themselves. The two men are defiant, and confident that they can overawe their fellow-villagers. The son, Wen-Te, is asked to explain his actions, and makes a rather mild criticism of his own actions. Then an old man, Ch'ou-har, remembers what Wen-te had done to him.

Before anyone could stop him, he strode to the spot where Wen-te sat on the floor, pointed a long quivering finger straight into the young man's face, and shouted with all the fury that was in him, 'You beat me! You almost killed me! I lay sick for weeks. And when you beat me you said, "If I beat you to death I don't care!"'

Ch'ou-har took another half step forward, raised his fist and made ready to strike. A score of men in the back of the Church rose to their feet. They began to move forward as if by command. Across the floor other men stood. Every person in the crowd strained to see the action in the centre. An ominous silence pervaded the whole vast space as a thousand eyes concentrated on Ch'ou-har's long hands. Wen-te, crouched and ready to spring, stared up at them also. If Ch'ou-har hit out, as he certainly intended to do, Wen-te would die in the next few minutes, for such was the feeling of hatred for him and his father that no power on earth could stop those peasants once Ch'ou-har galvanized them into action. The members of the work team stood as if hypnotized.

It was one of those moments when time stands still and every word and gesture is reduced to slow motion. A catastrophe was spontaneously being generated. I felt it, and the members of the work team felt it too. But no one moved.

'Tell me, who are the dogs? Who are the dogs?' said Ch'ou-har in a hoarse whisper.

At this Wen-te sprang erect.

'I never said that. I never called anyone a dog!'

His face was chalk white.

With a quick jerking movement Ch'ou-har reached out both hands towards Wen-te's throat.

A cry rang out.

'Make him stand back!'

It was Ch'i Yun. She ran forward and flung her arms down between the two men. Someone else – was it Hsieh Hung? – pulled Ch'ou-har back a foot or two. Then Little Li and Chang-ch'uer pushed him on into the crowd. He stood there looking helplessly at his cheated hands. They were still moving as if to throttle the wind in a human throat. He raised his eyes to meet Comrade Hou's and his eyes asked, 'Why? Why have you stopped me?'

Those men in the crowd who had stepped forward drew back a little.

With a shudder Ch'ou-har recovered control of himself. His arms dropped to his sides. He began to speak and suddenly felt the weight of his years crushing him. All his joints began to loosen, the muscles of his careworn face sagged, and the words came stumbling from his toothless mouth.

'I risk my life to accuse this man,' he said. 'If I should be murdered in some nameless place I only want to warn you beforehand. I put myself under your protection. All my life I have never beaten others or . . .'

He could say no more. Slowly he went back to his seat.[3]

[3] William Hinton, *Fanshen*, pp. 464-5.

It was the pent-up emotions and passions, the fears and aspirations, the restored hopes and joys, which found expression both in political action in the villages and counties, and in new community relationships and popular drama and literature. Not only the ugliness but the hitherto unexpressed kindness and friendliness, too, came out into the open. The new ethos was heavily for co-operation and forgiveness and against competition and self-destructive indulgence in revenge; this was not a *coup d'etat* but a revolution rooted in over twenty years of experience. The *economic* impact of the revolution on the Chinese countryside cannot be appraised without recognition of the fact that what was going on, especially in areas remote from previous Maoist activity, was a complex *human* drama charged with a wide range of conflicting thoughts and feelings. The need to pool resources was clear, but mutual trust and respect could not grow overnight on a soil sown for generations by man's inhumanity to man. People had lived too close to continual death too long not to hold irrationally on to what seemed like a chance of personal survival. Those who had not been assured of surviving the following winter had to learn how to think in terms of working for a vast China which would have to continue for generations.

But the land reform was not intended to return rural China to subsistence agriculture. In such a China the peasantry would be doomed as much as those who did not work on the land. To the leaders it was unthinkable that the rural sector should be primitive either politically or economically. But the plan to achieve steady progress towards modernization on both fronts ran into difficulties because of mistakes which were made both in Peking and at the provincial and local levels in some places.

In 1955 there was a sudden speeding up of the formation of producers' co-operatives throughout the country, the number of co-operatives increasing seven-fold in one year from the spring of 1954. Of the more than a hundred million peasant families in China, nearly 15 per cent had been co-operativized. By the end of 1955 that percentage had again been tripled. The following year the number of co-operatives began to decline, but the percentage of peasant households which were drawn into collectives increased fifteen-fold in six months.[4]

These statistics are quoted here just to give an indication of the problems that must have arisen at a time when co-operatives and

[4] For detailed information see Kenneth R. Walker, 'Collectivization in Retrospect: The "Socialist High Tide" of Autumn 1955-Spring 1956', *China Quarterly*, April-June 1966.
Dr Walker is one of the few non-polemical writers on the economy of contemporary China.

collectives, which imply advanced political and technological conditions, were formed before the ground had been prepared: some cultivators had not even learned to work in mutual aid teams before they became members of co-operatives; there was a dearth of leaders, and those who were capable were wasting their time trying to sort out the confusion which resulted from the rapid organizational changes. Investment also had been directed to heavy industry rather than to the type of industrial activity which could take agricultural development beyond the stage of improvements in irrigation to that of better fertilizer, better seed, etc.

The government benefited by the experience, and eventually made it a policy principle that agriculture would be the foundation, and industry the 'leading factor'. The socialist transformation of China could not, it was realized, be achieved on all fronts all at once. To reach where it wanted to go, revolutionary China must take account of where it was going from.

The most remarkable thing about the revolution in the Chinese countryside through the fifties (including the 'Great Leap Forward' and the formation of communes) was not the mistakes but the willingness of large masses of people to make experiments, to attempt innovations on a vast scale, and to learn by experience. The Chinese peasant had been transformed mentally and spiritually.

3. *Women and the Family*

It was reported after the revolution that sexual and family morals had fallen steeply. For example, it was said that women were shared in common; that attempts were made to separate husbands and wives, parents and children. This type of 'inside information' from 'experts' we need not waste time on: it tells us more about the mentality of the reporters than about anything that is likely to happen in China. What we need to ask is what are the direct as well as subtler effects the revolutionary changes in China have had on marriage, on family relationships and on the opportunities given to people to fulfil themselves as men and women in marriage, fatherhood and motherhood, and the family.

In the old China the family and clan were generally the basic unit of society. That is, it was not only the system of authority to which one was subject, but also, in the rural areas, the economic unit. Reverence for and obligations to one's forebears continued even after their death. The young were subject to the old, and young women and girls had no status at all of their own – daughters-in-law being little more than servants of their mothers-in-law. Women had no independent status in the village, and were subject to their husbands. The murder of infant girls was practised on a large scale. Children were often betrothed to each other. Concubinage was practised, and sexual relations before and outside marriage were common. Local village bosses had also the exercise of the 'right' known in Europe as *droit de seigneur.*

It was the position of women that was most interesting. Both girls and boys were bought and sold, as servants, or slaves, or factory labour. But girls were also sold by the tens of thousands, at an early age, for the thriving business of those who ran the brothels in the cities. One can read sober descriptions of how girls were collected, herded together and transported which read like some horrible fantasy. For Han Suyin, however, it is not easy to recall what she saw of the fate of her fellow countrywomen without feeling. In 1932 she was taken by a Belgian, Hers, who knew China well to see a high-class institution in Shanghai.

> Hers admired Chinese women, their figures, their wit. I learnt much then of the habits of European males on the coast looking for a sleeping partner, of the Nanking officials and their mistresses and their concubines, of the family relationships between the gangsters of Shanghai, their female protegees, regularly sent up, as 'fresh material', for the high officials of the Nanking government to inspect . . .
>
> But all the brothels and dance halls were not as high class as Hers averred. In the back streets prostitution was at fifty cents apiece; there were fifty thousand licensed and one hundred thousand unlicensed prostitutes, and many of them were girls from the countryside enticed there by gangsters. After the great famine of 1928, twenty-eight thousand corpses were picked up in Shanghai's streets, and in that year of 1932, thirty thousand.[5]

Two years later, during the New Life campaign of Chiang and his wife, Han Suyin, still a student, visits Shanghai again. She has been told 'You will see that the Chinese are worse to their own people than the Europeans', and goes to the Chinese section of the city.

> A small, rat-like man with glasses took me to a silk filature, in Chapei or Yangtsepoo, quite a way from the International Settlement. It was an area impossibly squalid, a slum of sagging huts, stinking unpaved alleyways. A barn-like structure, with a small courtyard in front, was the filature. Inside, great vats of boiling water, furnaces, and children looking about six but who the rat-faced man told me were all of fourteen, standing round the vats. It was hardly possible to see what they were doing with the steam rising from the vats, and it was suffocatingly hot;

[5] Han Suyin, *The Mortal Flower*, p. 227.

but they were plunging silk cocoons in bundles wrapped in fine webs of gauze in the vats. The children's eyes were peculiar, bright red with trachoma, their arms were covered with scalds, and they worked almost naked; the temperature outside was ninety-eight degrees, inside it was one hundred and three or perhaps more. The smell was bad, and I could not stand it and no one wanted me to stay very long . . .

From the famines, the floods, the civil wars, wave after wave of children would arrive with their parents. And they were sold by their parents, or hired out to work, as was done in England. The factories refused to employ men, they would take only women and children. From the refugee camps and the orphanages children would be bought. In crowded lofts, in rickety barns such as this, they were put to work; twelve, fourteen hours a day, no Sundays off; they made flashlight bulbs for the five and ten cent stores; they slept under the punch press machines; twice a day they ate gruel, and they died of beri beri, swollen with festering sores, within four months . . .

The foremen in the textile mills were armed with guns and whips. The girls, mostly from the countryside, were brought into the city in batches of thirty, worked fourteen hours a day and slept in lofts on floorboards. The prettiest were sold to the brothels . . .[6]

Foreign businessmen, who owned three-quarters of these textile mills in Shanghai, explained to the young Han Suyin that in view of the poverty and hunger, they were helping these women and children by employing them.

Whatever the services rendered to industry and in other ways by Chinese women and children, family life in the ideal sense did not exist except among the wealthier sections of the population.

Whether Chinese women 'wanted' to be emancipated or not might be a matter for discussion. But one of the first major acts of the revolutionary government was the passing of the Marriage Law of May 1950, which prescribed among other important acts of 'liberation' the emancipation of women from the lowly and servile position they had held.[7] Clearly, some mothers-in-law were affronted when their daughters-in-law were given a status as independent citizens with rights of their own; and some husbands could not have been pleased at the new-found freedom of their wives. The laws governing marriage and the family in the Chinese People's Republic strictly enforce the prohibition of the selling of daughters and wives,

[6] *Ibid.*, pp. 299-300.

[7] See Hinton's *Fanshen* for a description of the Yenan period; and Jan Myrdal's *Report From a Chinese Village*, Part Six. The text (translated) of The Marriage Law of May 1950, which affected the status of half of China's population, can be found in Albert P. Blaustein, *Fundamental Legal Documents of Communist China* (South Hackensack: New Jersey, Rothman & Co., 1962).

bigamy and concubinage, child betrothal and even arranged marriages. Under the 1950 reform people were encouraged to dissolve marriages under the old system into which they had been forced and which were a burden on either partner. For some people the sudden change (which for others had seemed long overdue) was too much to take emotionally and intellectually, and the reform was the cause of suffering for thousands, some even committing suicide. The enthusiasm of the reformers had later to be tempered by Peking.

Marriage is now a contract freely entered into by man and woman. The right to ask for a divorce belongs to both husband and wife, who have equal rights in family property and equal responsibility for the care of their children. Since women also have equal rights to education, equal pay for equal work, and in farms which are still privately owned equal share in the means of production, the position of women has been revolutionized. The closing down of the brothels and the rehabilitation of the prostitutes has given many victims of the old order the opportunity for a new start in life – education, respectable employment and even marriage. It is reported also that whereas there used to be people who formerly could not afford to marry, now everyone can afford to marry.

There are, however, safeguards against laxness. Family counselling of unhappy partners helps husbands and wives to overcome their difficulties. Sexual relationships before or outside marriage are disapproved of. Some observers consider that the disapproval of prurience and even flirtation is excessively puritanical. Certainly any word or action which implies that Chinese womanhood is there for the casual enjoyment of foreigners makes the Chinese very angry indeed. Brothels, night-clubs, and other forms in which sexual titillation aroused by the female body is commercially or otherwise purveyed are not tolerated.

The revolution has also struck at what many modernizers had regarded as the family-consciousness, the primacy of family loyalties, which was so much a feature of traditional Chinese life and a cause of its retarded development. The lack of a sense of belonging to, owing obligations to, the wider community or the nation was something that Sun Yat Sen had been concerned about and had criticized. Today, anything that savours of nepotism is not allowed. Since the welfare of all who are not counter-revolutionaries is the policy of the regime, people are encouraged to help all those in need of help in their work-place or neighbourhood, and not only someone who is a relation.

The care of the old and the nurture and welfare of children are considered as much the community's responsibility as that of the immediate family. Obviously, any attempts by parents to treat their children as chattels are prohibited. But there is evidence to suggest that old attitudes have not been rooted out, even among some highly placed officials and local cadres; and where the women and children do not for some reason assert their new liberties, the older generation and the believers in male superiority still exercise their 'tyranny'.

The new freedom of the young is seen best in the fact that during the Cultural Revolution the young were taken seriously. Whether their loss of reverence for their seniors is a good thing or not is a controversial question.

Are women there to be looked at, admired, worshipped, amused, played with as ornaments? Is it a case of 'He for God, she for God in him', as the poet John Milton believed, and as many, using more secular terms, believe? Do equality of status with men, late marriage, a career, make a woman less a woman? Questions like this, and more profound ones, are involved in an evaluation of the human consequences of marriage reform; and we must consider them later on. But there is no doubt that at the point of intimate, life-long relationships where people experience and exercise and perhaps discover their own humanity, as well as where the most primitive forms of belonging, and being loyal to one's group, exist, the revolution has brought about the end of traditional forms and values, and started to create something which is not to be found easily elsewhere.

7

The Revolutionary Impact on Chinese Politics

1. The Impact on Politics and Culture

HOW RADICALLY the status of women had changed in China was suggested when on 25 May 1966 seven members of Peking University, the premier university in China, challenged the establishment by violating a ban, and putting up a big-character poster, a *dazibao*, exposing the abuse of power and authority of leading Communist Party officials in the University administration – including the president of the University, the secretary of its party committee, and important representatives of the Peking Municipal Council. The leader of this group, whose activity in May, June and July was perhaps as much as any other single action to set in motion the forces of 'revolutionary rebellion' throughout the country, was a woman, Nieh Yuan Tzu. And their challenge to the whole apparatus of authority in Peking was the culmination of two years of struggle in the University.[1] Mao Tse Tung promptly realized the importance of what these people had done, praised their poster as the first genuinely revolutionary *dazibao*, and ordered it to be publicized throughout the country. The revolutionary group at Peking University had been supported by high school students, among them the 'Red Guards' at the school attached to Tsinghua University who on 24 June put up their own *dazibao*. In August and September Nieh Yuan Tzu and her colleagues were busy organizing a Congress to set up a Cultural Revolution Committee.

Already on 12 August the Central Committee of the Communist Party of China had issued a sixteen-point statement on the 'Great Proletarian Cultural Revolution'. In the months that followed China was seething with the activity of youthful 'revolutionary rebels' and 'red guards' – talking, arguing, putting up posters, investigating the activities of those in authority, travelling to meet one another from all over the country, exchanging experiences, and, in massive rallies,

[1] See *Peking Review*, 10 June 1966, and later issues.

attended by Chairman Mao Tse Tung and Vice-Chairman Lin Piao, expressing their revolutionary devotion and solidarity.

What happened in 1966 and 1967 would have been inconceivable twenty years earlier. Political discussion and activity of this kind was also quite unlike anything ever experienced or even comprehensible to people in Europe and North America. That it took place at all in China, and the way in which it did (and without lapsing into complete anarchy) was possible only because of the way in which the revolution made its political and cultural impact on the people of China.

What was China like in 1949? Throughout its long and sometimes great history China had as a whole not known any democratic activity. The 1911 Republic was suppressed before it could develop any liberal forms of democracy it might have wanted to. In the areas ruled by Chiang up to 1949 any form of popular democracy was out of the question, even at the provincial, local (*hsien*) or village level. To try from within Chiang's domains to organize politically in any way independently of Chiang's Kuomintang was to invite assassination or imprisonment. Elections and civil liberties were as unknown as they had ever been.[2] There was strict censorship, close supervision of the people by a secret police who had vast powers summarily to imprison and execute, and no independent courts. Chiang and his henchmen also instituted a system, called *pao-chia*, by which a group of households was collectively held responsible, and therefore could be punished, for 'crimes' with which the government charged any resident in the neighbourhood, and thus the price which one might have to pay for exercising the freedom to dissent was high.

In 1949, therefore, it was only in some areas which had been governed from Yenan that the people had had some experience of democracy.[3] It needs to be said, however, that 'free institutions' and 'democracy' in the sense of guarantees for foreign investment

[2] The reports by United States diplomatic staff members John S. Service and John P. Davies are quoted in *United States Relations with China*. See also the reminiscences of the pro-Chiang former Ambassador to China, John Leighton Stuart, *Fifty Years in China* (New York: Random House, 1954); Despatches to the *New York Times* by Brooks Atkinson, especially that of 31 October 1944; Joseph Stilwell, *Stilwell's Papers* (New York: Sloane, 1948); Carson Chang, *The Third Force in China* (New York: Bookman Associates, 1952); Theodore White and Annalee Jacoby, *Thunder Out of China* (New York: Sloane, 1947); Felix Greene, *A Curtain of Ignorance* (New York: Doubleday, 1964) especially pp. 17-42.

[3] First-hand accounts of 'Yenan China' are to be found in Harrison Forman, *Report from Red China* (London: Hale, 1947); Gunther Stein, *The Challenge of Red China*; Stuart Gelder, *The Chinese Communists* (London: Gollancz, 1946); Edgar Snow, *Red Star over China* (London: Gollancz, 1937).

and free enterprise, as well as in the sense of local capitalist forms of economic activity were known in pre-Revolutionary China. But these did not entail for the Chinese people experience of free political discussion, activity and the power to govern – except by insurrection.

The People's Democratic Dictatorship was conceived as a double process: the exercise of political power, by democratic processes increasing in effectiveness, and on their own behalf, by those formerly ruled over; and authoritarian exercise of governmental power over the minority (Chiang and his colleagues, Kuomintang officials and army officers, landlords, owners of large businesses and representatives of foreign agencies) who were deemed to have exercised the dictatorship before by oppressing and exploiting 'the people', and especially the revolutionaries and patriots – a dictatorship gradually ceasing to operate as various factors like conversion to revolutionary loyalties, punishment, the establishment of a new order leaving no room for an exploiting class, and changes in the world situation, made this exploiting class of negligible importance. It was to be government *of* and *for* the people initially, and increasingly and rapidly to be government *by* the people. In so far as there were people whose interests clashed with this aim, they had no political rights.

When it came to actual practice the subtle discriminations required for actually dealing with people were far from easy to make. The mighty had been brought low; the humble were to be exalted. But the members of the Communist Party of China and the non-Communist cadres who were to lead in the establishment of the new order (they had been the most politically conscious and daring among the masses) had in a narrower sense already been exalted before vast millions who were still to be 'liberated' from the shackles of the old despotic order. There were not thousands, or even hundreds of Mao Tse Tungs. There were more or less well-disciplined revolutionaries, with varying degrees of understanding of what was left to be done after China was 'liberated', who had to deal with people often from parts of the country they had never seen before and give them a lead. To the ordinary people of Shensi and Shansi they were heroes; but to the people of Szechuan and Kwangtung they had for years been presented by Kuomintang propaganda as ogres, and they in any case came not just as fellow-fighters against the Japanese or the landlords but as government officials. How were they to distinguish from the caution and suspicion of the people, from the confused and slow way in which they responded to suggestions for reform, who was the revolutionary and who the counter-revolutionary? Were not those who came promptly to their side, with the right words, friends, and those who had doubts, arguments or hesitations, enemies? They had been told to 'trust the masses' and to use persuasion and not coercion; they had also been told to smash the enemy and get on quickly with the job of work. For four decades life had been cheap in China. Moreover, most of the cadres had known of the role of government, of fathers and husbands, of village heads, and of leadership generally, very much in the terms in which China had conceived these for centuries. For some of them there was still the presence of the old ways and values within them to contend with. And among those who supported the old order and wanted to see it return there must have been some who were subtle enough to size up the problems of the new cadres, and to influence their actions.

The members of the People's Liberation Army and the Communist Party of China were an admirable body of men by all standards of the past. Even the most bitter opponents of Mao had remarked that these were men and women who were highly responsible citizens, and that they treated their fellow countrymen with consideration and respect. The revolution was overturning familiar Chinese notions of how a victorious army should behave. But the learning of revolutionary doctrine did not give the revolutionaries exemption from the temptations of power – a power whose exercise was sometimes not criticized by those who saw its abuse because there was to be found here and there the unscrupulous cadre who, far from the watchful eye of his colleagues and superiors, could threaten to deal with legitimate criticism of his actions as though it was agitation against the new regime. To be a Communist or a cadre was to be a member of the privileged elite, and some of those who joined the party after the beginning of 1949, when the worst was over, had jumped on the victorious bandwagon.

It is a fact that the achievements of the new revolutionaries were partly marred by injustices committed by officials from 1949 onwards. Offenders had regularly been reported and criticized in the official press. Policies laid down by the government were not always carried out; instructions on how to set about instituting reforms were ignored; officials on occasion collaborated with each other to prevent their tyrannical acts and other misdemeanours from being discovered and punished. There were occasions on which people on whose behalf Mao Tse Tung and the revolutionary forces who heard his call had sincerely fought to seize power in China were ejected from their land, arbitrarily subjected to enormous exactions, raped or imprisoned. It was discovered, quite early, that some of the Communist officials who had to deal with businessmen in the cities were conspiring with them to cheat the government and sabotage its economic measures.

2. *Serving the People*

It must be remembered that what the large mass of revolutionary workers had received in the way of training was, firstly, their own experience of what had been happening in their country, and, secondly, very simple teaching about what service to the nation and people meant. There was no abstruse and complicated doctrine. It is true that Liu Shao Chi, one of the chief associates of Mao, had written a book *How to be a Good Communist*, for the self-cultivation of Communist-Party members. But Mao's teaching was not in the least sectarian, and it did not encourage a sense of self-importance. His speeches and articles had either emphasized the realities of the historical situation in which revolutionary action was demanded or appealed personally to his followers in a very different style. This style was best exemplified in such pieces as 'In Memory of Norman Bethune'[4] (referring to a Canadian doctor who worked selflessly in Yenan and died there), 'The Foolish Old Man Who Removed the Mountains',[5] and 'Serve the People'.[6]

The last, an address given in September 1944, has become a major text of China's 'political philosophy' and is worth quoting in full:

Serve the People

Our Communist Party and the Eighth Route and New Fourth Armies led by our Party are battalions of the revolution. These battalions of ours are wholly dedicated to the liberation of the people and work entirely in the people's interests. Comrade Chang Szu-teh was in the ranks of these battalions.

All men must die, but death can vary in its significance. The ancient Chinese writer Szuma Chien said, 'Though death befalls all men alike, it may be heavier than Mount Tai or lighter than a feather.' To die for the people is heavier than Mount Tai, but to work for the fascists and die for the exploiters and oppressors is lighter than a feather. Comrade Chang Szu-teh died for the people, and his death is indeed heavier than Mount Tai.

If we have shortcomings, we are not afraid to have them pointed out and criticized, because we serve the people. Anyone, no matter who, may point out our shortcomings. If he is right, we will correct them. If what he proposes will benefit the people, we will act upon it. The idea of 'better troops and simpler administration' was put forward by Mr Li Ting-ming,

[4] In his *Selected Works*, II, pp. 337-8.
[5] *Ibid.*, III, pp 321-4.
[6] *Ibid.*, III, pp. 227-8.

who is not a Communist. He made a good suggestion which is of benefit to the people, and we have adopted it. If, in the interests of the people, we persist in doing what is right and correct what is wrong, our ranks will surely thrive.

We hail from all corners of the country and have joined together for a common revolutionary objective. And we need the vast majority of the people with us on the road to this objective. Today, we already lead base areas with a population of 91 million, but this is not enough; to liberate the whole nation more are needed. In times of difficulty we must not lose sight of our achievements, must see the bright future and must pluck up our courage. The Chinese people are suffering; it is our duty to save them and we must exert ourselves in struggle. Wherever there is struggle there is sacrifice, and death is a common occurrence. But we have the interests of the people and the sufferings of the great majority at heart, and when we die for the people it is a worthy death. Nevertheless, we should do our best to avoid unnecessary sacrifices. Our cadres must show concern for every soldier, and all people in the revolutionary ranks must care for each other, must love and help each other.

From now on, when anyone in our ranks who has done some useful work dies, be he soldier or cook, we should have a funeral ceremony and a memorial meeting in his honour. This should become the rule. And it should be introduced among the people as well. When someone dies in a village, let a memorial meeting be held. In this way we express our mourning for the dead and unite all people.

By the time this was spoken, in 1944, this statement of a theme frequent in Mao's thought, which must have been very moving in its total freedom from rhetoric, was the expression of a Chinese political tradition which was unlike any earlier tradition in Chinese history. A political ethic, in which humility, non-sectarianism, altruism and 'love' were important ingredients, had already then made its impact not only on a new political and intellectual elite, but on a good part of the heartland of China itself. One of its sources was the discipline which had moulded the People's Liberation Army and made it a school for revolutionaries, 'equivalent', in Mao's words spoken on 8 February 1949, 'to several thousand universities and secondary schools'.[7]

But because of the ruthless 'Annihilation Campaigns' carried out against the revolutionary nationalists by Chiang, and the decimation of the survivors of those campaigns during the ten-thousand mile Long March to Yenan very few of the people who in the 'twenties had had the kind of faith in and love of China's people

[7] *Ibid.*, IV, p. 338 (from the speech 'Turn the Army into a Working Force'). See also 'Manifesto of the Chinese People's Liberation Army', IV, pp. 147-52; and 'On the Reissue of the Three Main Rules of Discipline', IV, pp. 155-6.

expressed in Mao's teaching had survived physically. But life in Yenan, behind the Japanese lines, and during the last stages of the Civil War, had been made possible for thousands of revolutionaries because of the deep, spiritual significance Mao had given to living and dying in the service of the oppressed and in the cause of national salvation. Thousands of the old and new cadres who had survived the anti-Japanese resistance died during the last struggle with the Kuomintang; thousands more (among them Mao's only son) were recalled from reconstruction work in 1950, to fight and die in Korea.

Already in February 1949, after the decisive battle of Hsuchow, Mao had, in giving instructions (see Chapter Four above) for quick demobilization, underlined the fact that new tasks in the rural areas would be 'fundamentally different' from work in the old 'liberated areas'.

> Therefore rural work must be learned afresh. However, as compared with urban work, rural work is easy to learn . . . If our cadres cannot quickly master the administration of cities, we shall encounter extreme difficulties.

With the ranks of cadres who had been well-tried and long-orientated to the new ethos thinned by death, the revolution had to be accomplished in policy-making and action on such matters as public finance, the creation of a national administration, technological and scientific research and development, educational policy, national security in an age of nuclear weaponry, etc. for a China which wanted to stay independent and become and stay modern. The ethic of *Serve the People* had to be put to the tests of a society which experienced the whole gamut of the moral and political problems of the modern world.

All the instances of tyranny, abuse of power and privilege, corruption and sabotage that came to light in the first decade of the new order were a small part only of what went on in China. And they were often discovered and punished. The 'rectification' of those who had responsibility for revolutionary leadership throughout the country was the constant concern of the top leaders. But the lapses, which were magnified and sensationalized and exultantly publicized by China's enemies abroad, showed how much the Chinese who had been trained as representatives of the new values and forms of behaviour could not only antagonize the people and create disaffection where it had not existed before, but also carry and spread the infection of the old order – which in the new jargon was referred to pejoratively as 'capitalist', 'bourgeois' and 'feudal'. These failings, evident also among some senior members of the Party, showed what the difficulties were in depending on the Communist Party's virtual monopoly of power to achieve a democracy based on the initiative and responsibility of the broad masses. For Mao, who in the years after 1949 probably did not have control over the Communist Party apparatus, anything which savoured of indifference to or contempt for the masses (which is what some cadres showed) was anathema. It was a firm Maoist assumption that it was only with the masses that the 'greatest creativity' and the 'greatest wisdom' were to be found to exist, and that isolation from the masses would destroy all that China's revolutionaries were working for.[8] How seriously, then had the new China's leadership been corrupted by 'capitalist' and 'bourgeois' ways?

If the struggle to create a new China in the period up to 1949 was the first Maoist revolution – by which the revolutionary forces among the masses were successfully mobilized to seize power – the socialist construction in the following years of a new order for that large proportion of the world's poor and oppressed who lived in China could be described as the objective of the second Maoist revolution. In January 1940, when the success of the revolution seemed quite far off in time, Mao published an extensive discussion of political aims in what was then one of the most important political documents to come out of colonial Asia, 'On New Democracy',[9] it was contribution to a new journal, *Chinese Culture*, published in Yenan.

Victory in 1949 took the Maoists beyond the point of new-democratic culture and practice. In the years that followed many obstacles, natural and human, were encountered; but the work went on, and the process by which a new China was established in place of the old seemed, to those who deplored it as well as to those who acclaimed it, an irreversible process. Measures to disperse political power and initiative throughout the country and root it in local communities were begun as part of the people's democratic dictatorship by which the old order would be eradicated. The principle of election based on universal suffrage was introduced throughout China for the first time. Elections at village, district and provincial level led to the formation of the National People's Congress, composed of both Communist-Party

[8] See his 'Be Concerned with the Well-being of the Masses', *Selected Works*, I, especially pp. 148-9, 'Problems of Strategy in China's Revolutionary War', I, especially pp. 190-2; 'Win the Masses in their Millions for the Anti-Japanese National United Front', I, especially p. 291; 'The Role the Chinese Communist Party in the National War', II, 'The Chinese Revolution and the Chinese Communist Party'; II, 'In Memory of Norman Bethune', II, pp. 337-8; 'Rectify the Party's Style of Work', III, especially pp. 35-52; and 'The Present Situation and Our Tasks', IV, especially p. 166.

[9] Mao, *Selected Works*, II, pp. 339-82.

members and others; and this congress discussed and adopted in 1954 a new constitution for the Chinese People's Republic. By 1956 an effective administration on the new principles for the whole of China (excepting Tibet where the old order was allowed to continue) had been organized. The foulness and chaos of important cities like Shanghai had been replaced by a new decency and order. Land reform had been completed. It certainly looked as if the political culture of feudal and semi-colonial China was dying under the impact of the 'thought remoulding' campaign, and that the few who had to wait to receive their political rights in the new order, and who had been feared as possible restorers of the old order – those who were labelled the 'reactionaries' and counter-revolutionaries – were under control. There was an atmosphere of political relaxation and a mood of optimism among revolutionary nationalists. With a 'People's Government' firmly in power, some of them thought, everything was well for the people. Only the reactionaries, it was felt, had cause for dissatisfaction, or felt deprived.

In February 1957, Chairman Mao made one of the most important of the speeches he has made in the last eighteen years. It was not one of his 'prophetic' utterances, but a long and careful analysis of policy, addressed originally to members of the Supreme State Conference. Entitled *On the Correct Handling of Contradictions Among the People,*[10] it was published and thus addressed to the whole country. It soberly made assessment of the new China's development up to that point. Mao began:

> Never before has our country been as united as it is today. The victories of the bourgeois-democratic revolution and the socialist revolution and our achievements in socialist construction have rapidly changed the face of old China. A still brighter future for our motherland lies ahead. The days of national disunity and chaos which the people detested have gone, never to return. Led by the working class and the Communist Party, our six hundred million people, united as one, are engaged in the great task of building socialism. The unification of our country, the unity of our people and the unity of our various nationalities – these are the basic guarantees of the sure triumph of our cause. However, this does not mean that contradictions no longer exist in our society. To imagine that none exist is a naïve idea which is at variance with objective reality . . .

After explaining the different kinds of social contradictions, especially the two main types, 'antagonistic' and 'non-antagonistic', whose conception was fundamental to his analysis of society, Mao continued:

[10] Published by Peking: The Foreign Languages Press, 1957. The following quotations from Mao are taken from this work.

Our People's Government is one that genuinely represents the people's interests, it is a government that serves the people. Nevertheless, there are still certain contradictions between the government and the people. These include contradictions among the interests of the state, the interests of the collective and the interests of the individual; between democracy and centralism; between the leadership and the led; and the contradiction arising from the bureaucratic style of work of certain government workers in their relation with the masses. All these are also contradictions among the people. Generally speaking, the people's basic identity of interests underlies the contradictions among the people . . .

The Chinese were also reminded that the people's democratic dictatorship's function was first 'to suppress the reactionary classes and elements and those exploiters in (the) country who resist the socialist revolution . . .', and secondly, 'to protect (the) country from subversion and possible aggression by external enemies'.

(It was) to protect all our people so that they can devote themselves to peaceful labour and build China into a socialist country with a modern industry, agriculture, science and culture. (But it) did not apply within the ranks of the people. The people cannot exercise dictatorship over themselves, nor must one section of the people oppress another . . . Our Constitution lays it down that citizens of the People's Republic of China enjoy freedom of speech, of the press, assembly, association, procession, demonstration, religious belief, and so on . . .

Democracy, it was important to be clear, 'sometimes seems to be an end, but it is in fact only a means . . . Within the ranks of the people, democracy is correlative with centralism and freedom with discipline . . .' Mao then went on to warn that . . .

. . . all attempts to use administrative orders or coercive measures to settle ideological questions or questions of right and wrong are not only ineffective but harmful . . . The only way to settle questions of an ideological nature or controversial issues among the people is by the democratic method, the method of discussion, of criticism, of persuasion and education, and not by the method of coercion or repression . . .

After going into other related questions, he said:

While welcoming the new system, the broad mass of the people are not yet quite accustomed to it. Government workers are not sufficiently experienced and have to undertake further study and exploration of specific policies. In other words, time is needed for our socialist system to become established and consolidated, for the masses to become used to the new system, and for the government workers to learn and acquire experience . . .

In regard to planning the country's development, too, Mao made it clear that those responsible should think in terms of China's six hundred million as a whole. (The sheer size of China's population was a special problem in achieving a socialist democracy. One of the consequences of difficulties and set-backs in achieving progress on a broad, national front is the resort to ways of contracting the definition of 'people', the resort also to short cuts which by-pass the more intractable social and political tasks. If it is democracy and service to the people that is desired, who are the people? Once a higher standard of living and greater liberties had been achieved for some, it would be a temptation to concentrate on raising gross national income in statistical terms, and to postpone the satisfaction of the rest. Democracy for a particular section of the people – a class, a sector of the working population, a nationality, or a party – was comparatively easy to achieve, as the rest of Asia was showing. And some leaders in China were clearly interested in giving priority to the development of a managerial class, a new elite, and party members.) Mao made it clear what he wanted to see was the well-being of *all* Chinese ensured.

In drawing up plans, handling affairs or thinking over problems, we must proceed from the fact that China has a population of six hundred million people, and we must never forget this fact. Why do we make a point of this? Is it possible that there are people who are still unaware that we have a population of six-hundred million? Yes, everyone knows this, but when it comes to actual practice, some people forget all about it and act as though the fewer the people, the smaller the circle, the better. Those who have this 'small circle' mentality resist the idea of bringing all positive factors into play, of uniting with everyone that can be united with, and of doing everything possible to turn negative factors into positive ones so as to serve the great cause of building a socialist society. I hope these people will take a wider view and really recognize that we have a population of six hundred million, that this is an objective fact, and that it is an asset. Our large population is a good thing, but it also involves certain difficulties. Construction is going ahead vigorously on all fronts and very successfully too, but in the present transitional period of tremendous social change there are still many difficult problems. Progress and at the same time difficulties – this is a contradiction. However, not only should contradictions be resolved, but they definitely can be. Our guiding principle is overall planning and proper arrangement. Whatever the problem – whether it concerns food, natural calamities, employment, education, the intellectuals, the united front of all patriotic forces, the minority nationalities, or anything else – we must always proceed from the standpoint of overall planning which takes the whole people into consideration and must make proper arrangements, after consultation with all circles concerned, in the light of the specific possibilities of the particular time and place. On no account should we complain that there are too many people, that they are backward, that things are troublesome and hard to handle, and so shut the problems out. Does that mean that the government alone must take care of everyone and everything? Of course not. In many cases, they can be left to the care of the public organizations or of the masses directly – both are quite capable of devising many good ways of handling things. This also comes within the scope of the principle of overall planning and proper arrangement. We should give guidance to the public organizations and the masses of the people everywhere in this respect.

Considering what had been normal in the country as a whole less than ten years previously, these were norms for government planners and workers which may have seemed very demanding in the way of political consciousness and an awareness of the complex social and other conditions in the country. Mao's words were not addressed mainly to the more arrogant and high-handed cadres and civil servants. Millions of humble and dedicated people must have experienced the same sense of exasperation and even despair when they realized that the Maoist injunction *Serve the People* meant not a general ideal but the eradication of the political, economic and social backwardness which impoverished the lives of actual people in the midst of all the diversity and inequality and 'contradictions' of Chinese society as it really was. There were people whose tardiness in giving up feudal and bourgeois ways and values, and accepting reforms, was not due to any sinister or subversive intent; but their conservatism was an obstacle to progress and change, it seemed. Mao's norm of political equity in the midst of radical change, of practical respect for needs and interests of all groups, must have asked for profound changes in the way some even of the most enthusiastic of those who exercised state power looked at their responsibilities.

For China's revolutionary nationalists, the right of the Chinese Communist Party to form the government in 1949 could not have been doubted by the other anti-Kuomintang forces. Further, given the goals and policies of the People's Republic, with its Maoist assumptions and values, it was again the Communist Party of China that could play the leading role in it. The victorious and ruling Communist Party could grow in membership for a number of reasons; but could it be said as time went on that it maintained its position of leadership not only because it represented the interests of the masses economically and politically, but also because its view of life, of human possibilities, of truth and justice, of the future of China, and of the world situation carried conviction? China need not have become a democracy in order to industrialize or become a strong power; but since she was proclaimed as one it is pertinent to ask if there was free and vigorous discussion on fundamental issues not only between the Maoists and others in the Communist Party of China but, equally important, discussion and criticism between the Maoists and other Chinese patriots who supported government policy but did not share the fundamental Marxist assumptions.

Apart from the Communist Party, there are a number of very small political parties in the People's Republic. Most of their members are the liberal-democrats among the intelligentsia and well-to-do who found Chiang's Kuomintang unacceptable, and who represented the rare anti-imperialist and democratic elements among the westernized middle class. In 1956 two slogans – 'Let a hundred flowers blossom, let a hundred schools of thought contend', and 'long-term coexistence and mutual supervision' – heralded a period of political experiment in China. It appeared to be designed partly to encourage criticisms and suggestions to emerge from among the people, whether they had complaints to make or ideas on how things might be done better, and partly to restore intellectual sharpness and vigour to revolutionary political thinking and to ensure that the ascendancy of Maoist thinking was not due to its being the new orthodoxy. Mao explained,

> Questions of right and wrong in the arts and sciences should be settled through free discussion in artistic and scientific circles and through practical work in these fields. They should not be settled in summary fashion. A period of trial is often needed to determine whether something is right or wrong. Throughout history, new and correct things have often failed at the outset to win recognition from the majority of people and have had to develop by twists and turns in struggle. Often correct and good things have first been regarded not as fragrant flowers but as poisonous weeds . . . In a socialist society, conditions for the growth of the new are radically different from and far superior to those in the old society. Nevertheless, it still often happens that new, rising forces are held back and rational proposals constricted. Moreover, the growth of new things may be hindered in the absence of deliberate suppression simply through lack of discernment. It is therefore necessary to be careful about questions of right and wrong in the arts and sciences, to encourage free discussion and avoid hasty conclusions . . .

Marxism, Mao pointed out, has as a mode of approach to human problems itself 'developed through struggle'.

> The proletariat seeks to transform the world according to its own world outlook, and so does the bourgeoisie. In this respect, the question of

which will win out, socialism or capitalism, is still not really settled. Marxists are still a minority among the entire population as well as among the intellectuals. Therefore, Marxism must still develop through struggle . . . What is correct invariably develops in the cause of struggle with what is wrong. The true, the good and the beautiful always exist by contrast with the false, the evil and the ugly, and grow in struggle with the latter. As soon as a wrong thing is rejected and a particular truth accepted by mankind, new truths begin their struggle with new errors. Such struggles will never end. This is the law of development of truth and, naturally, of Marxism as well.

Mao's conception of the importance of 'struggle' was central to all his thinking, and to the kind of democracy which he, and those who thought on similar lines, wanted to see in China. It was a process, a means, by which a 'truth' could be identified, a good decision made, a sound policy adopted, the account of those in authority correctly rendered. It was believed that after passing through the fire of intense discussion and criticism only what was true and honest would survive.

'Marxism' was the prevailing ideology. But what Mao was saying was that it must be put to the fiercest test by those who were not Marxists and asked to give an account of itself and the role it was playing. On the other hand, those who are Marxists must challenge those who are not. Mao said,

Ideological struggle is not like other forms of struggle . . . *The only method to be used in this struggle is that of painstaking reasoning and not crude coercion. Today, socialism is in an advantageous position in the ideological struggle.* The main power of the state is in the hands of the working people led by the proletariat. The Communist party is strong and its prestige stands high. Although there are defects and mistakes in our work, every fair-minded person can see that we are loyal to the people, that we are both determined and able to build up our motherland together with them, and that we have already achieved great successes and will achieve still greater ones. The vast majority of the bourgeoisie and the intellectuals who come from the old society are patriotic, and are willing to serve their flourishing socialist motherland; they know they will be helpless and have no bright future to look forward to if they turn away from the socialist cause and from the working people led by the Communist Party.

People may ask, since Marxism is accepted as the guiding ideology by the majority of the people in our country, can it be criticized? Certainly it can. Marxism is scientific truth and fears no criticism. If it did, and if it could be overthrown by criticism, it would be worthless. Marxists should not be afraid of criticism from any quarter. Quite the contrary, they need to temper and develop themselves and win new positions in the teeth of criticism and in the storm and stress of struggle. (italics mine)

It is not clear what degree of resistance to Mao's radical views there was in the Communist Party leadership, and how much he was at that time in a position to over-rule opposition.[11] But in June that year the 'Hundred Flowers Campaign' was brought to an end. It had failed to produce the serious and profound 'struggle' suggested by Mao, but had only shown how much discontent there was at a more trivial level. Articles and letters complaining of the arrogance and incompetence of some Party officials did not say much that had not already been said. Some of the most articulate critics were westernized intellectuals who resented the curbs on the liberties they associated with democracy. The criticisms were the occasion for a thorough shake-up within the government. But some of the critics found themselves 'struggled with'. It could be that the Communist Party of China took fright at the publication of such criticism, though day after day during the campaign and even after it was officially ended letters and articles attacking the government or asking for more freedom for counter-revolutionaries were widely publicized. In view of the new developments in the next few years the reasons for the decision cannot be discovered fully. There was, in 1957, a rural 'socialist education movement' and a campaign to dispel attitudes of contempt felt by the intelligentsia (the scholar class) for manual work. Then came the mass upheaval which created the communes and the fantastic drive to increase production called 'the Great Leap Forward' of 1958, which were followed by the period of dreadful national disasters until 1961. It was not till 1962 that China as a whole was able to settle down to a period of comparatively quiet reflection, and to digest its unprecedented experiences.

'Of all things in the world,' Mao Tse Tung had said to contradict Dean Acheson in 1949, 'people are the most precious.' Most cadres and party members were selfless and dedicated men engaged together in an enormous task of construction which perhaps no previous ruler of China had entrusted to his officials. If on account of the misdemeanors and incorrect notions of a few all cadres had been harassed by frequent scolding, harsh punishments, discouragement of initiative and excessive supervision they would have lost confidence in themselves, and been unable to face up to the tremendous tasks before them. Worse than that, if the numbers of cadres fell off, and if the initiative was monopolized by the centre, and if the villages and farms were left to their own devices, the hope of developing purposeful mass initiative in intelligent decision-making

[11] In his *Speech at the CPC's National Conference on Propaganda Work* on 12 March 1956 Mao made *his* position very clear to the Party.

and action would have to be given up. The central government's contact with villages, communes, factories, towns, would have been lost, and China would become a bureaucratic state.

The problems of the uncompleted revolution were too many to be solved all at once; what was remarkable was not that perfection had not been achieved but that out of what had been regarded as the dregs of Chinese society, the coolies, such magnificent material emerged. The problems were there not just because, let us say, there is always the problem arising from the need for an administration and the need at the same time to avoid bureaucratic methods: the problem was there because the essential nature of the continuous process of revolutionary transformation in a vast and poor country made great intellectual and moral demands on officials which did not have their counterparts elsewhere. It was so much easier for revolutionary leaders to go as fast as the most impatient members of the proletariat wanted to go, than to learn to wait for those others who, once they came to see the way that was being opened before them, would patiently and single-mindedly go much farther on the 'journey of 10,000 li (miles)' which Mao had described as the revolutionary road.

Mao in 1943 had written on behalf of the Party's leadership the document 'Concerning Methods of Leadership'. At one point it said:

> In all the practical work of our Party, all correct leadership is necessarily 'from the masses, to the masses'. This means: take the ideas of the masses (scattered and unsystematic ideas) and concentrate them (through study turn them into concentrated and systematic ideas), then go to the masses and propagate and explain these ideas until the masses embrace them as their own, hold fast to them and translate them into action, and test the correctness of these ideas in such action. Then once again concentrate ideas from the masses and once again go to the masses so that the ideas are persevered in and carried through. And so on, over and over again in an endless spiral, with the ideas becoming more correct, more vital and richer each time. Such is the Marxist-Leninist theory of knowledge.[12]

There have been since 1953 several elections for congresses at the grass-roots level, and as less than one per cent of the population over eighteen years of age are disqualified on grounds of counter-revolutionary activity, undefined status, insanity and so on, the revolution has therefore, as we noticed, clearly brought the first experience of elections, voting and representative government to most of China's population. But the holding of elections was not in

[12] Mao, *Selected Works*, III, p. 119.

itself the objective of political change. Politics as the business of bureaucratically organized political parties and interest groups contending for legislative and executive power was not in the line of China's present development. The belief in 'From the masses, to the masses' as an article of faith in China led in the fifties to the movement for the formation of co-operatives and collectives in agriculture, but wrong procedures were applied in some cases to people who were not as convinced about the changes as the activists were. The tremendous upsurge of enthusiasm, wild enthusiasm, at all levels in 1958 which led to the formation of people's communes and to the Great Leap Forward showed how fluid the political situation was. But in some places cadres, carried away by the activists' belief that a great breakthrough into a new era would be achieved by jettisoning carefully laid plans, exceeded their authority in coercing more cautious and circumspect elements among the masses. Some of them later compounded their error by indulging in wishful thinking and sometimes deliberate falsification in their statistics of increased production, thus serving the masses very badly indeed; their action was a set-back for Maoism in China.

3. *The Struggle between the 'Proletarian' and 'Revisionist' Lines*

It was not ordinary human failings – lack of foresight, over-enthusiasm, impatience and others – which were regarded as the greatest dangers for Communist-Party members. It was the corrupt and selfish use of power, the acquiring of special privileges, the suppression of the masses, the belief in material incentives, the introduction of a caste system, and others, which would bring in again the hatred features of the old regime.[13] It was believed that once revisionism – the bourgeoisification of the proletarian attitude – took over, the revolutionary salt would have lost its savour. The belief that much had been achieved already, that those who represented the revolutionary government should be respected because they were in authority, that the experts knew best what was good for the country was a danger. And it became one of the main reasons for the launching of the Great Proletarian Cultural Revolution. But this simplified explanation does not convey the nuances and subtle-

[13] The interpretation of contemporary China which follows is based on an analysis of a good deal of Chinese and foreign material from the spring of 1966 onwards. The documentations will be provided in a fuller account of the 'Cultural Revolution' which is in preparation. There are, of course, many other interpretations of current events in China. A rare visit by an American editor to China, late in 1966, was the occasion for Dave Dellinger's 'Report from Revolutionary China' (*Liberation*, January 1967).

ties either in the 'revisionist' views of the leading office holders who came under attack early in 1966, or in the debate which must have been going on between Mao and non-Maoists. For example, the criticism of cadres who had been bureaucratic and high-handed was apparently used over the years by some people in authority to tone down the radical and proletarian character of the revolution, and to introduce more respectability and 'order'. They encouraged a reaction in a bourgeois direction – somewhat in the way the Soviet Union had moved since the Bolshevik Revolution – and not from the standpoint of the mass line. The economic disasters, especially food shortages, between 1958 and 1961, Mao's relinquishing of the position of head of state to Liu Shao Chi, and his relative obscurity at this time: all this seems to have contributed to a certain unrevolutionary trend in the early 1960's.

By any standards Mao Tse Tung was a man whose personality and abilities marked him out as a leader of the most exceptional genius. There was also a whole galaxy of highly able men and women in the leadership who were not as prominent as they might have been if they had not been outshone by him. They had all made very valuable contributions to the revolution, and commanded great respect. Because of the collegiate system of leadership in China some of Mao's colleagues had considerable authority in their own ministries or areas. Some of them seem, however, to have thought of China's development, of national prestige and strength and greatness, in terms which are characteristic of the 'bourgeois world'. They have undoubtedly been strongly patriotic, but their notions implied assumptions which were highly controversial. The seemingly ceaseless discussion of fundamentals was inevitable.

But the Maoists felt alarmed by the trends within the leadership. If it was good and admirable to be great in the sense of rich, strong and powerful, then it could be assumed that the rich are *ipso facto* superior to the poor, the strong to the weak and the big to the small. China had changed so much that these assumptions seemed to be highly questionable. The values implicit in these assumptions were all of a piece with a belief that it is better to be clever than true, or to be 'expert' than 'red', or even to be erudite than wise. The Revolution had certainly introduced into China – a nation with rich intellectual traditions – a capacity to perceive and sharply distinguish nuances within the political culture to which most people outside China who are sophisticated about political issues are not normally sensitive. This acute awareness of what appear to be subtle distinctions of ultimate assumptions has played an important part in shaping China's political development. For the Maoists the acceptance of certain assumptions of their colleagues meant that a door was being opened to what was termed a 'restoration'. This 'revision' of the proletarian revolutionary assumptions was greatly feared, as it must lead to a counter-revolution which was more deadly than anything that the old 'feudal-capitalist' elements or 'imperialism' threatened China with. Hence the serious character of the struggle which went on over the fundamental aims of policy, and over fundamental questions about what human dignity and worth consisted in. The academics and dignitaries were not interested in these questions, but they were vital to the future of the Chinese masses. If it was better to seek to be rich than to live frugally, why should it not be considered 'better' and more sensible to be rich and not quite free rather than poor and free? The development strategy which gave the highest priority to a quick rise in material standards would be valid if certain moral and spiritual values followed from affluence. But did they? If it was better to have the 'experts' rather than the revolutionaries (or 'reds') directing the country's affairs, did not several other choices follow? That, for example, the modernization of China and her people by the Maoist strategy – that is, revolutionary transformation of human attitudes, relationships and values as well as of the social structure, laws and so on, which all together formed the social and cultural and psychological environment in which human freedom is exercised, and which in their old form had been responsible for the backwardness, oppression and dehumanization of the old society – had better be exchanged for her modernization by the bourgeois strategy – that is, the modernization of her technology. Did it not also follow that engineers and economists knew more about what was good for the country and what could be done for her than a politically conscious and organized people who knew what, with their intelligent understanding of the situation around them, they could achieve through organized and clearly directed community action? These were issues which could not be left undecided in China. And there were other issues as well.

If armed forces trained and equipped in the modern way (and perhaps forming part of a defence alliance) were held to be more efficient for the country's defence than a militia and People's-Liberation-Army-type army, what was implied in this notion of efficiency? To many Chinese it was not just an argument about two alternative methods of doing the same thing. Such a view would seem to the Maoists to betray an insensitiveness to crucial questions about what it was that the Chinese Revolution was about. For what a militarily powerful, well-armed and 'professional' army by itself can defend and secure is fundamentally different from that which needs for its defence the intelligence, vigilance, loyalty and courage of every citizen and his untiring determination never to allow the new China to be destroyed. To begin to rely on others is to end up depending on and serving others. Against this the more conservative forces could argue, firstly, that a defence responsibility shared by the whole community would be inefficient against modern weapons and not act as a deterrent against foreign attack; and, secondly, that it was disorderly and untidy. But what did they mean by order? Similarly, the arguments about seemingly alternative methods of achieving high productivity are held to exist on entirely different planes: in one case there is the dependence for productive 'efficiency' on material and monetary incentives; in the other case people work hard, firstly, because it is taken for granted that the life of the community continues only because of hard and efficient work in which all must share, secondly, because work is part of the revolutionary transformation of the world, and thirdly, because work is an expression of community relations, and the worker is rewarded by its social and political results, not by what he sells his work for. It is not just that the two conceptions of 'incentives' are part of different political philosophies. One represents a way of life labelled 'revisionist' which totally contradicts the way of life, 'proletarian', which the other represents. For example, widely differentiated monetary and material rewards can act as incentives only if it is desirable and prestigious for an individual to possess many things, and also if culturally it is regarded as a superior achievement for a man and his family to live less frugally, in a more affluent style, than most of the rest can afford to do. Was it going to be a society in which there were ranks, or an egalitarian society, in which wage and status differentials remained as narrow as they had become in China? In any case, was not the idea that man needed either a carrot or a stick a libel on humanity? The Maoists might ask.

The battle of alternative policies raged back and forth through the years. The absolutely fundamental cleavage between the two ways of life is related to the fact that China's newly-found 'democracy' did not allow for a 'government party' and 'opposition parties'. The two roads seemed to the Maoists to lead in opposite directions; it was revolution versus restoration, as they saw it. Their opponents believed they had good sense and a sounder rationality to support their case. Many members of the new elite, personally honest and able men and women, must also have felt the appeal of what was best in the Confucian scholar-bureaucracy. There is evidence that 'struggle', in the Maoist sense, continued for years before some attempt to make a decision was made. But it was also a debate about what China's people were capable of, and the issues were, apparently, understood by people at all levels. There must have been conservatives and revolutionaries in debate throughout the country.

The People's Liberation Army underwent a change of policy when Marshal P'eng Teh Huai was Minister of Defence. It had once been unique among armies in not having an officer corps;[14] yet it had produced 'leaders' who had been brilliant both in guerrilla and in conventional warfare. It was out of this school of leadership that there 'graduated' the able top administrators and political organizers who were needed by Chou En Lai and Liu Shao Chi after 1949. Soon after the Korean war the process of 'modernization' began, and the army became more 'professional'; there was now an officer corps, with the usual hierarchy of ranks, and the observance of distinctions between officers and men, and between the military and the political. It was not only in the People's Liberation Army (which had been highly regarded in the country) that there was opposition and criticism on account of this change in what was regarded as an anti-democratic direction. People also observed the army's growing alienation from the masses; and its growing remoteness from the revolutionary process. The first dangers of militarism were apparent. Criticism increased in intensity, especially as there had been parallel trends in industrial management. In 1958 Chu Teh declared:

> There are people who advocate an exclusively military viewpoint, who have a one-sided regard for military affairs and look down upon politics, have a one-sided regard for vocation and technique and look down upon ideology, have a one-sided regard for the role of individuals and neglect the collective strength of the Party and the masses. They only deal with tactics and technique, but not strategy; they only want the army but neglect the function of masses of the people; they only pay attention to national defence, but not to the significance of economic construction to national defence. In essence this is a kind of manifestation of bourgeois military ideas.[15]

The policy was then reversed, probably because Maoist criticism of it won support. The role that non-professionals could play in the country's defence through the militia was emphasized. There was an 'Everyone a Soldier' movement in late 1958, and by 1959 over two hundred million citizens had enrolled in the militia. The issue of whether it was man or weapons which could defend a revolutionary people came to the fore. Late in 1959 P'eng Teh Huai, who was opposed to some of the changes, lost his post of Minister of Defence,

[14] The title 'Marshal' was not created till 1955.

[15] Quoted in John Gittings, *The Role of the Chinese Army* (London: Oxford University Press, 1967), pp. 174-5.

which was then filled by Lin Piao. The role of the People's Liberation Army as a training school for revolutionaries in the widest sense was revived, and by 1964 the Maoists, who seemed to have lost influence within the Communist Party of China were able to launch a country-wide 'Learn from the People's Liberation Army' campaign. The following year the notion of an officer corps was given up. The People's Liberation Army played an important role in the launching of the Cultural Revolution. During the period when revisionists and proletarians fought the issue out, the latter encouraged the masses to believe that what the experts and professionals knew was not beyond their capacity to acquire.

A second example, and perhaps a more momentous one, concerned the future leaders of a revolutionary China. What kind of preparation and training did they need? Did they have to be Communist? And who was a 'Communist'? How was 'democratic centralism' related to 'democracy'? What should a minority which holds the truth do? The issues in the 'struggle' in this case may appear indistinguishable to most foreign observers. But it needs to be remembered that in a country whose millions of newly educated people were being encouraged to 'make revolution' and 'put politics in command', most literature in Chinese was either of a pre-revolutionary and feudal kind, or the material put out by the Communist Party of China. People who wanted to know what it was to be revolutionary had no traditional body of thought to go to. But was the type of Party writing available good enough? The 'struggle' which developed over this eventually focused itself as an attack on the 'top Party person in power', Liu Shao Chi, Mao's successor as head of state, and on Teng Hsiao Ping, Secretary-General of the Communist Party of China. It was broadly an attack by the exponents of the mass line on the party apparatus men.

Liu Shao Chi had in the Yenan period written a manual for the 'self-cultivation' of Communists: entitled in English: *How to Be a Good Communist.* This manual, in which the term 'self-cultivation' was repeated hundreds of times, reads indeed rather like a book of instructions for seminarians or monks who aimed at personal salvation by spiritual exercises in the acquisition of right thoughts and right actions. It could produce only self-conscious, self-centred, self-righteous and very sectarian 'Communists', such as are to be found in most places. Liu Shao Chi's book was reprinted[16] and used, and there is no doubt that the kind of 'ideological self-cultivation' it enjoined turned out from the party schools hundreds of intellectu-

[16] In 1962 as a special edition of *Red Flag.*

ally arid, dogmatic and vulgar Communists – fanatics who held certain abstract ideas to be sacred, but had not learnt how to live and work among other people. Liu in his book had told them, 'Members of our Party are no ordinary people but the awakened vanguard fighters of the proletariat' and 'A member of the Communist Party should possess the finest and highest human virtues'. Liu's view was strongly criticized, one critic pointed out in 1967,

> A person with such a view of life must be filled with vulgar interests, an utterly selfish man with a selfish soul. Such a person will definitely fear and oppose revolution, and become a stumbling stone for the revolution.

Liu had done valuable service for China. It is a matter for controversy whether the 'slavishness' he enjoined and insisted on in his book, as well as his ideas on economic policy, showed that he had become distant in spirit from the motive force of the Chinese Revolution he had helped to lead. But when it came to influencing the future development of China his type of 'vulgar Communism' could only be regarded as a pernicious influence by those who wanted to have nothing to do with 'self-cultivation'. The remnants of the old feudal and capitalist China would cease to exist. But a new kind of elite was being created who would carry on and entrench bourgeois selfishness and individualism in a new form. The kind of obedient, colourless man or woman who had been trained to 'submit' to the party and 'deny' his human interests in order to cultivate himself would tend to be an inhuman tyrant in dealing with the heathen over whom he was placed in authority. Instead of building up a world in which people would be outspoken, independent in spirit, unafraid and rebellious, this new priesthood of the Chinese Revolution would produce meek and submissive subjects. Indeed unquestioning obedience to authority was already part of the heritage of the old China. For these and other reasons, we gather, the campaign was launched to save the Communist Party of China from continued infection by 'revisionism' and from taking the road to a restoration of the values of the old order. But, some Maoists believed, the revisionists were using their positions of high authority to suppress criticism, therefore it seemed that only an attack against those who had the greatest authority could restore proletarianism.

By the end of 1965, therefore, the tremendous pressure of discontent with what Maoists regarded as the general laxness seems to have been built up. Leading intellectuals – 'philosophers' like Yang Hsien Chen, economists like Sun Yeh Fang, historians like Wu Han, educationists, literary critics and others – were felt to have entrenched themselves in key positions, and to be spreading a 'bourgeois' ideology. They were apparently under the protection of highly placed anti-proletarians, and in a position to deny their rivals or opponents opportunities for refuting them. Therefore there came the call, printed in the newspaper *Renmin Ribao* (*People's Daily*) of 3 June 1966, to proletarians to 'capture the positions' 'seized' by the bourgeoisie and the 'royalists'. The 'Paris Commune' spirit was invoked. In Peking University students and teachers had observed how the socialist 'work-and-study' programme had been ignored, and they had also been powerless to prevent students from a proletarian background from being discriminated against by the President of the University. The University authorities were so much in league with the party authorities that the self-correcting process which was devised had been corrupted. A mood of rebellion was growing at 'Beida' (Peking University). Those who were outraged by injustices and corrupt practices were not allowed to demand change. When the Proletarian Cultural Revolution began, the young rebels took their cue, and their struggle against the power apparatus helped greatly in the exposure of its increasingly conformist and totalitarian character.

It was the young, many of them children of once illiterate peasants who had grown up in the pre-revolutionary environment, who were most roused by the establishment's demand for 'order', respectability and 'moderation' to strike the hardest blow for the renewal of the revolutionary spirit. We have already referred to the *dazibao* of 24 June 1966 which was put up in support of Nieh Yuan Tzu and her colleagues by the students of the school attached to Tsinghua University in Peking. Since it was partly in this school that the Red Guard movement had its beginnings, their poster must have made a tremendous impression on young people throughout China. It said:

> Revolution is rebellion, and rebellion is the soul of Mao Tse Tung's thought. We hold that tremendous attention must be paid to the word 'application', that is, mainly to the word 'rebellion'. Daring to think, to speak, to act, to break through, and to make revolution, in a word, daring to rebel, is the most fundamental and most precious quality of proletarian revolutionaries. This is the fundamental principle of the proletarian Party spirit! Not to rebel is revisionism, pure and simple!
>
> Revisionism has been in control of the school for seventeen years. If we do not rise up in rebellion today, when are we going to?
>
> Some bold people who were against rebellion have, today, suddenly turned coy and shy, humming and hawing incessantly about us being too one-sided, too high and mighty, too rude, and going too far.

All this is rank nonsense! If you are against us, then say so. Why be bashful about it?

Since we want rebellion, the matter has been taken out of your hands! We are going to make the air thick with the pungent smell of explosives. Toss them over, grenades and stick bombs together, and start a big fight. 'Sympathy', 'all-sidedness', out of the way!

You say we are too one-sided? What then is your all-sidedness? Your all-sidedness looks like 'two combining into one', eclecticism.

You say we are too high and mighty? We are high and mighty. Chairman Mao has said: 'And those in high positions we counted no more than dust.' We are going to strike down not only the reactionaries in our school, but the reactionaries of the whole world too. Revolutionaries consider the transformation of the world is their task. How can we not be 'high and mighty'?

You say we are too rude? We should be rude. How can we be soft and clinging towards revisionism or go in for moderation in a big way? To be moderate towards the enemy is to be cruel to the revolution!

You say we are going too far? To put it bluntly, your 'avoid going too far' is reformism; it is 'peaceful transition'. You are day-dreaming! We are going to strike you down to the dust and keep you there!

And there are some who are scared to death of revolution, scared to death of rebellion. Sticklers for convention, obsequious, curled up inside your revisionist shells, as soon as there is a whiff of rebellion in the air, you get nervous and afraid. Recently, heartless censures have every day been poured into your ears and, daily, your hearts beat with fear. Don't you feel it insufferable? Hasn't life become unbearable?

Revolutionaries are Monkey Kings, their golden rods are powerful, their supernatural powers far-reaching and their magic omnipotent, for they possess Mao Tse-tung's great invincible thought. We wield our golden rods, display our supernatural powers and use our magic to turn the old world upside down, smash it to pieces, pulverize it, create chaos and make a tremendous mess, the bigger the better! We must do this to the present revisionist middle school attached to the Tsinghua University, make rebellion in a big way, rebel to the end! We are bent on creating a tremendous proletarian uproar, and hewing out a proletarian new world!

Long live the revolutionary rebel spirit of the proletariat!

Red Guards
Middle School Attached to
Tsinghua University
24 June 1966.[17]

As in the case of all translations, the English version of this declaration perhaps does not convey what it means to Chinese listeners and readers. Apart from the allusions which are lost unless one has followed earlier controversies in the Chinese People's Republic, the expressions when taken literally can lead to *bona fide*

[17] Quoted in *Peking Review*, September 1966.

mistakes about 'calls to beating, robbing and killing' (see p. 33). The revolutionary rebels met with opposition and counter-attacks from persons in power who were, or were likely, to become targets of criticism, as well as from the kind of dogmatists who had been expert at 'self-cultivation'. It is certain that in some places some rebels initially had a very hard time at the hands of the Communist Party of China leadership. There were undoubtedly cases where Red Guards exceeded the limits set by the sixteen-point Central Committee decision of 8 August 1966. Repeated appeals by the Maoist leaders against bullying and violence showed that Mao's teachings were not always followed. But considering the nature of the upheaval throughout the country, and the remoteness from Peking of some areas where there was Communist-Party opposition, the minute proportion of incidents of violence or physical coercion which occurred, and the orderliness of the proceedings in the country, showed how far China had progressed since the last days of the previous era.

The use of the posters for a vigorous political discussion meant that the Chinese people now had a freedom of expression which was immediate and real. There were occasionally silly posters, conveying or based on inaccurate information; there were some which were less original or less gracefully worded than others. But the manifestations of 'instant democracy', which can call officials to account publicly, and which encourages the immediate public expression of political views in the *dazibao*, were signs that China was on the way to a democracy which was as peculiar to her as was her revolution.

At the end of its plenary session in the summer of 1966, the Central Committee of the Communist Party of China issued a communique, in the course of which it said:

> The Plenary Session holds that the key to the success of this great cultural revolution is to have faith in the masses, rely on them, boldly arouse them and respect their initiative. It is therefore imperative to persevere in the line of 'from the masses, to the masses'. Be pupils of the masses before becoming their teachers. Dare to make revolution and be good at making revolution. Don't be afraid of disturbances. Oppose the taking of the bourgeois stand, the shielding of Rightists, attacks on the Left and repression of the great proletarian cultural revolution. Oppose the creation of a lot of restrictions to tie the hands of the masses. Don't be overlords or stand above the masses, blindly ordering them about.

Matters of the highest importance for China have for months been fiercely argued throughout the country, and groups and organizations formed and re-formed. The close contact that Mao has had with the older generation of 'rebels' in Kiangsi and Yenan has been made with their children's and grandchildren's generation by massive rallies and widespread distribution of the printed selections of his teachings and analyses of events.

The Proletarian Cultural Revolution has in no ordinary sense been a 'struggle for power'. Through it the 'revolutionaries', who long chafed at the bourgeois and Russianizing trends of the political apparatus, have reinstated Mao in his role as the sage of a modern, world-conscious China which has broken with the past, the prophet of proletarian humanism, the conscience of the Revolution, and the champion of the 'new man'. The Party functionaries were not to be dismissed or supplanted by other functionaries, but put through an ideological and spiritual purgation through 'struggle' with revolutionary rebels, and through collaboration with them in the revolutionary Triple Alliance. This had to take place in every province, municipality, factory and college. Mao has not been trying to seize power; but, rather, to get *the people* to control and supervise its use through proletarian political and economic organizations. With the old order less than twenty years away it was an act of great daring to try to scale the heights of socialist democracy in a country where people in their tens of millions are dispersed throughout a vast area. There has been confusion. But mass organizations have had the burden of identifying, in the light of true revolutionary doctrine, the leadership capable of sustaining a moral and ideological challenge to men legally in power. They are being challenged to change, not accept, the world of today.

The 'revisionists' have, however, stood their ground. They had evidently been able, whether innocently or tactically we cannot say, to get themselves into strong positions, at the centre and in the provinces. It is possible that the Maoists' insistence on strict abstention from intervention in Vietnam may have helped their opponents. There are many subtleties – personality clashes, regional factors, variations in the pace of change, etc. – in the dispute which most non-Chinese can hardly understand. The way in which the rebels among workers and students and peasants have freely created new structures and organizations is truly amazing. The re-publication in June 1967 of Mao's *On the Proper Handling of Contradictions Among the People*, with its six criteria for judging 'non-antagonistic' contradictions, indicates that what he had hoped to see develop in 1956 was constructive mass-democratic activity of the kind which has characterized China, and confused the China-watchers, in 1967.

8

The Human Implications of the Revolution: for the World

1. The Emergence of a Major New Force

IN THE October of 1948 a part of the People's Liberation Army was grouped in the area of the city of Hsuchow. About two hundred miles to the north of them was the highly important Peking-Tientsin area held by Chiang Kai Shek's armies; at the same distance to the south-east was Nanking, to which the Kuomintang regime had moved its capital back from Chungking after Japan's defeat; to the south-west, higher up in the Yangtze valley, was the important urban complex of Wuhan-Hankow. Not only Hsuchow but also the other cities and towns in the area were under the control of Chiang's troops, who had been trained and were 'advised' by the Americans, and equipped by them with tanks, heavy artillery and other modern weapons.

Just after the second World War the conservative nationalists had been in a very strong position. Japan's surrender had given them a great boost, even though they had contributed little to it, and some of them had in fact collaborated with the Japanese. The representation of themselves to the world as *the* independent government of all China and leading partners in the war-time alliance had been accepted almost throughout the world, whereas the cave men of Yenan had hardly been heard of. But in the three years since Chiang had decided to renew his campaign against the revolutionaries, the fact that he had never commanded the allegiance of all China had become much clearer than it had ever been when the old censorship had been effective. The world was becoming aware that China had not been the kind of country it had been made out to be. The men and women who fought, first against the pre-war Kuomintang dictatorship and then against the Japanese and their puppet 'government of China', were now fighting, with increasing effectiveness, against a renewed attempt by the Kuomintang to assert its authority over all China. In the summer of 1948 things had been happening very rapidly, and the once-meagre forces of Mao's peasant fighters, armed with a motley assortment of captured weapons, had been greatly expanded by volunteers from the Kuomintang areas and deserters from its armies. As the Communist-led troops grouped for an attack in the Hsuchow area, Chiang's generals knew that they had either to hold or to destroy the People's Liberation Army in order both to protect the vital region of central China and to ensure Chiang's continued hold over his own subjects and his forces. What would happen if the People's Liberation Army were able to cross the Yangtze could have immense consequences. On the other hand, if the revolutionaries were being over-confident in going over to the offensive, and were badly defeated, they would lose a good part of their best troops.

When Mao Tse Tung, who had earlier been driven out from the caves of Yenan, gave the People's Liberation Army commanders (among whom was General Ch'en Yi) orders to launch their major offensive there began the first part of what is known as the Battle of Hsuchow, or the Hsuchow campaign. Although few people outside China had during that autumn caught up with the swift progress of events in China at that time, or knew what was happening, this battle was to be one of the decisive battles not only in Chinese history, but in world history. To understand how its issue could affect our own destinies we must go back a few years to view those events in context. In fact we are now, about twenty years later, in a much better position to see the history of the post-war years in true perspective than were people in the forties, who did not have the record of the specific discussions and policy-considerations of major political leaders, and for whom the objective pattern of events was obscured both by current propaganda and by emotion. For us, fortunately, the so-called 'Cold War' has been demythologized.

The second World War had been frightful in what it cost mankind. Tens of millions of people had been killed, homes and cities and industries destroyed, previously unrecorded cruelties practised on a large scale, and the whole course of civilized existence distorted. It was not accidental that the immediate cause of the war was the aggression against their rivals of the two later-comers on the scene of the major imperial powers of the nineteenth century, Germany and Japan. To the ordinary people of the world, who had personally paid the cost of the war, it was inconceivable that there should ever again be another World War. The weapons of indiscriminate mass destruction developed towards the end of the war, even before the atom bomb was exploded, indicated what kind of war a third World

War would be. It is true that among the victors in the conflict there were some who self-righteously and hypocritically aimed to make moral capital for themselves and their interests out of the aggression committed by the Fascists, and there were others who had calculated the political and material gains which victory would bring to those who survived. But the overwhelming desire to achieve as quickly as possible a return to peace and stability, and to prevent the recurrence of the aggressive and expansionist ways of the past, was uppermost in the minds of those for whom there was clearly no glory or gain but only suffering and shame in war. To Roosevelt, who saw how much the rivalries of imperialism, with its false notions of 'prestige', racial superiority and the mission to rule over alien nations, bred aggression, the mercenary aims of the old imperial nations were obvious; to Stalin, who had seen his country ravaged, security against another attack of the same kind from Germany demanded continued collaboration with her war-time allies. The war-time conferences at Cairo, Teheran and Yalta were a sound basis for the kind of consensus among the 'big powers' and especially between the two 'super-powers', which would guarantee a stable and peaceful post-war order. The United Nations was devised as the instrument through which they could do this. To the peoples of the world's industrialized 'north' this promise of a continued collaboration during the period of post-war reconstruction was very welcome. Nearly the whole of the 'south' had been ruled or controlled by the northern powers, and it was taken for granted that the 'powers' would gradually call into being in the 'backward' continents politically autonomous states which would respect the interests of other countries, accept the basis of the new world order, and work together in the United Nations and its various organizations.

However, as we know now, things did not quite work out as the optimists had expected. On Roosevelt's death President Truman had initiated a tougher policy towards the Soviet Union.[1] On the strength of America's possession of the new nuclear weapon, he had tried, but without success, to intimidate an exhausted Russia into climbing down from her position of equal partner, and into withdrawing from positions she had secured in Eastern Europe. Stalin, not easily intimidated, got equally tough. Though the collaboration in setting up the United Nations continued, there developed the mutual antagonism between the two blocs of nations – 'the first world' (the international free-enterprise, capitalist society)

[1] Gar Alperovitz, *Atomic Diplomacy* (New York: Simon & Schuster, 1965); see also James P. Warburg, *The United States in the Post War World* (London: Gollancz, 1966).

under North Atlantic leadership and the 'second world' of East European communists under Soviet Russian leadership – which led to their joint attempt to polarize or interpret in terms of United States-Soviet rivalry and competition the politics of the rest of the world. This rivalry, interestingly enough, did not prevent a good deal of collaboration between the 'big powers' where the rest of the world was concerned. The big two, or the big four (the United States, Soviet Union, Britain and France) were united in the assumption that it was by agreement among themselves that any developments would occur in the new world order. Russia, in return for her veto powers in the United Nations Security Council and her sphere of influence in Eastern Europe, had to agree to a United Nations General Assembly in which the Americans could automatically command a majority of votes to get resolutions passed.

To the governments of the Big Four – all of them old imperial powers – had been added a fifth, that of Chiang Kai Shek in Nanking. This arrangement had given the West four of the permanent votes in the Security Council, and it was generally believed that the government of China had been accorded equal status with the others. She was the only one outside the 'northern' hemisphere, or the developed world of Euramerica, to be accorded this status. China, formerly the victim of all these nations, had been the first victim of attack by a Fascist power, and the resistance of her people to Japan had played an important part in the War as a whole. However, apart from the period 1937-8 when Chiang's armies were allowed to fight the Japanese, and sometimes fought extremely well, the Kuomintang forces had come very near to coexisting with Japanese-ruled China; it was undoubtedly in the areas in the north where the revolutionary forces were based that there had been effective political-military resistance to Japan, as well as enthusiastic support for the worldwide alliance of anti-Fascist forces. But though Chiang himself was known to have a Fascist ideology and to be 'soft' towards Japan, he had, ever since his kidnapping and release at Sian in December 1936, been built up as a symbol of a *national* resistance, a united *Chinese* resistance to Japanese imperialism. Owing to the national emergency, Mao had wanted Chiang's government to be the international representative of China during the War.

When the War drew to a close, major issues about their own country which had since 1927 not been settled among the Chinese came to the fore. Japan surrendered, her puppet administration in China collapsed and it became an urgent matter to decide how the Chinese people as a whole could get the kind of good government they had yet to see. Mao had gone to Chungking in 1945, and for the first time since they had worked as colleagues in the old, revolutionary Kuomintang, Mao and Chiang met. But the meeting produced no results. Any voluntary diminution by Chiang and his associates of their dictatorial powers and the formation of a national government for all of China seemed out of the question. What then were the Chinese people, who had suffered much, going to do about their country's future? What government did they want? Who was to be given the task of decolonizing China and reconstructing her, and according to what programme was she to be rebuilt?

Before these questions could be decided by the Chinese, their future was being decided in Washington and Moscow. The rule of Chiang for the whole of China was by big-power consensus to be part of the post-war world order and stability. And Chiang had in return made concessions to Russia and America at China's expense which obviously he had no authority to do.[2] This raised for the Chinese questions and issues of colonial history which had still not been settled. The allocation among themselves by the northern powers of the right to promote certain national interests abroad revived the clash of China's own interests with those of the interests and authority of the Euramerican nations in China.

What was it that was decisive in the legitimization of a government in the southern world? Was it its approval and adoption by the major Euramerican powers, or the mandate its nationals gave it by their choice and consent? This question must seem irrelevant and absurd to us, especially if we are Europeans or Americans. But it has dominated the minds of politically-conscious peoples in the colonial and semi-colonial world for many years. The Chinese, who had fought the war as a semi-colonial people, mobilizing all their anti-imperialist feeling in the resistance to Japanese rule, shared the same anxieties as other Asian peoples. Like the other Asian and like the African and Latin-American peoples they had been deeply humiliated and angered by what they saw as the racial discrimination which had legitimized what the 'whites' of Euramerica did to the 'coloured' peoples, and which assumed that the latter were 'right' only when they got the approval of the whites or abided by the 'law' and 'order' which they created. What was felt as even a greater oppression and affront than the economic limitations imposed by colonialism was the racial insult implicit in the assumption that not only in their own lands but throughout the world outside Euramerica 'white' interests, loyalties and values took priority or precedence over those of the 'coloureds'. Coloured peoples, the Chinese

[2] See the White Paper published by the United States Government, *United States Relations with China*, p. 95.

among them, had regarded with scepticism and hostility the Euramerican condominium which was called international law and order.

Before the end of the first World War the consensus of the imperial nations of Europe, together with the United States and Japan, determined the fate of other peoples; it constituted the basis of 'international law' and of normality and order. Colonial governments were the legitimate ones; foreign conquests by one or another were recognized, provided there was no trespass by one into a sphere of operations assigned by this consensus to another power.

This was the way of the world. During first World War there had been the Allies' insistence on the disgorging by 'aggressors' of their foreign conquests, and the self-determination of peoples who were under foreign rule. But the Zaghlul Pashas and Ho Chi Minhs, who had set out for the Versailles Conference of 1919, and the Sun Yat Sens and Mohandas Gandhis, who had taken this principle to apply to them at home, discovered that their peoples did not enter into the purview of international relations. The war was a war among the imperial nations. The empires of the vanquished were broken up; the victors acquired more territory than they already had.

The Chinese found that part of the Chinese territory which Germany had treated as if it were her colony was assigned by the Treaty of Versailles to Japan; and they made their views known in the May 4 movement. The Arab lands, which had nominally been ruled by Turkey, were partitioned, and not given back to the Arabs. What from the Asian and African point of view was the humiliating position and degraded status of the coloured peoples, continued to be an essential part of the international order up to the outbreak of the second World War.

The creation of the Soviet Union, and the subsequent rise to power in it of Stalin, created a world situation in which, on the old assumptions of Euramerica's right to rule the world, two imperial systems had to share the spoils of war, and achieve some kind of consensus in order to prevent the world order from breaking up. Magnificent things had been written and spoken during the War about human freedom, the end of rule by force and terror, the evils of racialism and the non-recognition of the 'right' to seize by conquest. But it was discovered that neither Roosevelt's so-called Four Freedoms,[3] nor the declared aims of the allied leaders about the liberation of subject territories, was meant to be taken seriously by

[3] I.e. freedoms of speech and expression, of worship, from want, and from fear. (These freedoms were meant to be realized 'everywhere in the world'.) It was delivered in his Message to Congress, 6 January 1941.

the subject peoples of the world who for generations had sought to regain the freedom to rule themselves: these solemn declarations neither implied the restoration of national liberty nor precluded the acquiring of more territory by the victors in a war. The last of the great empires, Japan's New Asia (or Greater Co-Prosperity Sphere, as it was called), had fallen. Her subject peoples found that they had been wrong to assume that with the defeat of the ruling imperial power in such countries as Indonesia, Annam, China and Burma, the indigenous anti-Fascist forces would have the countries restored to them. In Europe and Asia Russia annexed vast territories, and also extended her power by a new type of colonial device – the creation of puppet states. The United States and Britain did the same. Allied commanders ordered the vanquished Japanese to take up arms and resist the Asian nationalists who were taking over or had taken over from the Japanese in north China, Vietnam, and Indonesia. Korea did not go to the Koreans, but was partitioned between the Russians and the Americans. To Asians who were determined not to be bound by what Europeans or Americans thought of their 'inferiority' and 'unfitness for democracy', it seemed that the Churchills, Trumans and Stalins, whose minds had been formed in the pre-war era, had not been changed by the struggle against Fascism. But could the Asians do anything about it? Would they take the initiative?

Some nationalists had never accepted their inferior or subject status, and had continued to struggle all through the colonial period. The Vietnamese were a proudly independent nation, and they made up their minds that the Japanese would be the last of their imperial rulers. Japan surrendered in August 1945. That same month the Vietnamese, who had carried on an anti-Japanese resistance, organized the revolutionary seizure of power, and created their independent republic. The Japanese puppet, Emperor Bao Dai, abdicated. But by September the first shots in a new worldwide struggle had already been fired. This new struggle was in a real sense a continuation of the struggle of which the second World War of the history books was an important part. It was directed against all the political evils (which Germany and Japan had manifested in the most extreme form) – foreign rule and exploitation, the belief that might is right, the claim that certain races or nations had the mission to be world rulers or rulers over other races, local traitors who had collaborated with foreigners to oppress their own fellow-citizens.

And so it was that citizens of the new Democratic Republic of Vietnam, who had assumed that with Japan's surrender they had finally freed themselves from imperialist rule, found themselves fighting against Japanese, British, French, Indians under British command, and Africans under French command.

It is essential to understand the actual course that history was taking at this time. It is not the history in the history books of Western countries, but it was none the less what most non-westernized Asians are convinced did happen. And it was in that context that what was happening in China was crucial for the power of the big four to keep revolutionary nationalism in Asia and other parts of the Third World in control, and to ensure peaceful transition. Chiang, who in fact was not the ruler of all China, had been recognized as the sole ruler of China by the governments of Russia, the United States and Britain. The Russians were convinced that no initiative which was not taken by the big four would have any significance. The Soviet Foreign Minister, Molotov, had spoken contemptuously of the Chinese revolutionaries under Mao. The continued rule of the Kuomintang in China was essential to the interests of the powers which now dominated world affairs: it would secure the kind of order they had guaranteed in the world, and it would be a government of China which was obliged to both the United States and Soviet Union, and too weak to be a challenge to either of them in Asia and the west Pacific. Chiang had had close contacts with Moscow as well as with Washington.

The resumption of the civil war between the two Chinese regimes created new problems. Mao and his colleagues were not concerned about what non-Chinese wanted in China. Faced with the attempts of Chiang, with vast armies, American training and equipment, to subdue or to annihilate them, they had to fight for control of China. The war did not go as Chiang had expected. By the summer of 1948 Lin Piao's brilliant campaigns in Manchuria had made it clear who was to control that vital region. Things were moving too quickly for conservative forces outside China to know what to do, and in any case, it was becoming too apparent that Chiang had no support in China. The battle of Hsuchow was going to decide very important issues (cf. pp. 171-2). If it ended in the defeat of the People's Liberation Army or in a stalemate, Chiang and his backers would still have time. A thoroughgoing clean-up of his Kuomintang administration, perhaps with some other acceptable person in Chiang's place, would have made more direct Western intervention feasible. Chiang was certainly much chastened by the Manchurian *débâcle*. If the kind of policy of more massive support for the Kuomintang, which some of the later critics of America's China policy had wanted, had been followed, it may have roused Soviet opposition, and forced Moscow to offer help to Mao's forces. The more practicable possibility was, of course, a partition of China which would have the United States-Soviet Union-backed Kuomintang in control in Nanking, with North China, temporarily, abandoned to the revolutionaries; Yenan's China would be more extensive than it had been before, and have its capital in Peiping; but it need not have been given any international status or security.[4]

But when the battle of Hsuchow ended in January 1949 the Kuomintang's defeat there was so complete that all hopes of a stalemate were destroyed. That same month Chiang withdrew into the background, and under General Li Tsung-Jen, one of the few honest Kuomintang leaders, an attempt to begin peace negotiations was made. But Mao and his colleagues could not see how without certain minimum changes, including land-reform and the end of the Kuomintang dictatorship, China could be at peace. His conditions for peace were rejected, and the civil war continued, with the People's Liberation Army crossing the Yangtze and taking Nanking. There was no going back to the pre-war situation. And there was not going to be a part of China left for Chiang. It is suggested that Mao was advised by Stalin and others not to cross the Yangtze, and not to eliminate the Kuomintang regime. But Mao did not heed the advice. The whole of China except for Taiwan and the offshore islands where United-States-protected 'China' moved, was 'liberated'.

The Chinese Revolution had radically altered the situation in the Third World, and thus had been the most disastrous blow to the Euramerican 'big-power consensus'. The people of China had taken an initiative in making history which had just not been provided for in the plans for the post-War world. They had acted in the face of big-power opposition, and had shown that they had the power to decide the role that China was going to play, whether or not that role was approved. Could it be played in the context of the world order they had defied? This was the question that the new China faced the outside world with.

It was the self-confidence, the independence, the dynamism and the aggressive disregard of the new China for the status quo that were to show the kind of impact she was going to make. Quite clearly she was, by her history and her experience, anti-imperialist, and made that fact plain – though what is really meant was not yet clear. The Soviet Union had affected an attitude of contempt for the Communist leaders of China's revolution. Their Embassy had

[4] In view of the Western intention of disregarding the 1954 Geneva Agreements on reunification in Vietnam, this was roughly what was achieved when the Democratic Republic of Vietnam forces defeated the French at Dien Bien Phu.

followed the Kuomintang remnants even to Canton in 1949. But Stalin accepted the inevitable. If Russia was to get special privileges in China it would have to get them from Mao, not from Chiang. If the rest of the world recognized the new government what would happen? On 18 November 1949, China's new Foreign Minister, Chou En Lai, wrote from Peking to the United Nations Secretary General Trygve Lie informing him of the change of government, and, in terms of the United Nations Charter, of the fact that the old delegation sent by Chiang did not represent China. This could only mean that one of the most important delegations at the United Nations, with a veto power in the Security Council, was going to be nominated by Chou En Lai. But the world never had the opportunity to find out how the United Nations would have worked in 1950 and onwards with one of her Permanent Members a new government from the Third World, anti-imperialist, independent, resolutely opposed to the 'consensus'.

For the Western governments, who had preponderance in the United Nations, the main threat to the conservation of the old order was the danger of the nationalist movements combining into an anti-imperialist movement. Some of the radical proposals made at the Asian Relations Conference in 1947 were rejected because the Conference Organizers were the more conservative Indian nationalists. For the West the real problems in the Asian region was how to placate the leaders of the nationalist movements while retaining the Western position in Asia. The refusal of the Vietnamese to compromise any more than they were willing to do in 1946 had been enough of a problem. Any doubts about whether China would follow India and respect Western interests in Asia did not last long. In January 1950 the Democratic Republic of Vietnam, fighting for her life against the French, who had American and British backing, was given diplomatic recognition for the first time by China.[5] At the same time as she manifested her total disregard for the Western powers' special position in Asia, China made her new priorities clear in other ways. She was in no hurry about exchanging ambassadors with Great Britain but established cordial diplomatic relations with other Asian countries. Her insistence that strict equality, mutual benefit and mutual respect[6] would in future be the basis for friendly relations with other countries, including those who had done as they pleased in China before, was also dangerous in its implications: for

[5] Russia was forced to follow suit, though for years she had not done anything to help the Vietnamese. It had been part of the war-time 'deal' that each major power would keep to its own sphere of influence.

[6] See p. 72 for Mao's statement on this.

it established a standard by which the unequal relations between the 'big powers' and the rest would be tested and found wanting.

In the first months of the new regime 'imperialists', who had intervened in China's domestic affairs, or who were unwelcome for some other reason, were deliberately treated with a minimum of courtesy. There was a policy of making the Americans and Europeans who had treated Chinese as inferiors 'lose face', so that the 'white man' would never more be held in awe by the Chinese people. The leaders knew how deeply-rooted and habitual this fear and awe was, and the techniques used were meant to be effectively therapeutic. 'Foreign devils' who had indulged in practices which were normal and 'common in Kuomintang China were detained or imprisoned for 'criminal activities' in a manner which both infuriated and frightened Europeans and Americans in China. With great determination the new government set about rooting out attitudes of Chinese inferiority or servility to Europeans and North Americans, and restoring faith and confidence in things Chinese.[7]

With equal aggressiveness and fervour the new leaders set about dispelling any notions that, for what they wanted to do, Chinese needed the approval or permission of foreigners, or that their achievements had to be judged by the standards laid down by the Americans, British or Russians. In China the Chinese challengingly proclaimed, by their actions, henceforth Chinese authority and Chinese interests would be paramount and absolute. The Chinese were also to decide their own future for themselves. The British government's action in sending warships up the Yangtze River into the heart of China as the People's Liberation Army was advancing on to Nanking in 1949 had greatly angered the Chinese revolutionaries. In the fighting which ensued the People's Liberation Army suffered casualties, and the frigate *Amethyst* was damaged. Winston Churchill, then in opposition, wanted one or two British aircraft carriers sent into Chinese waters to retaliate. In the past if Chinese had anywhere in their country crossed the path of any national of an imperial nation they were taught a lesson. But this was no longer the case. With characteristic intensity of purpose the new leaders set about making the ordinary Chinese forget the lessons of the Opium Wars, of the Boxer War and of similar punishments.

The determination of the Chinese leaders to root out, emotionally and psychologically, any awe and fear of 'imperialism', and the methods used, were deeply offensive to the West, and the Chinese knew it. The revolutionary leaders wanted to make it impossible for any Chinese faction to allow foreigners to be arbiters of China's

[7] For a fuller account see William Sewell, *I Stayed in China*.

internal affairs, and also to make the traditional paternalism and attitudes of racial superiority of Europeans and Americans in Asia untenable. This was decolonization with a vengeance, and an unmistakable indication that the debunking of what revolutionary nationalists in Asia regarded as the 'imperialist myths' would be relentlessly pursued. The Americans and Europeans realized that the People's Liberation Army victories had brought into being a China 'fanatically' hostile to their position in Asia.

The revolutionary change of status of the Third World achieved by the resurgence of China without aid or authority from others was not the only problem. There is also the effect of the new China's ability to survive and grow in spite of all the measures taken against her by the West and, later, by the North Atlantic and Soviet blocs together. Whatever the Chinese have wanted to do in their country they have been able to do, with the possible exception of exercising the sovereignty they have claimed over Taiwan. The harassment and propaganda from abroad they have found inconvenient, but, on the other hand, their ineffectiveness has shown up the impotence of those who took it upon themselves to do something about China's resurgence. This aspect we must examine again later in greater detail.

2. *A Quarter of Mankind*

We are assessing the consequences for the world as a whole of the course that events have taken in China under Maoist leadership. Before we begin to look at direct Chinese influence and activity outside China, we must notice the universal significance of what, in spite of opposition from abroad, China has been able to achieve.

The Chinese form nearly a half of Asia's population (if we exclude Japan). Though sociologically pre-revolutionary China was not typical of all Asia, she shared with her neighbours many of the features of a highly developed pre-industrial culture, a largely peasant population, a colonial economy and a dependence on Western techniques for modernization. She had a variety of peoples within her, and one cannot think of what happens in China without at the same time thinking about the whole Asian continent. Secondly the Chinese also form one-third of the world's poor. More truly than in the case of any other single country, what is done or not done for them is done or not done for the world's proletariat, if by 'proletariat' we mean those who while bearing the burdens of toil have had no status or power in their societies. Thirdly, the Chinese peasantry constitute a large part of the peasantry in the 'underdeveloped' world.

China's problems then, have been a substantial part of the problems of the poor, of the subject peoples, of the peasantry, of the world. They also, as the peoples of the other great Asian nation, India, will not mind acknowledging, represent the most important of the problems of modernization and resurgence for the great Oriental civilizations of pre-industrial times. The sheer size and scale of the problems to be identified and solved make success or failure within China a large part of success or failure in the whole world. We could have learnt a great deal about the plight of man in the twentieth century by studying what was going on in China in the past. We can now learn a great deal about the unusual human implications of China's resurgence simply by looking within China, at what is happening to men, women and children there. As we suggested earlier, if it is true that, in a country as potentially great (because of the quality of her past achievements) as China is, there have been increased misery, disease, starvation and so on as some of the 'experts' report,[8] it would have been a set-back and a disaster for the world. Fortunately, for those who are concerned about the welfare of the poor, these reports are untrue, on the contrary, China's standard of living is rising. And every thirty-dollar increase in the per capita income in China raises the per capita of the world's more than two thousand million poor by ten dollars.

There are problems other than those of ending the conditions which bred poverty. A nation composed of a variety of ethnic groups or nationalities, some of whom are minorities considerably more backward than others, is a common feature in Asia, as well as in Africa and Latin America. How equity can be achieved, and inequalities eliminated, in the process of modernization, is a question which has not been answered in most countries. There are also problems of how the masses can organize to exercise democratic powers, which need to be discussed separately.

China, as her top leaders have said very clearly, has a long way to go before her people can reach the goals set by the revolution. The predominance of the 'revisionists' will probably mean that economic growth – in the sense of the rate of increase of the gross national product – will be greater, but it also implies that within the country inequalities will remain or increase, and more autocratic methods of rule will be restored. The Maoists will probably invest much more effort in China's now seven hundred and fifty million people, and economic growth in what they would regard as the narrower sense would be less spectacular than it would be under the others. But China's progress on all fronts has already been unprecedented

[8] See Chapter Two above.

among countries with similar economic problems, and she is at present well set on the road to a steady improvement in living conditions for every Chinese. An important aspect of the impact of the revolution on the world is that the task of alleviating a large part of the burden of gross poverty, ignorance, disease, debility and low productivity which blights the consciences and lives of mankind has been taken over by the Chinese people, and appears to be in competent hands. Furthermore, in an area where natural disaster brought destruction to hundreds of thousands of people, and little was done before to prevent it, it is now clear that remedial and precautionary measures are being taken by people with intelligence and foresight. It is now possible for that part of the world which is genuinely concerned with the evils of poverty and human misery not only to concentrate on a smaller area of work elsewhere, but also to feel encouraged by what has been achieved already in just a few years.

Not least of all the implications of the scale and thoroughness of the transformation of man and his man-made environment in China is what it has begun to achieve for the vast urban areas. Any sensitive person who contemplates the problems of Calcutta, Djakarta, Lima and similar cities must feel a terrible despair. But Shanghai was perhaps in an even worse condition. Its transformation from a typically overcrowded and miserable colonial city to a well-organized, clean, urban, industrial centre, in vital relationship with the rest of a rapidly developing economy, gives hope to such cities as Calcutta. Not all of Shanghai's problems have been solved. But it is in the decisive change of direction taken by it that its value as a model of meaningful urban development lies.

The fact that Mao's belief that 'of all the things in the world people are the most precious' has turned out not to be just pious sentiment but to function in practice which throws new light on what is called the problem of overpopulation. If this practical application meant what one Pekinologist described – the killing off deliberately by Mao of millions of his own people so that their bodies could be used as manure for Chinese agriculture – the Chinese 'solution' would not perhaps be very relevant. But the Chinese seem in fact to have alternative ways of dealing with the problems of a single national economy which has had to function partly under conditions of siege, supporting the needs of seven hundred and fifty millions. The elimination of gross malnutrition, cholera, plague and numerous other scourges which seem to be chronic in the southern hemisphere and the strict ban on infanticide has not only reduced what this expert would consider potentially useful fertilizer, but raised the rate of population growth. In spite of this population growth educational opportunities are expanding, food supplies are equitably distributed, production is increasing, slums are being eliminated, and there are more opportunities for Chinese to marry and have families than there were in the colonial era.

China's present population is equivalent to what the population of the whole world was two hundred years ago. The ideas which occur to Mr Harrison Salisbury about how China might solve her food problem do not, fortunately for her neighbours, appear to have occurred to her revolutionary leaders. In bad times, as in the period of the terrible natural disasters of 1959-61, the Chinese have tightened their belts and lived on strict rations, everyone, including those who formerly lived well, taking a share of the hunger. In normal times most of them seem to be eating better food than they have ever eaten before; they are healthier, and, one presumes, working better. It seems as though while people elsewhere have been talking frantically about the 'population explosion' those in China have in half a generation been showing that rational action is more to the point.

China's vast population seems then to have been turned into an asset; and the way her 'population problem' has been dealt with makes her progress equivalent to the solution through a single programme of one-third of the problem of the world's rapidly proliferating poor. But it is more than just a solution for the Chinese. The need of her vast population, now that China is making steady progress, makes the vastness of her size an encouraging factor for her neighbours. Most normal people would not quite think in Mr Salisbury's manner. The Vietnamese might argue that if they had escaped their present dreadful fate, the rice they might still be producing would not only be supplying adequate amounts of the staple cereal for the whole nation, but its surplus would have found a vast market in China. So might the Thais. The Japanese know that there is a growing market for their goods in China. The American diplomat in the nineteenth century who commended the work of the missionaries by calculating what a demand for textiles they would create if every Chinese were taught to wear a shirt was stating an important principle. The Chinese are today still wearing, with a new dignity, much patched clothes; they need cheap textiles; they also need rubber, some metals, petroleum and other products. Whereas the markets of the developed world are not open to the products of India, Ceylon, Vietnam, Burma, the Arab lands, and the rest of Asia, the biggest part of Asia's population has begun 'a journey of 10,000 li' towards a decent, dignified and independent existence. In so far as other developing countries have a vested interest in the growing prosperity of China it may be true to say that China by her revolutionary transformation of her economy has decisively reversed the vicious downward spiral of poverty in the under-developed world. China has created a sizeable industrialized sector within her. This kind of impact would have been inconceivable twenty years ago.[9]

3. *Creating the New Man*

But the Chinese revolutionaries were not just humanitarian leaders. They strongly oppose humanitarianism. The revolution took place in a country where in the past a great deal of much-advertised philanthropy was practised by non-Chinese. It therefore set itself to eliminate the attitudes of philanthropy as part of the vicious order which bred the specific evils of the 'feudal' and 'imperialist' societies. Its precept and practice amounts to the doctrine that it is only when the proletarians – those who have had no claim on the means of life – are roused by their oppression to political consciousness and disciplined, revolutionary action to win control of their destiny, and are self-reliant and hard-working that there will be success. Feudal man, capitalist-bourgeois man, colonial or neo-colonial man, with the limitations and inhibitions he sanctifies, cannot break out of his oppression, lethargy and helplessness. He must criticize himself first, and release himself from the shackles of the old order of exploitation.

Mao had written in June 1949 in 'On the People's Democratic Dictatorship'[10] why there would have been no tolerable future for China if she had taken the path shown by the imperial powers.

> From the time of China's defeat in the Opium War of 1840, Chinese progressives went through untold hardships in their quest for truth from the Western countries. Hung Hsiu-chuan, Kang Yu Wei, Yen Fu and Sun Yat Sen were representative of those who had looked to the West for truth before the Communist Party of China was born. Chinese who then sought progress would read any book containing the new knowledge

[9] It has been one of the aims of the West to strangle China economically; or, failing that, to isolate it from the rest of its natural region of economic co-operation and trade. The Economic Commission for Asia and the Far East excludes Asia's major economy, and includes several imperialist countries which are thousands of miles away. The so-called Asian Development Bank is one of several schemes to prevent the Asian countries from realizing the tremendous economic potential in China's remarkable growth.

[10] In his *Selected Works*, IV, pp. 411-24. The quotation that follows is to be found on pp. 412-3.

from the West. The number of students sent to Japan, Britain, the United States, France and Germany was amazing. At home, the imperial examinations were abolished and modern schools sprang up like bamboo shoots after a spring rain; every effort was made to learn from the West. In my youth, I too engaged in such studies. They represented the culture of Western bourgeois democracy, including the social theories and natural sciences of that period, and they were called 'the new learning' in contrast to Chinese feudal culture, which was called 'the old learning'. For quite a long time, those who had acquired the new learning felt confident that it would save China, and very few of them had any doubts on this score, as the adherents of the old learning had. Only modernization could save China, only learning from foreign countries could modernize China. Among the foreign countries, only the Western capitalist countries were then progressive, as they had successfully built modern bourgeois states. The Japanese had been successful in learning from the West, and the Chinese also wished to learn from the Japanese. The Chinese in those days regarded Russia as backward, and few wanted to learn from her. That was how the Chinese tried to learn from foreign countries in the period from the 1840s to the beginning of the twentieth century.

Imperialist aggression shattered the fond dreams of the Chinese about learning from the West. It was very odd – why were the teachers always committing aggression against their pupil? The Chinese learned a good deal from the West, but they could not make it work and were never able to realize their ideals. Their repeated struggles, including such a country-wide movement as the Revolution of 1911, all ended in failure. Day by day, conditions in the country got worse, and life was made impossible. Doubts arose, increased and deepened.

The process by which China had become aware of the harsh realities as well as the possibilities of the world outside her traditional sphere of influence had been long and painful. During the nineteenth century there had been continual failures on the part of the decaying Chinese empire to withstand the impact of the rising world powers of Europe and America. The technology and social organization which had led to the penetration of European and American expansion into China had for some centuries been building up the foundation of European strength and prosperity. And China, in the things which she needed in order to enforce her own laws or command respect, had clearly fallen behind even minor European nations, though the elaborate, mediaeval pretences of the Ching courts and its mandarin bureaucracy for years sustained itself on empty gestures of superiority. The uninvited guests were more and more getting profoundly implicated in China's economic, cultural and administrative affairs, and had to be kotowed to by Chinese officials and gentry. At the same time they on their own part did not show for the law, civilization or the social order (which the Chinese had believed to be supreme and universal) any of the respect which the Chinese had traditionally expected even from those who conquered China. At first the Chinese acted outwardly with deference towards their conquerors, while among themselves they affected to despise them. Later they did admit to one another that something was wrong with China. The loss of confidence in things Chinese, and the sheer need for the survival or independence of China (which was still identified with the traditional social order) had made some scholars turn to the West. Western power had effectively humiliated one of the great Oriental civilizations. Something similar had happened in India, too.

The first series of attempts by the guardians of the social order to save China, which were carried out not by looking into China's own resources but by imitation of the 'superior' industrial and capitalist societies, were viewed with suspicion by the Manchu court. These reform proposals were essentially conservative, since the new developments were to be grafted on to the existing tree. Later, towards the end of the nineteenth century, there were some outstanding thinkers who proposed fairly far-reaching changes in China. The examination system was criticized, and Western forms of education were admired. Changes in military training, the manufacture of armaments, a ship-building programme, more study of science, more industrialization and foreign commerce were proposed. The parliamentary form of government then practised in countries like Britain and the United States were commended. Associated with the Westernization movement of the end of the century were names such as Kang Yu Wei, Huang Tsun Hsien, Liang Chi Chao, Yen Fu, Tan Ssu Tung and Wang Kang Nien. People who were later to be prominent in republican China, like Sun Yat Sen and Chen Tu Hsiu, were much affected by this Westernizing trend. But the search for salvation in Western models saved neither the Manchu Dynasty nor the dominant position of the Confucianist elite; and it did not give China a nationalism with the will, the strength, or the ideology which could withstand the increasing power of the Europeans, Americans or Japanese. The basis of Chinese society – the Chinese peasantry – had been untouched by it.

The decade following the collapse of the new Republic had been years when some, at least, of the realities of China's situation came home to her patriots, and when a rapid reappraisal of 'the West' produced two clearly noticeable trends. One was negative: Yen Fu, who once had been one of the great advocates of radical Westernization, wrote:

The culture of Western countries since this European war has been corrupted completely . . . I feel that the three great centuries of the progress of their races have accomplished four things, that is, to be selfish, to kill others, to have no integrity, and to lose the sense of shame. When we recall the doctrines of Confucius and Mencius, they are really as broad as heaven and earth and their influence is extended to the people all over the globe . . .[11]

This attitude is almost similar to the negative reactions of a much earlier period, and provided no clue to what China could *do* to survive and flourish in the changing modern world. It left the continuing westernizers unconvinced. The reappraisal of the West led also to a second result. In place of the vague notion of an idealized 'West' which lumped together the European and American peoples, their bourgeois liberalism, capitalism, philosophy, literature, religion and others, a new conception emerged. Both the 'imperialist' nations and Chinese institutions and traditions were viewed at from new angles. The reappraisal involved for people like Sun Yat Sen[12] new convictions about the relation of westernization to China's 'subjection' by imperialist forces, about the historical role of the popular mass movements like the 'Tai Pings' and the 'Boxers' which tried to throw out the foreigners. It was understandable that the son of a peasant in the 'progressive' province of Hunan should during this period come to see the Chinese nation's greatness as the greatness of Chinese *masses* and not of the rulers. Under the impact of 'the West' and the exploiting ruling class the Chinese people had been reduced to a proletariat. But one would have to see China's powers of recuperation and rejuvenation as a great nation in the dynamism and creativity of her common people, not in outside forces.

Thus Mao and other young Chinese of his generation had, as he explained, been convinced of the correctness of their appraisal by the way the Russian masses in October 1917, led and organized by the Marxist Lenin, had overturned the autocratic, feudal order, and had been persuaded to adopt the proletarian world outlook as the instrument for studying the nation's destiny and considering anew their own problems.

Follow the path of the Russians was their conclusion. In 1919, the May 4 Movement took place in China. In 1921, the Communist Party of China was founded, Sun Yat Sen, in the depths of despair, came across the October Revolution and the Communist Party of China. He welcomed

[11] Quoted in Teng and Fairbank, *China's Response to the West*, p. 151.
[12] See Chapter Three above.

the October Revolution, welcomed Russia's help to the Chinese and welcomed co-operation with the Communist Party of China.[13]

Mao (who in 1921 had been one of the eleven people, among them Chen Tu Hsiu, who had decided on the inspiration of Lenin's example to found a Communist Party to carry out a revolution in China) then gave an account of the rise of Chiang Kai Shek, the second World War, and American backing for Chiang against 'the Chinese people'. 'Thus Western bourgeois civilization, bourgeois democracy and the plan for a bourgeois republic have all gone bankrupt in the eyes of the Chinese people.'[14]

In saying this, Mao was expressing a conviction which other Asian nationalists were to have in the years that followed. This frontal attack on the Western belief in its own superiority and sufficiency for all men naturally provoked angry reactions. The French writer, Robert Guillain, in *The Blue Ants* wrote:

> He did not realize that this statement rebounded against the Chinese. True it accuses the West, but does it not also incriminate China, by inadvertently admitting that she had been unable to make good use of Western teaching, and that she demolished or corrupted everything that had been brought to her by the West? Is this not tantamount to saying that for the Chinese liberty was a gift which they were not yet worthy to receive, or, at any rate, not ready to use for the good of their country? When, on the other hand, the system of totalitarian dictatorship in the Marxist form arrived, the Chinese recognized at last the method which suited them.[15]

This reaction of resentment, the argument that, far from the Western models and lessons not being good enough for China's needs, the Chinese were not good enough to benefit by what the West gave, is understandable. Some of Mr Guillain's points had already been answered by Mao in September 1949 in the piece of scathing and witty polemic which he directed towards then United States Secretary of State Dean Acheson's version of Chinese history.

> The reason why Marxism-Leninism has played such a great role in China since its introduction is that China's social conditions call for it, that it has been linked with the actual practice of the Chinese people's revolution and that the Chinese people have grasped it. Any ideology – even the very best, even Marxism-Leninism itself – is ineffective unless it is linked with objective realities, meets objectively existing needs and has been grasped by the masses of the people . . .
>
> Since they learned Marxism-Leninism, the Chinese people have ceased

[13] Mao, *Selected Works*, IV, pp. 413-4.
[14] *Ibid.*, p. 414.
[15] Guillain, *The Blue Ants*, p. 223.

to be passive in spirit and gained the initiative. The period of world history in which the Chinese and the Chinese culture were looked down upon should have ended from that moment. The great, victorious Chinese People's War of Liberation and the great people's revolution have rejuvenated and are rejuvenating the great culture of the Chinese people. In its spiritual aspect, this culture of the Chinese people already stands higher than any in the capitalist world. Take U.S. Secretary of State Acheson and his like, for instance. The level of their understanding of modern China and of the modern world is lower than that of an ordinary soldier of the Chinese People's Liberation Army.[16]

If indigenous *Chinese* culture was not to be 'looked down upon' any more, then everything that had prided itself on its 'superiority' to Chinese culture, and perhaps to other Asian cultures, was brought to naught. Western institutions, the missionary 'contribution', Western education and culture and Western criteria were regarded by the Chinese as unsuitable and unnecessary for China's progress, for which the resources of a 'rejuvenated' indigenous culture and enterprise would be adequate. The Chinese soon set about proclaiming their achievement in Asia's major country of a 'new man'; whereas, they seemed to say, the Chinese who wanted to see their country's resurgence as a modern, democratic, secure and great nation had in the past repeatedly found the bourgeois West inadequate, and even an obstacle, now find their own anti-imperialist nationalism, enriched and inspired by the achievement of the Marxists-Leninists in Russia in 1917, had proved adequate. Mao had pioneered a way of 'liberation' for the vast area of the world in which the colonial and semi-colonial peoples bore the burdens of 'imperialism'. If the standard of living, the quality of life and the status of the colonial peoples was to be raised, the organization and strategy by which this was to be achieved, and the assumptions, values and ethos of the new order to be created, were of vital importance. But to plan and build on specifications offered by the 'imperialist' (or 'revisionist') powers was to invite frustration and failure. A correct reading of history would have made this as clear as it was 'to an ordinary soldier of the People's Liberation Army' when he was struggling for China's freedom.

This kind of nationalist argument was a direct challenge to the authority, prestige and interests of those who had to maintain the continued presence of Europe and North America in the rest of the world. Because it was a challenge presented boldly and aggressively by such a resolute and dynamic new force as China had shown herself under Mao's leadership to be, it became the most serious chal-

[16] Mao, *Selected Works*, IV, p. 458.

lenge the West and Russia had ever faced from Asia, Latin America and Africa. If it came to be widely believed that China's ability to deal with the problems of poverty, economic underdevelopment, social evils, ignorance, disease, disorganization and political liberty was not just accidental, and not due, as Acheson had suggested, to 'the impact of the West', but could only have been achieved by the Maoist reading of history, strategy, organization and aims, then, there was cause to fear that the whole of the Third World, already strongly anti-imperialist in the non-westernized (or, in Latin America, the non-Americanized) sector, would become an enormous problem.

As the years went by it became evident that the new leaders of Asia and Africa to whom power had been transferred were much less critical about 'imperialism' than the nationalist movements had been before independence had been granted. The 'rights' of the Western powers in their territories were recognized, and these new governments showed the hoped-for sense of their international responsibilities by making it part of their function to protect the economic interests of European and American concerns. 'Development', too, was undertaken in terms of Western analyses of the causes of underdevelopment and of the world-historical situation, and often with Western advice, technical assistance and capital. Except in Vietnam, and later in Cuba and to a lesser extent in Guinea and Tanzania, there was no radical restructuring of the economy or shift of political power. The transition seemed to be much more peaceful than had been feared. The Cold War also helped, by making it possible for people to see the issues and choices not as the Chinese and those who agreed with them saw them, but rather as one between loyalty to the Anglo-American leadership and loyalty to Soviet leadership. The problem for the West was that highly pro-Western regimes like those in Brazil, Thailand, Indonesia and the Ivory Coast were too much like Chiang's for comfort.

For those Europeans and Americans who have uncompromisingly claimed a universal jurisdiction for 'the West' and their 'consensus' condominium – equating progress and modernization with westernization, international order with Western authority, freedom with the free market economy, and so on – China's xenophobia has continued to be a problem. Whereas the Chinese had had their confidence in the sufficiency and universality of their civilization undermined in the nineteenth century, it is the West that has lost its self-assurance in recent years, as its moral superiority, its model of progressive man, its ideal of justice and freedom, its conception of democracy, its intellectual superiority, its omnipotence, are all questioned and challenged. Nor has the liberalizing trend in Russia increased the appeal of the Soviet Communist variant of Euramerican society. The attractiveness of the Chinese ideal of the 'new man' is a serious threat. China has shown, the Maoists would claim, that in the Third World's break-through into a more just and progressive order imperialist influence had made no contribution. Revisionism, too, could not solve China's problems, the Maoists will explain. How, then, have there been among a people, who were recently almost at the end of their long history, the tremendous release of energy, the enlargement of human possibilities and the dynamism which are demonstrable? How have ordinary, obscure people come to perform acts of heroism? How has the laboratory synthesis of insulin or the manufacture of a cheaper hydrogen bomb been achieved in a seemingly backward and non-westernized country? How has production been increased? Was it competition? No, they would answer. Was it the individual's ambition to achieve greatness? No, they would answer. What was it then? It was 'the thought of Mao Tse Tung'; in other words, it was that devotion to the service of mankind that enabled one to scale hitherto unattainable heights. It is man everywhere, rebellious, daring, unselfish man, and not Western man or Chinese man who can overthrow oppressors and renew society, they would claim. What the Chinese have done in China other liberation movements can do in their own countries.

In the light of these claims, China as a potential model for the rest of the Third World is then doubly a menace. Firstly, she destroys the big-power consensus, ridicules the 'balance of terror', and generally ignores the polarization of the world between the United States and the Soviet Union. She puts them both together *vis-à-vis* the Third World, and points out to other options in a polycentric world. Secondly, she throws into question the assumption that the United States and the Soviet Union are in the vanguard of progress. Both Khrushchev-Kosygin and Johnson-Wilson are rejected as those who will lead mankind into a more attractive future. 'The new world,' as *Renmin Ribao* said in 1966, 'needs a new Man to create it.' The Canadian Norman Bethune (see p. 148) or the Chinese Chang Ssu-teh (see pp. 148-9) are examples.

> This kind of man is a noble man, a pure man, a man of moral integrity, a man who has left coarse tastes behind, a man of use to the people. He is a man with no selfish interests, heart and soul for the people.[17]

Large numbers of these are needed in every society, in any part

[17] These words echo Mao's own epitaph to Norman Bethune who died in 1939. This became one of the basic texts of Maoism.

of the world, before a new world without oppression and injustice can be created.

4. The Pressure for Change

The belief that the emergence of the People's Republic would be a threat to the stability of the post-War international order proved to be justified. The preference by China of a Chinese 'proletarian' model of her own devising over 'Western' and 'bourgeois-democratic' models for modernization was a rejection of the assumptions about Western superiority, her exercise of an independent initiative in creating a new state of affairs in East Asia argued for the irrelevance of the sanctions and prohibitions implicit in the super-power consensus. But the direct confrontation by China with her traditional enemies from Europe and North America, now able to use the United Nations against her, puts the future of the prevailing international order, with its mode of power-politics and conceptions of war and peace, in doubt. For China, with a literalness and forthrightness which by the standards of diplomatic behaviour seem crude and brutal, has insisted on certain changes in the prevailing system of relations between states and peoples. It is as if China's experience of the modern world, and the thinking and work which has arisen from China's own struggle, have created a force for the end of the old order not only in China but in the whole Third World, not only in the Third World but universally. Let us once again look at China's viewpoint.

From the beginning the principle of absolute equality among nations was strictly insisted on – though early in 1950 even Mao Tse Tung got a little less than equality for his country when the treaty of friendship between China and the Soviet Union was first negotiated. If China had been able to get her way and have her principle accepted the whole international system to which the pre-revolutionary order belonged would have been overthrown and the ensuing tensions between the old and the new would not have formed a part of the international scene. For she was unwilling to speak as a 'big power' speaking the special language which 'major powers' used among themselves. She sought to introduce a new language into international politics. Universally applied, the triple principle of equality, mutual respect for each other's sovereignty and territorial integrity and mutual benefit would ultimately imply the withdrawal within their own boundaries by all countries of their political, economic and cultural dominion; it would mean that the benefits which the militarily powerful countries enjoyed in what the Chinese, like most Asians, would regard as colonies or neo-colonies would have to be reciprocated; it would imply that all foreign holdings or operations sought after would as a rule be costed in nationalist terms, and corresponding benefits be secured. Since there is also underlying this the assumptions that the resources of a country are inalienable the property of all her people, and that sovereignty over them belongs to all the people as a whole, it is understandable that China's revolutionary demands are not taken seriously. The principle of mutual benefit, respect for territorial sovereignty and integrity and equality in relations of Euramerica with the peoples of Africa, Latin America, Asia and Eastern Europe would have turned the world upside down. Why should the big powers suddenly apply China's revolutionary nationalist principles to the whole world? There was no reason why the Americans should relinquish their hard-won mastery of the whole of the Pacific Ocean, nor why the integrity of Korea should be respected. In spite of their demands, the Chinese themselves were not able to get the Americans to withdraw from their territorial waters or from Taiwan, since the United States government believed it was in its national interest for them to secure this area. They were not able to prevent their *de facto* expulsion from the United Nations. The United Nations' decision, which implied that they, *the Chinese*, could not decide unilaterally what the government or social system of China was to be, made it very clear that their challenge to the post-War big-power consensus about the international order did not extend beyond the Chinese mainland. In fact they are outside the United Nations (as the Democratic Republic of Vietnam had been since 1945), and would have to fend for themselves. China's challenge to the international system was, as was to be expected, met by a counter-challenge: her power to inaugurate her new anti-colonial order in China had been secured not only by appeals to rational thought or consciences, but also out of the victories of the revolutionary armies; now she has to face the fact that the law and order she has outraged and sought to supersede could be restored in China also by the power that could grow out of the gun-barrels down which she looked when she looked out at the world she hoped to see changed. Troop bases, naval bases, air bases, missile bases, aircraft carriers, nuclear submarines seemed to be aiming at her from her own waters, from South Korea, Japan, Okinawa, Taiwan, the Philippines, South Vietnam, Laos, Thailand, Guam and the enormous Seventh Fleet. Far from being hailed as the shining knight in white armour, she finds herself the pariah of the international community.

Quite clearly the Maoist model of revolutionary change – whether one calls it democratic, nationalist, socialist, Communist or all these together – is a do-it-yourself one. Lin Piao's famous pamphlet leaves no room for doubt what the Maoists believe on this point.[18] But would China's own revolution be able to survive beyond one decade, two decades, or even three? If a large country like China could not fend for herself in the tough modern world, which is tougher for revolutionary peasants than it was thirty years ago, how could other countries which want to take the same path do so? It is necessary for those whose interests Maoism threatened to knock the 'new man' off his feet, or to make him appear unattractive, 'phoney'. China could be pressured into coming to terms with the existing order either by calling off her support for opponents of the existing world order, or by adopting big-power politics herself – and there are both the cautious type and the belligerent type in the Chinese leadership. Some of these questions are still unanswered, but how has China faced up to them so far?

The Russians had thoroughly looted the highly industrialized region of Manchuria in 1945, and had secured special rights there from Chiang. Mao was able to put an end to this, after two years' grace being given to the Russians, presumably for rather meagre low-interest loans for China's reconstruction. But the more important question which arose from the revolutionary nationalists' denunciation and repudiation of the unequal treaties was this: would restitution of territories annexed under these treaties be part of the Chinese demand? The answer to this was not very clear at the beginning, but it was to come in time. Till the end of the second World War and even later, Mao and his colleagues knew very little of what was going on within China's giant neighbour, the Soviet Union. Western accounts of what was happening there would naturally be disbelieved; whatever accounts they got from Moscow or the Comintern – and these would be highly idealized – would more likely be believed, even though Yenan itself had little use for Stalin's agents. It seems to have dawned on the Chinese Communists and their supporters only later that the picture of 1917 of a Russia in which masses had under Lenin's party ended oppression, imperialism, and other evils, and were the vanguard of a new millennium, was a highly idealized picture, and had no relation to the realities. It was not only the Chinese like Sun Yat Sen, who had admired the anti-imperialism of Lenin, who would have found the truth – that the Soviet Communist Party had framed and killed all the old Bolsheviks, that Stalin had restored all the cruelty, oppression, obscurantism and imperial pretensions of Tsarist Russia, that the murder of 'Lenin-

[18] Lin, *Long Live the Victory of People's War*, pp. 41-2.

ists' in Western Europe was a speciality of the Russians, that lies and fears prevailed in Russia – so far from the idealization that they would have dismissed it as propaganda, but, as Chou En Lai, and especially Mao, in a conversation with a Japanese correspondent who in 1964 asked him about the Russian annexation of Japan's Kurile Islands were to reveal, the Chinese leaders were outraged by the annexations made by Russia in Rumania, Poland, Germany and other parts of Europe. And they had not forgotten that 'the account' for the enormous Chinese territories annexed by Russia had not been presented. The Chinese had come to experience what from their point of view was the Soviet Government's calculating and mercenary attitude in her relations with China, her vanity as a 'superpower', her intrigues in the province of Sinkiang, and her attempt in the late fifties to wreck China's reconstruction programme. Her passionate support for revolutionary nationalism in the Third World brought China into conflict with Soviet conservatism.

Chinese foreign policy had three aspects, which, in Foreign Minister Chen Yi's words were:

> to develop the principle of proletarian internationalism, relations of friendship, of mutual aid and co-operation between the countries of the socialist camp; to struggle for peaceful coexistence between countries of different social systems on the basis of the five principles and against political aggression and imperialist war; and to support the revolutionary struggle of all oppressed peoples . . . These three aspects are linked to each other.[19]

China's disillusionment with the 'socialist camp' has been growing. How far her fraternal criticisms of the Communist Party of Soviet Union's lapse from the 'Leninist principles' of 'proletarian democracy and brotherhood' have had an effect on the rest of the socialist governments is difficult to say. Some of them may have found her polemic too radical and too strident for their liking. But with her socialist neighbour Vietnam China has generously shared her meagre resources.

The transformation of China on socialist lines is the main priority in Chinese strategy. But an attack from what is termed 'United States imperialism' has increasingly been feared. The realities of politics being what they are, China's enemies must, if they are to meet the revolutionary threat from China, wreck or disrupt her reconstruction programmes, attack her, and misrepresent her in the eyes of the world. If she is provoked into war it would suit their purpose. It is this fear of an attack which seems to worry China's

[19] Quoted in K. S. Karol, 'Marshal Chen Yi Speaks', *New Statesman*, 28 May 1965.

leaders. For China is vulnerable to nuclear attack, and, it was made clear to her by the fate of Vietnam, where the bombing had as its aim the systematic destruction of 'the great economic achievement and the sense of national unity', she will, if attacked, get neither protection nor help from either the United Nations or from any other country.

In January 1966, United States Secretary of Defence McNamara, while giving evidence to a Senate sub-committee to justify his policy of reducing dependence on bombers in favour of long-range missiles, explained by a reference to China how effectively the striking capacity of United States missiles was deployed. After referring to the readiness to strike at the Soviet Union he is reported to have said:

> A considerably smaller number of weapons detonated over fifty Chinese urban centres would destroy half the urban population – more than 50 million people – and destroy more than one half their industry. Such an attack would also destroy more of the key governmental, technical and managerial personnel and a large proportion of the skilled workers.

How well could a China as yet in the early stages of modernization continue her revolution, and at the same time give her citizens protection against new, deadly forms of attack? Of the kind of planning going on in the Pentagon and the State Department in Washington the Chinese could be in no doubt. The United States spent much more than China's gross national income on her military budget, and probably fifty times as much per head of population as China did. A 'people's war' of the kind waged against Japan was much simpler than any struggle that China's militia would have to undertake. What Mr McNamara had disclosed was the strength of the initial nuclear strike for which the United States was in continued readiness, if war should break out. Population density in the agricultural areas was quite high, and subsequent nuclear attacks could be effective. Further, it was plain that the weapons being tested on the Vietnamese would be very effective on the Chinese. Newer and deadlier forms of napalm were continually being perfected. Bombs ('cluster-bombs') which had maximum effect on rural populations had been developed: the 'lazy-dog' had been improved into the 'guava' bomb; and then there had come the 'pineapple' type anti-personnel bomb, which was believed to be effective against people hiding in ditches – causing maximum suffering before death, and thus destroying morale. Chemical-biological warfare not only could nullify the effect of China's health programmes; but could also decimate the population. Crops could be destroyed on a large scale;

new crop-destroying organisms and disease organisms resistant to known methods of treatment are available.[20]

Altogether a 'people's war' of resistance would not be anything like the struggle against Japan's new order and her pacification programme. The Chinese must know from the widespread approval given to the use of chemical and biological weapons and anti-personnel bombs that they would get hardly any sympathy; and that such an attack against 'Chinese expansionism and aggression' would not be opposed abroad unless it was made very costly, which the Chinese would not be able to do. What power, then, had the possibility of severe action against 'the Yellow Peril' to deter the Chinese revolutionaries from their 'struggle against political aggression and imperialist war', and their determination 'to support the revolutionary struggle of all oppressed peoples'? If it did not deter them, then the instability which has characterized the international situation since 1949 will continue.

Chen Yi, Vice-Premier and Foreign Minister, in September 1965 issued a 'tough' statement of resistance to United States imperialism (effort was made to distinguish as usual the American people from U.S. imperialism). That same month Defence Minister Lin Piao had his article on the twentieth anniversary of the Japanese surrender published in *Renmin Ribao*. This declaration of China's solidarity with all peoples fighting against imperialism and oppression was published as 'Long Live the Victory of People's War'.

The world situation, according to Lin Piao (who has since become 'Vice-Chairman'), today resembles China's before the revolution. And the cities of the world, the highly militarized affluent societies, are being encircled and beleaguered by the rural areas, the peasant masses. Where does China stand in all this?

Our attitude towards imperialist wars of aggression has always been clearcut. First we are against them, and secondly, we are not afraid of them. We will destroy whoever attacks us. As for revolutionary wars waged by the oppressed nations and peoples, so far from opposing them, we invariably give them firm support and active aid. It has been so in the

[20] An American scientist, Dr Ralph E. Lapp showed in an article in *Life* (28 May 1965) how, using B 52 bombers, the United States was in a position to make a nuclear attack on China which would kill 350 million Chinese, and cripple a hundred million more. Trustworthy American accounts of how the anti-personnel cluster bombs work are to be found in 'Report from the Tribunal' by Dave Dellinger (*Liberation*, April 1967), and ' "And Blessed be the Fruit" ', by Don Duncan (*Ramparts*, May 1967). A scientist's account of the 'weapons' of Chemical and Biological Warfare which are being perfected by research in universities, and are being manufactured, is to be found in 'Chemical and Biological Warfare: I, The Research Programme'; II, 'The Weapons and the Policies' (*Science*, 13 and 20 January 1967) by Elinor Langer. *Science* is the journal of the American Association for the Advancement of Science.

past, it remains so in the present and, when we grow in strength as time goes on, we will give them still more support and aid in the future . . . Of course, every revolution in a country stems from the demands of its own people. Only when the people in a country are awakened, mobilized, organized and armed can they overthrow the reactionary rule of imperialism and its lackeys through struggle; their role cannot be replaced or taken over by any people from outside. In this sense, revolution cannot be imported. But this does not exclude mutual sympathy and support on the part of revolutionary peoples in their struggles against the imperialists and their lackeys. Our support and aid to other revolutionary peoples serves precisely to help their self-reliant struggle.

The following May, with the possibilities of a direct United States confrontation with China on the increase, Prime Minister Chou En Lai restated the government's policy towards the United States:

(1) China will not take the initiative to provoke a war with the United States. China has not sent any troops to Hawaii; it is the United States that has occupied China's territory of Taiwan Province. Nevertheless, China has been making efforts in demanding, through negotiations, that the United States withdraw all its armed forces from Taiwan Province and the Taiwan Straits, and she has held talks with the United States for more than ten years, first in Geneva and then in Warsaw, on this question of principle, which admits of no concession whatever. All this serves as a very good proof.

(2) The Chinese mean what they say. In other words, if any country in Asia, Africa or elsewhere meets with aggression by the imperialists headed by the United States, the Chinese Government and people definitely will give it support and help. Should such just action bring on U.S. aggression against China, we will unhesitatingly rise in resistance and fight to the end.

(3) China is prepared. Should the United States impose a war on China, it can be said with certainty that, once in China, the United States will not be able to pull out, however many men it may send over and whatever weapons it may use, nuclear weapons included. Since the 14 million people of South Vietnam can cope with over 200,000 U.S. troops, the 650 million people of China can undoubtedly cope with 10 million of them. No matter how many U.S. aggressor troops may come, they will certainly be annihilated in China.

(4) Once the war breaks out, it will have no boundaries. Some U.S. strategists want to bombard China by relying on their air and naval superiority and avoid a ground war. This is wishful thinking. Once the war gets started with air or sea action, it will not be for the United States alone to decide how the war will continue. If you can come from the sky, why can't we fight back on the ground? That is why we say the war will have no boundaries once it breaks out.[21]

[21] Chou En Lai, *Peking Review*, May 1966.

'The Chinese mean what they say.' Except for two occasions – the entry into Korea in 1950, and the time when their counter-attack against the Indian troops in the border war took them into disputed territory – Chinese troops have never crossed their borders. But an American attack on China would lead to the Chinese advancing to American bases on the Asian mainland. A China under American attack is by her own admission a 'threat' to the governments which have provided the bases for aggression.

Further, foiled in their repeated attempts to get their call for universal nuclear disarmament taken seriously, or even a declaration from the nuclear powers that they would not use nuclear weapons against non-nuclear nations the Chinese began developing their own 'nuclear deterrent' – becoming the first Third World nation to do so. They have no stock-pile of hydrogen bombs and missiles, yet. But, clearly, their emergence as a 'nuclear power' puts them in a position to make two new moves: first, to bargain more effectively for nuclear disarmament; and second, to threaten the bases, including the huge Seventh Fleet, with nuclear retaliation when the Americans attack. Apart from Chou En Lai's statement quoted earlier (and similar policy declarations by Ch'en Yi) there is nothing on record to suggest that the Chinese are preparing for any war outside their borders. One can only speculate that the Chinese are not interested only in the symbolic value of having developed their own hydrogen bomb; some deterrent against the kind of attacks which the Vietnamese have to bear, and worse, may be intended in the long run.

But 'the spiritual atom bomb' is what the Maoists, in their vision of a new man, see as the weapon which will change the world. For that reason, coexistence between a China which will not stop denouncing 'oppressors' and 'imperialists', and a United States which defines her national interests and prestige as her government has been doing since Roosevelt's death, seems to be impossible.[22]

[22] Professor Owen Lattimore, in a piece published in the *New Statesman* (24 February 1967), has some pertinent observations.

'Our problem, trying to understand China from the outside, is to make sense of the way in which internal developments in China gear in with the Maoist analysis – not our analysis – of the menace from America.

(The Chinese) conviction that the Americans are ugly customers is hardened by the Vietnam record . . . The Chinese are further convinced by the hate that is being shouted at them and about them from behind the barrage of bombing in Vietnam and the huge American build-up in Thailand. The American fear and hatred of China, and the dangerous extremist and 'preventive war' aggression to which they could lead, are very much under-reported in Britain. In the press and on TV and wireless there is repetitive identification of China as the source of America's woes . . . Suggestions that Asians be 'bombed back into the Stone Age' and demands that target restric-

What of the future? It is probably true to say that Mao got to know China better than anyone else ever did. He was a Chinese, knew his country's history, had lived through most of the events which made modern China, and knew his own countrymen intimately because of his intense interest in their lives. But China is not the world in which non-Chinese live. And the Maoists' understanding of the experiences and frustrations which constitute the lives of the rest of the world is clearly defective in some important respects. This is not very serious, since Maoist China has no wish to be active on its own account in the history of other countries. But in communicating their own fears and aspirations, their own achievements and failures, their ideas, the Chinese have sometimes failed to carry convictions because they have not been aware enough even of other people who share the same outlook. The lesser Maoists are often humourless, officious, tiresome, behave too much in the way that Christian communities used to behave in 'heathen' lands. This, more than any hostile act of the Chinese government, may isolate China from the less pious and idealistic world outside, and reduce the revolutionary impact of China's unique proletarian humanism.

---

tions for bombing in Vietnam be lifted are of course monitored in China . . . (The) Chinese can hardly be blamed for assuming that inevitably, two or three escalations from now, the U.S. bombing will spill over into China . . .'

Professor Lattimore then goes on to present the alternatives for China as the 'revisionists' and the Maoists see them.

9

What Kind of Dragon?

DESPITE THE developments we have been describing, the campaign of condemnation and denunciation by Western governments and journalists and scholars continues unabated, as do the arguments which justify war against China. It would be difficult for anyone to believe that the base from which all this is mounted lacks foundations. This base is built on what is taken to be historical fact, moral righteousness and political necessity. Surely, it will be argued, it would have collapsed long ago if it had had no substantial foundations! If it were not for the aggressive and subversive activities abroad of the Chinese, ambitious to dominate the whole world, would not the world as a whole be the peaceful and orderly place that the governments of the United States, the Soviet Union and Britain have wanted it to be? However plausible Chinese claims to justice and security may look when her actions and preoccupations are explained and rationalized from her own viewpoint, will not an objective study of the facts and arguments on both sides, the Chinese as well as the anti-Chinese, reveal, first, that the world is in a state of great and intolerable turmoil, violence and anxiety, and, second, that China's intransigence, lawlessness and love of violence are the main cause of the trouble?

There can be no dispute that since 1945, when the 'war to end war' came to an end, the international order has been in a very troubled state. And there is, equally, no dispute that the fact that in the course of 1967 too many events took place in and around China calls for more explanation than we have had in the last few chapters. For example, there are the more rowdy activities of the so-called Red Guards. Even if much of the reporting and comment on contemporary events in China are mischievous in intent there is a core of truth in accounts of hysterical Red Guard behaviour towards foreigners in China and of the contemptuous dismissal by the Maoists of those who want a compromise with the West as appeasers and cowards. Further, even if China is now concerned only with developing a military capacity to defend her land and to strike at the bases from which she expects nuclear and post-nuclear types of attack to be launched, her growing strength is potentially a menace.

The violation of diplomatic immunity and, beyond that, the physical assaults on and bullying of foreign diplomats, their wives and children, as well as other foreign personnel – all of them in China with the permission or at the invitation of the Chinese government and guaranteed its protection – cannot be easily explained away by the reluctance of the Maoists to suppress the enthusiasts. These acts of savagery belie the Chinese claim to be taken seriously; their connection with the way foreigners behaved in China until 1949 was most tenuous; and they could not be excused by the acts of violence and insult against those of Chinese race and against Chinese diplomats encouraged and even organized by anti-Chinese regimes and agencies abroad. Even the intrusion of these visitors and guests into China's rather delicate internal political struggles and problems, indisputable in some cases, did not justify anything more than expulsion; it could not explain the coarse and insolent actions of political activists who were claiming to be fighting for high principles of political freedom. The Chinese government has continually invoked on behalf of its own representatives abroad the very diplomatic immunities it has allowed its citizens to violate with impunity in China. Further, the tone of the government's communications with foreign governments calls for severe criticism.

Is it not China, for all her professions, which is responsible for the disturbed state of the world? And, even if some of the Yellow Peril charges are based on fabrications, are not many of them valid?

That the world for these last twenty years and more has been in an unhappy state we cannot dispute. There were hardly any areas of the world in which countries were spared not merely strife and bloodshed, but also the aggressive, expansionist or subversive activities or 'pressures' of ambitious foreign powers. If we were to attempt to chronicle the bloody or treasonable events which occurred from Aden and Afghanistan to Yugoslavia and Zambia it would take us a long time. The student of contemporary history, checking through the material he has gathered, can only hope that the past quarter of a century is an unusually disturbed period, and can be seen in proper perspective only as part of a phase of history which is far from over. In Afghanistan, on China's border, the higher administrative posts have effectively been infiltrated by agents of a foreign power. The efforts of the Arabs to again achieve unity, complete independence from domination of their politics and resources, and their own dignity as a modern nation, have been frustrated or opposed in various ways, particularly since 1947 – the attempt to invade Egypt in 1956, and overthrow the government of President Nasser, being only one of many complex moves. In the newly independent Congo massive foreign intervention took place, and the Prime Minister was 'liquidated' in the interests of foreign powers. In 1961 Cuba was invaded with the intention of overthrowing her too-independent government, and attempts to strangle Cuba economically and to assassinate her Prime Minister appear to be continuing. Many years previously Czechoslovakia had been occupied by foreign troops and agents, by whom her government was brutally overthrown; and for years her people were terrorized by the same forces. In 1962 the elected, highly popular democratic government of the Dominican Republic was overthrown, with the backing of a foreign power, and an indigenous attempt in 1965 to restore constitutional rule was promptly met by the invasion and occupation of the capital Santo Domingo by foreign troops. In between these two events the elected government of Brazil was overthrown by a military *coup*, with obvious foreign backing, just before it could introduce universal adult suffrage. In 1967, not long before a general election could take place, as it seemed very likely to, in an orderly way, to give a clear expression of the popular will in Greece, there was a military-monarchical *coup*, endorsed by foreign embassies, which ended democracy in Greece. The elected government of Guyana was overthrown through strikes and communal riots organized by a foreign power. In 1954 one of the most popular governments Guatemala has ever had was overthrown by an invasion organized by a foreign power. In the previous year the highly popular government of Iran was brought down by foreign interests whose stake in Iran was threatened. In 1958 a foreign attempt to overthrow the government was foiled in Indonesia, as also was an attempt to assassinate President Sukarno. In Laos in 1958 foreign intervention prevented the election results from taking effect; the country has been heavily bombed for years, and it is heavily infiltrated by soldiers and other agents of foreign powers. And there are many other similar cases.

All this gives us an idea of the patterns which characterize the post-War world. The contemporary world certainly appears to be one in which national security is not assured for most people, and neither self-determination nor democracy is respected. We may not like things as they are. We may believe that these things have to be the way they are if our own interests are to be promoted or protected. We may decide that it would be unrealistic to expect things to be other than they are. But the point is that China has absolutely no responsibility for the events we have chronicled. As far as we know, there is no foreign government which China has overthrown or tried to overthrow. There are countries which keep as much as a million troops and vast fleets in foreign soil or foreign waters, far remote from home, but China does not appear to spend a single fen on maintaining any troops in foreign countries. One can only reach the conclusion, for whatever it is worth, that China has not contributed to the state of things which we have indicated by the examples given.

As for the specific charges (they are listed in Chapter Two above), they are a matter for the reader to investigate for himself. For example, the saying about the power that grows out of the barrel of a gun can easily be studied for its intended meaning and historical significance in the context of the original work of Mao. The Sino-Indian border conflict should be examined in the light of the history, the maps, all the official documents on both sides, the press cuttings and reports, and the work of impartial experts. The question of Tibet raises issues of a different kind. Historically and legally Tibet has been part of China, as even the United States State Department's 'White Paper' of 1949, with its map of China, recognized. But 'separatist' arguments are not based on the rights established by the status quo: the American Civil War a century ago arose out of the right claimed by the Southern landowners who refused to give up traditional practices and accept radical changes. The French Canadians have even more impressive arguments than the Confederate states. The Nagas have stronger claims to autonomy than even the Welsh. In the literature condemning the Chinese government for instituting and then enforcing radical changes in feudal and lamaist Tibet there is very little discussion yet of the issues: the justice of the policy of breaking the power of the Tibetan lords, liberating the serfs, and modernizing Tibet is one issue; whether the administration of the Tibetan Autonomous Region has been humane and equitable and efficient is another. Perhaps we need to suspend judgment until we get more reliable information than is supplied for us by a body like the conservative and highly pro-Western International Commission of Jurists, which receives the the sponsorship of the Central Intelligence Agency, and which issues a 'report' which grossly underrates the intelligence of the public.

What about 'aggression'? Those who are interested should try to find out why the United Nations Charter does not include a definition of what 'aggression' is. For whose benefit is aggression not defined? By what process did this term, not recognized in the United Nations Charter for some strange reason, come to be applied to China when she went to the rescue of North Korea, and interposed her forces between the Chinese border and the forces advancing towards it? There are many questions like this which need to be answered.

To take up all the charges made against China would be tiresome and unprofitable. We should first be clear whether or not there is a fanatical, irrational and racialist element in all what we say and do in regard to China, before we try to decide what these allegations mean. It would be incredible if there were not actions and policies of Chinese people and the Chinese government which were found to be deserving of criticism and censure. Just as much as the portrait of the 'totalitarian monster', responsible for most of the contemporary world's troubles, is too bad to be true; so a China which wears the halo of perfection both at home and abroad would be too good to be true. We must recognize that much of the campaign of easily exposed lies and slanders designed to mobilize us in the great anti-China campaign takes for granted that we are ignorant, gullible and racially prejudiced. We are challenged as readers to think rationally and realistically – to demythologize the myth of the Yellow Peril.

There can be no doubt that what is happening in China, and China's policies and actions in her relations with other countries, are affecting and will continue increasingly to affect our own lives, however far away we are from China. Over those events, and over those policies and actions, governments in the West have tried to get control in the past. They have not been successful. The revolutionary nationalism of Mao not only has a dynamism and creativity which are confronting us with ideas, institutions and practices which we find difficult to cope with intellectually and politically; its uncanny attraction for those who believe themselves to be oppressed by 'imperialism' and 'neo-colonialism' – its character as the Red Hope of the poor in the Third World – challenges the leadership and authority of the West, and threatens revolutionary changes in the whole world order. It is difficult for us to be rational about what we mean by the term *China*. Should we have destroyed it? Should we have come to terms with it? Should we agree with the military men who want China to be attacked? Should we make the effort to respect it?

Is the problem *we* are having of living in the same world with a resurgent China the real *China Problem*?

10

Questions from China

WHAT WE have been attempting to do thus far is to mark out the relevant area of ground that needs to be cleared, so that we can begin the urgent and important task of working out the implications for the world of China's resurgence under Maoist leadership. The confusion of rumours and wild allegations which so thickly cover the real features of the China reality makes intelligent talk about China almost impossible. Even though the discussion so far has only been sketchy, it has still taken a good deal of time to get to the point of seeing in outline what we mean when we talk about contemporary China. The reader, of course, has had to do much of the work of clearing away the tangle of fantasy and misrepresentation which prevents us from recognizing China for what she is – neither a 'hell' peopled with 'snarling' dragons, nor the new Jerusalem, in which all poverty and injustice has been ended. It is only another country, but one in which highly exciting and puzzling (sometimes inexplicable) events and changes are taking place. It is also a country in which the destinies of a great part of mankind are being worked out.

No attempt has been made to be either systematic or comprehensive in what we have discussed so far. There is much that we have hardly touched on. A new industrial base has been created for China, there has been a leap forward in China's technological and scientific consciousness and achievement, China is composed now of about seventy thousand communes, primary and secondary education has been expanded and adult literacy increased, there have been new developments in communications and transport, and so on. To get a comprehensive picture of contemporary China one needs to discover how her factories and industries are organized and administered; what the communes are; how the difficulties of suddenly expanding education (the provision of teachers, the provision of books, the replacement after the Cultural Revolution of the old by new textbooks) have been met; and a host of other matters. But our interest here has been focused on the radical and disturbing nature and the enormous scale of the changes which Chairman Mao and his revolutionary colleagues have set in motion.

We have now done with the preliminary clearing of the ground, in the hope that it may make it easier for readers to get down to beginning a more substantive discussion about China's achievements, failures and problems.

People who think of themselves as makers of history, or as morally responsible persons, or as scholars in search of true knowledge, and are therefore seeking a sober and critical understanding of the world in which they have to make decisions and to act, will find that the 'China Problem' cannot be considered to be disposed of simply because the Yellow Peril arguments can be shown to be false. The moves to isolate China from the rest of mankind, to 'contain her' and harass her are going on all the same. And no action to stop them can be taken; nor can the slanders on the Chinese people be replaced by more truthful reporting, until the actual reason for the official 'Western' attitude to the Chinese are explained and discussed. For it is likely that we are being deceived about China, and attempts are being made to stifle her voice, simply because she has something to say which is deeply disturbing to most of us who would like the world to go on in the way it has been going for the last century or two. On the other hand, it may be that having disposed of the ridiculous charges against China of 'expansionism', 'aggression', and what not, we may be able to make more honest and more substantial criticisms of her conduct since her resurgence under Maoist leadership.

China is indeed a profoundly disturbing element. She has stirred up controversy and challenged the established order in a way which has few parallels in history. Perhaps one has to go to the past, not modern history, to find comparable episodes in human affairs. China, Vietnam and Cuba are seeking to re-establish a new world order on political and ethical principles which are unacceptable to Europe and America. Are we entering a period of world history comparable to the fifth century B.C.? Mao and Maoism are overturning a world order secured with power such as has never before been dreamed of. How is it done? Can we find some help in looking at the 'threat' that Paul and Christianity, or Mohammed and Islam, or Luther and Protestantism, represented to the established order of their time?

If Mao Tse Tung were merely a theorist, a philosopher, a sage, he would not compel immediate attention. Many of the questions he asks have been asked before. Some of his prescriptions could have been regarded as optional, and could have been politely ignored – as perhaps they were in China itself in the early sixties. But there are two practical reasons why we must take seriously the challenge of Mao. One is the fact that he has shaped and is shaping what, if others don't prevent it, may become the world's leading nation in the coming century. The other is the fact that he seems to be speaking for a vast majority of the world's people when he questions the existing order and its values, and points to them the way to establish a new order. Added to these as reasons for our undertaking to do some serious and fundamental reflection on the issues that arise is the need for an intelligent basis from which to make a critical appraisal of contemporary China.

But it is not only the practical reasons that are important. May we not, we must ask, be better off intellectually for trying to answer some of the questions and to clarify the issues which Maoist China stirs up in the world? Should we not make sure whether the disturbance caused by China is good for us, even if we are living, as we may think, in the best of all possible societies?

The issues and questions which surround the 'China Problem' are many. Their nature will become clear if we take some examples of the more important ones, and briefly elaborate them. They are all interconnected, and we must consider later what all the questioning amounts to. These notes and questions may be taken as variations on a single theme.

1. 'What a piece of work is Man?'

One of the fundamentals of Maoism is the coming into being of the 'new man'. The new man is the man without human status, the proletarian, who sets himself free from his condition of slavishness and impotence, and transforms the not-yet-truly-human situation into one in which good, just and loving acts are normal. His strength issues from a confidence in the potential superiority of the human spirit over all adverse and dehumanizing circumstances, and over all the weapons, gadgets and other instruments of man's inhumanity to man. This superiority or heightening of human capabilities is realized by the study and application to difficulties as they arise of the 'thoughts of Mao Tse Tung'. The new man is a rebel against all forms of authoritarianism, all attempts to deprive the people of their freedom to think, speak and act; in the struggle between oppressor and oppressed he is unambiguously a fighter for the oppressed, and not a neutral.

Superficially, studying and applying the 'thought of Mao Tse Tung' appears to be another kind of yoga; or, more likely, akin to

Buddhist practice. But it is very simple. Just as, let us say, the athlete who has to hurl a great weight a given distance braces himself against the weight of the missile, concentrates on taking a clear and sober view of what he has got to do, tests his own strength against the requirements of the feat to be performed, trains for his task, waits patiently till he can do what he sets out to do, and finally, without false throws or rash trials, accomplishes his task – so the Maoist acts in society in accomplishing the humanizing of his environment. The process of the humanization is very complex, and some necessary tasks may have to be performed in historical circumstances, economic, social or physical conditions, which are most unfavourable to them. But the 'new man' takes a clear-sighted view of the objective situation, not so that he may be deterred if things seem difficult, but in order to summon enough of the resources – physical, spiritual, intellectual, psychological and social – needed for what he knows has to be done. Any man, however limited his personal inheritance, can perform heroic deeds. He does not need to be a member of a hand-picked elite which has undergone complicated and abstract exercises in self-cultivation; he needs to face up to his ordinary tasks in the light of the knowledge of the revolutionary human situation in which he is placed. The accomplishment of the Chinese revolutionaries in liberating China in virtually impossible circumstances was a supreme example of this.

That seems to be the gist of the Maoist conception. But its meaning becomes clearer and more specific when we see references to it in the context of Mao's writing. In general, the new man is a superior being, as an ethical person, as a political participant or maker of history, as an economic performer or worker, and in other ways, too; he is not self-regarding, assertive and cruel.

The celebration of the new man in a major country like China, which itself had great traditions in the past, raises a number of questions about the nature and being of man some of which at least we need to state.

Firstly, is the 'new man' just a bit of political clap-trap? If his existence is sincerely and genuinely believed in, is the belief realistic? What in fact are the dimensions of Man? Do we need to think again about what we mean by 'normality' in people?

When the Chinese masses seized power in their country and 'stood up', most of the old institutions and ways whose weight had pressed down on their heads and shoulders was, as it were, overthrown or overturned. But the seizure of power did not itself create the new man. Even later, after the Cultural Revolution had got going, weren't people just as mean, small-minded, inconsiderate of the sufferings caused to others, resentful, greedy and cruel as they had been under the old order? Or was there a change? Was Maoism truly transforming China into a land where authoritarianism, subservience, and pessimism were disappearing? It may be that formerly obscure people performed new feats of skill and miracles of social transformation. But did they exhibit new moral powers, power to act more responsibly and humanly in regard to others? How are these questions to be answered?

Can one 'serve the people' except out of a personal freedom and love of the people? Is there any tendency to frighten or otherwise coerce people into 'serving'? If so, does not service become corrupted into subservience, one of the marks of the old order? Again, in what sense is Maoist revolutionary rebellion different from old-style anarchism?

Secondly, generally speaking, in Europe and North America, and the small sectors of the Third World over which they have influence, there has been established a certain conception of what people are capable of, and what the end of human existence is; it implies what a 'normal' human being's needs, wants and possibilities are, and what human excellence is. Would it be correct to call this man bourgeois man – one who has characteristically bourgeois needs and wants, and has a bourgeois ideal? Whether it would be or not, does the conception of man and his powers prevalent in Europe and North America take into account all the resources on which the human spirit can draw?

The new man challenges the conventional Western view in more than one way. It regards 'bourgeois, capitalist man' as vulgar and 'slavish'. Its view of what ordinary people can do if they had a mind to it exceeds the excellence of liberal bourgeois 'humanism'. In the perspective of the new thought and action – if it is taken as real – bourgeois man is made to appear vulgar and trivial in his preoccupations, delights and goals, mean in his evaluations and puny in stature. Instead of being self-reliant and courageous, he looks for support to wealth, weapons, the opinions of others, and so on. On the other hand those who are judged thus in their turn reject, deride and attack the Maoist conception of the new man; rather than watching it with interest, they seek to prevent its being taken seriously.

But there is some incontrovertible evidence of the genuineness of the Maoist achievement. The last nineteen years in China have for their achievements been without a parallel in the history of any other country. But that, perhaps, is not the point. Rather it is this: *what man demonstrably can be and do, man everywhere ought to do.*

We might say that there is an ethical 'imperative' implicit in our taking seriously the historical emergence of the Maoist 'new man'; that is, if ethics is concerned with being fully human, or, rather, with being as human as we can, in the circumstances, be, then no one outside China can help being judged by the new stature that 'ordinary' man has realized.

Thirdly, with the Maoist 'promotion' of the new man there has been a carelessness about some matters to which the rest of us in any well-run society pay great attention; and this has shocked or offended people. In the late fifties, when even China's most implacable enemies were acknowledging that remarkable stability and growth had been achieved under Maoism, the Maoists seemed to throw away all this achievement by approving mass initiatives which resulted in the communes and the Great Leap Forward. In 1966 the Great Proletarian Cultural Revolution was launched, seemingly disrupting order, weakening authority, wasting a year of schooling and so on. Was this boldness and daring, or was it rashness? What is lost and what is gained? Do wealth, formal education, 'birth', and material power really make a person greater than one who lacks these? What goes into the formation, or inspiration – the making – of 'new' men, women and children? Is 'the thoughts of Mao Tse Tung' the best basis for education for people who have to pull down what has to be pulled down, change what has to be changed, create what needs to be created, and speak what needs to be spoken? Or are people cultivated on 'the thoughts of Mao' uninstructed, ignorant and unfit for the demands of modern life?

Fourthly, the Maoist new man reminds one of the 'new man' in Jesus Christ, which was one of the original conceptions of Christians. One is reminded very strongly of this fact when reading the three simple essays: *Serve the People*, *In Memory of Norman Bethune*, and *The Foolish Old Man Who Removed the Mountain*. (It does not matter here that this Christian humanism is officially very much a dead letter. It is no less valid today than it was for Paul of Tarsus).

The great social, intellectual and political contribution of Western-Missionary-Christianity to China is one of the myths which for a long time prevented people from facing up to the realities of what historically the missions were part of and what their impact was on the non-Western peoples and their traditions. But unfortunately Western Christianity, and the Christians in the Third World still to be freed from the ideology, financial organization and bureaucratic structures of a West-centred Christianity, have remained hostile to China and Chinese Christianity; and no creative discussion has taken place outside China. Meeting in Bangkok two months after the Chinese People's Republic was proclaimed, 'top' representatives of this type of Christianity examined the 'Christian Prospect in Eastern Asia'. The American Chairman of the International Missionary Council cast Mao's China in the role of anti-Christ. He was perhaps correct when he spoke of his and Mao's as 'the two rival systems in East Asia today',[1] but between Asian and other Christians and the Maoists can there be any such 'rivalry'? At that high-powered conference at Bangkok the General Secretary of the World Council of Churches was moved to give an authoritative exposition of 'Communism'; he concluded, according to the official summary: 'Communism has an answer, although a wrong answer, to the problem of the masses . . . We can combat it only by giving a better answer.' The 'Communist' new man naturally was not inclined to learn from such examples, or to believe in the possibilities of a meaningful dialogue with Christian 'revolutionary rebels'. But Mao wrote,

> We must all learn the spirit of absolute selflessness from him (i.e. Dr Norman Bethune). With this spirit everyone can be very useful to the people. A man's ability may be great or small, but if he has this spirit, he is already noble-minded and pure, a man of moral integrity and above vulgar interests, a man who is of value to the people.

What an irony! For what would those who extol what Western Christians have done in China and are doing to Vietnam say about Norman Bethune? Are those who see in the condemned and outcast Jesus Christ the model and inspiration of the 'new man' going to 'combat' and speak ill of the ideal of the new man in the new China?[2] Or will they 'serve the people' rather than those who resent the fact that the Chinese people have 'stood up'? What Chairman Mao has called 'the patriotic people in religious circles' cannot feel disappointed at the standards of honesty, devotion to the service and welfare of the people which the Maoists have achieved. Have they anything to say which will be considered relevant about Mao's call for selfishness, humility and tolerance as highly-valued personal qualities? Finally, if Asian followers of Christ believe they have something of value to strengthen and sustain the 'new man', must

[1] *The Christian Prospect in Eastern Asia – Papers and Minutes of the East Asia Christian Conference* (New York: Friendship Press, 1950), p. 108.

[2] There were Christians, including missionaries, who were appreciative of revolutionary China even in the Yenan days. See Gunther Stein, *The Challenge of Red China*, pp. 188ff. For a good selection of *Chinese* views of the Christianity represented by the missionaries see Jessie G. Lutz, ed, *Christian Missions in China* (New York: Heath, 1965) esp. Ch'en Tu Hsiu, 'Jesus the Incarnation of Universal Love'; T'ang Liang Li, 'Missions, the Cultural Arm of Western Imperialism'; Hsu Pao Chien: 'Christianity, A Religion of Love Spread by Force'.

they not dissociate themselves from those elements in Western Christianity which approved and still approve what is being done in East Asia by imperialist forces, and what Saigon, Bangkok and Taipeh stand for?

2. *What does it mean for a whole community to be liberated for mutual service to the people?*

There appear to be interconnections between the 'new man' on one hand and national liberation on the other. There also appear to be interconnections between national liberation and the creation of a truly human community. What are these relationships?

When Stuart and Roma Gelder, two British writers, asked Mr Chou En Lai in 1960 if individuality was being destroyed in China, he replied: 'We aren't trying to destroy individuality. But we are certainly doing our best to destroy individualism. It's a policy of "No man for himself and every man for others", if you like to put it that way.'[3] The 'personality type' in every form of society reflects and reinforces the social ethos. What kind of social order does this type serve?

What is involved in the freeing *of a nation*, as distinct from the freeing of individuals? Fundamentally, there appears to be at issue the integrity of a people to be its true self; to live and grow untrammelled by that which is alien to its being as a creation and a creator of history; to be in touch with, or, rather, to be able to draw freely on, the sources of the means of a dignified and meaningful existence.

One nation rules over another, or manages its political, social, cultural and economic affairs, or in subtler ways controls the way in which it lives and acts, mainly to serve the dominant one's interests. This principle applies as much to anything else as to programmes of providing 'aid' and of educating the young of the 'victim' nation in such a way as to ensure continued dependence. For the nation which is ruled over or managed or controlled by another, the most obvious first step to take towards actual freedom is that of ending the formal and constitutional aspects of subservience or subjection. That act is important only if it is a conscious break with a false legality which is part of the ideology by which imperial ruler-nation and colonial subject-nation are assured that their relationship is a normal one. If the bonds of subservience are not burst as a result of the assertion of one's freedom to exercise freedom,

[3] Stuart and Roma Gelder, *Long March to Freedom* (London: Hutchinson, 1962), p. 133.

but, rather, if their loosening is derived from or part of, the legality of the old order, then can there be said to have been even the first step towards liberation? In other words, what is known as 'the transfer of power' at the will of the imperial administrators to native administrators (what is also known as the 'giving' or 'granting' of 'freedom') still takes place within, and maintains intact, the order of servitude. A nation must liberate *itself* if it wants freedom, it cannot be liberated. One says 'must' and 'cannot' here because, plainly, what comes out of the free choice of the 'rulers' or the 'managers' is the history that they in *their* freedom have made. It liberates them. It liberates them, that is, from the outworn, out-of-date imperialism of the days before the revolt of the coloured and subject peoples, gives them a future to create. It extends their freedom at the expense of the subject people, for whom the trammels on their integrity and freedom become only less visible. Indeed, is it not true, and a lesson of history, that whereas those nations who are unwilling and rebellious subjects or subordinates know that they cannot be despised, those who are grateful for the pseudo-freedom which is prescribed for and allowed them by other nations come to despise themselves for what they are? And that, consequently, the soul-destroying effects of subjection – loss of self-confidence, a tendency to see oneself in the false mirrors of the rulers, a sense of racial inferiority – are heightened?[4]

And, then, there is the phenomenon of those in the subject nation who collaborate with the rulers. Is the consolation afforded the collaborators that they have freed themselves as a class or as individuals not a delusion? The impression has sometimes been given that to become part, let us say, of the dominant Euramerican system either by cultural assimilation or by the playing of the appropriate political and economic roles in it amount to an emancipation from the shame and inferiority shared by a people who do not have the freedom or the dignity to create an authentic history of their own. But is this a valid impression? Can we remove a racial or national stigma by a migration into the dominant racial or national group? Is this kind of migration by cultural assimilation or transfer of

[4] Those who are inclined to believe, reading press 'reports', that Africans who reject 'white' domination and domination by those whom they regard as neocolonialist elites are not speaking out of a newly found dignity and freedom but are victims of Chinese 'subversion', should ask themselves if Africa is still a 'dark continent' to them. See Mamadou Dia, *The African Nations and World Solidarity*, E. T. (London: Thames & Hudson, 1962); Frantz Fanon, *The Wretched of the Earth*, with Preface by Jean-Paul Sartre (London: McGibbon & Kee, 1965); Nelson Mandela: *No Easy Walk to Freedom* (London: Heinemann, 1965). The notion that Africans have no longing for freedom and dignity is a thoroughly racialist one.

political allegiance in fact a means to emancipation from inferior status? These are some of the major questions in the study of race relations, and cannot be answered in simple terms. But there seem to be good reasons for saying that one of the essential means to the emancipation of anyone from the despised and discriminated-against nations or peoples (the non-white races in general) is total national liberation, and the realization of a corporate, racial dignity. A corollary of this is the likelihood that every attempt by a member of an inferior nation to 'emancipate' himself regardless of or at the expense of his compatriots is not only futile but also adds to the insult and the injury done to his people.

Is not patriotism, and nationalism in a country which is still seeking to liberate itself, of a different order from the nationalism of a people ruling or seeking to rule over or manage others? The same words are often used: are the moral, political and spiritual realities not totally contradictory? Further, what can be said of the emigrants (not using the word in the physical sense) or the so-called 'refugees', who do not merely and selfishly contract out of the national liberation task but in fact seek a rapid rise in status in the alien system which has adopted them by joining the neo-colonial apparatus which is trying to obstruct or forcibly suppress the emancipation of their people? What evaluation must we make of the 'collaborators' in a neo-colonial or neo-imperialist apparatus – not just in appreciation of their service to the interests of the 'free world' but in terms of an ethic which values highly a people's corporate freedom, their integrity and their need to be free to make their own history? In some situations these collaborators act as mercenaries of the alien power in a military, or cultural, or political role; and they get the satisfaction of exercising some power, of receiving monetary rewards, and of winning the approval of the dominant or would-be-dominant nation. Is it right for them to be so employed – not only to their own moral degradation but also when it exposes them and their families to the worst penalties that the revolutionary justice of national liberation metes out? What evaluation in terms of social ethics can one make of the role of these 'native' agents of the foreign opponents of a popular national liberation struggle?

We must move on to other issues. It has been suggested here that one may not be able to live a truly responsible and human life unless the freedom, dignity, self-respect and creative powers one enjoys are shared as a right by the whole community. There is a certain given-ness about human life; and much of what we can have to give and receive in interpersonal relations we must draw from the collective resources of the nation. Have we adequately discovered what it is that we are given thus to use and enjoy through the nation's having the freedom to live in its own way?

We have reason to wonder if the 'freedom' of liberal individualism is not a false one. Is it not true that human-ness is such that one can exercise an authentic liberty only if one's acts are thereby not curtailing the liberty of others? And can we go further and say that the test of genuine freedom in thought and word and action is the fact that it liberates others as well as ourselves? If we can, then the claims of the liberal ideal to high ethical status is pretentious. 'No man for himself and every man for others.' Is this ethos false or is it a truly human one, which judges, among other things, humanitarianism as something which constricts and degrades? On the other hand does not altruism as a normal feature of life make personal acts of generosity impossible, paradoxical as this may seem? Does the openness and candour of the society of the new China destroy a very necessary privacy? There may be valid grounds on which family loyalties have been subordinated to patriotism and to loyalty to the whole community of which one is a member. But there are certain moments when even in a socialist democracy privacy is a necessary condition of personal integrity, if man is not to live like a beast – for example, the secret openness of lovers to each other; the personal enjoyment of nature and society; one's reaching out to appropriate something beyond the stream of history, from which one draws sustenance and in the name of which one serves the community; the appropriation of the situation in which one lives in terms of the rhythm and style of one's own thinking and feeling. Is the selfish individualism and the narrowness of the old being destroyed in order to set people free for this necessary privacy, among other things? Can a genuine and sincere search for national liberation and a shared, humble existence with one's fellowmen be a factor constricting or even destroying certain values; for example, genuine personal humility, a real joy in working for others, truthfulness in relationships, the complex personal life in which alone one can as a person grow and bear fruit mentally, emotionally and spiritually? To this last question the thought and work of Mao Tse Tung gives a clear 'Yes' as an answer. But is his warning taken seriously in China? And how do these issues look in a different context from that of contemporary China?

If a humanity of greater dimensions than we had believed possible can be realized in certain forms of community we are faced with new ethical problems. Higher standards inevitably imply more demanding obligations from those who create and work in social institutions. If our consciousness and consciences encompass what we know to be achievable goals which lie beyond our conventional or customary ones, we as men of goodwill find ourselves on the threshold of a revolutionary situation. We have the effective choice of realizing by action new roles for the intellectual in society, a new morality for business, a new doctrine of what freedom is, a new evaluation of the existence of extremes of power and wealth and status for social groups within the same community, a new evaluation of parasitic modes of living, and so on. If the new institutions of Mao's socialist society are richer in human content, more just and more 'efficient' than the Western bourgeois ones, rebellion becomes justified! Talcott Parsons, the sociologist, in one of his books states his belief that modern American society is the model of the goal towards which all modernizing societies are moving.[5] The existence of another historical model, possibly more richly human, more dynamic and more exciting even, does pose difficult problems for those who share his faith. These problems may be solved, perhaps, only at great cost to what we cherish dearly.[6]

3. *Must Western Dominance of the World Come to an End?*

Why is it that the West feels threatened? During the forties it looked as if the imperial powers, not only Japan but also Europe and America, would have to withdraw completely from the positions they had occupied in Asia in the colonial period. At that time it was the Indian nationalists who appeared to be the leading force in the national liberation movements. Although it was done with his characteristic vagueness and fumbling, Nehru's summoning of the Conferences of 1947 and 1949 were partly the basis of 'Afro-Asian' anti-imperialist solidarity, which found its clearest expression at the Bandung Conference. To Asians, generally, it was then a vital need that their subjection, and the foreign possession and exploitation of their homelands, should effectively be brought to an end; Western dominance had, they felt, destroyed their self-respect and self-confidence, retarded their modernization and looted their economic resources. Most Europeans and Americans did not agree with this adverse view of the way they had carried out their 'mission'. But

[5] *Social Structure and Personality* (New York: Free Press of Glencoe, 1964), p. 164.

[6] C. B. MacPherson's *The Real World of Democracy* (London: Oxford University Press, 1966) is a valuable contribution to a badly needed discussion, even though it shows little knowledge of contemporary China. The same remarks would apply to Peter Worsley's *The Third World* (London: Weidenfeld & Nicolson, 1964.

it did seem as if world history would take the course decided on by Asian nationalists who wanted to be sovereign over their own homelands and their resources just as the British or French or Americans were over theirs, the burden which the coloured people had borne of their supposed racial inferiority would be sent back to its sources.

But somewhere on the way to the attainment of the goal of liberation from Western domination something seems to have gone wrong. The intensely-held hopes of those years have not been realized, except by China and in a very tragic, 'spiritual' sense by Vietnam. And this failure has had important consequences. One of the most important facts of the present time is the deep despair and cynicism of most of Asia, the sense of impotence and shame. Most of Asia is still part of the Western system established in the colonial period, but modernized and made much more efficient than it was in the horse-and-buggy period of colonialism which ended in 1941. The fight for social justice and modernization on the one hand and the fight to reject Western tutelage and control on the other have become fused into a single struggle for many 'patriots'.

For people in the West it is naturally most difficult to enter sympathetically into the sense of hopelessness, of aimless drifting, of dull resentment, of a loss of identity, of shame, which the most sensitive Asians feel. It is also difficult for them to recognize the fact of Western domination. Though there has been a 'communications revolution', they do not, for reasons which we shall discuss later, receive any authentic communication on this matter from non-westernised Asians, or, for that matter, from non-westernized Africans and Latin-Americans either.[7]

[7] The great Brazilian humanist and scholar, Josue de Castro, former President of the Food and Agriculture Organization, and author of the famous *The Geography of Hunger*, has pointed out 'the essential characteristic of colonialist economic development, quite different from authentic economic development of a nationalist type. Colonialism has promoted, here and there in the world, a certain sort of progress, but always at the exclusive service of the colonizer's profits. At most it is associated with a small group of the privileged, who have lost interest in the future of the nation and the political, social and cultural aspirations of the majority . . .' ('The Brazilian Dilemma: Bread or Steel' in Ignacy Sachs, ed., *Agriculture, Land Reforms and Economic Development* (Warsaw: Polish Scientific Publishers, 1964). After the pro-Western military *coup* of 1964, he is in exile. Another distinguished Brazilian liberal economist Celso Furtadol, has demonstrated that 'development-minded doctrine takes the shape of an ideology of national development, calling for a process of national individualisation, within the framework of the world economy. To develop a country one must, at the same time, individualize, i.e., individualization is not a simple consequence of development but an autonomous factor. Autonomy in decision-making is, thus, of great importance, and without it there can be no authentic policy of development . . . The new ideology of

That does not matter, since Western domination of the non-Western world is an objective fact, available to sociological study, and not a subjective fantasy of anti-colonialist Asians. It is the assumptions underlying the thinking of those of us who live in the West which more than anything else prevent us from recognizing the realities. In this context 'the West' does *not* mean democracy, or science, or the music of Mozart, or the Gospel of Jesus Christ, or civilization, or even ordinary men, women and children in Europe and North America. It means contemporary Europe and North America, in so far as they intrude into, destroy and 'asphyxiate' the rest of the world with their power, wealth, their social structure, their objectives and their operative values.[8]

No one doubts that Western civilization is one of the very great civilizations the world has ever known. It is unlikely that its greatness or power of survival is increased by the imposition of Europe and North America on the rest of the world. For such great things as Europe and America in their creative phases have contributed to the progress and welfare of mankind tribute will undoubtedly be paid to them by the people who will take these things and use them and even develop them. The confining of the power and rule of Europe and America within Europe and America is not going to impoverish the world. Why then does the West, as represented by Dean Rusk or Harold Wilson, feel threatened by the democratic spirit in the Third World?

Is not the intrusion of the countries of 'Euramerica' outside their homelands something divorced from the truly great values which developed within the West? Even if we speak in all charity can we see *any* aspect of what is good in the Western tradition represented by the efforts of those who now command its fire-power to try to intimidate and its money to try to corrupt those who want to see Europeans and Americans, like others, exercise dominion over their own resources at home and not abroad?

national development takes it for granted that the possibility of hampering the progress of the country by decisions taken abroad by groups whose interest might collide with those of the national economy, should be reduced to a minimum. ('An Analysis of the Economic Development of Brazil' in Ignacy Sachs ed., *Planning and Economic Development* (Warsaw: Polish Scientific Publishers, 1964) p. 152. See John Gerassi: *The Great Fear in Latin America* (New York: Collier-Macmillan, 1965); and Frederick Pike: *Chile and the United States 1880-1962* (Notre Dame: University of Notre Dame Press, 1963), pp. xxi-xxiii.

[8] The National Assembly of Cuba used the term 'asphyxiate' with telling effect in one of the two Declarations of Havana it issued in 1960 and in 1962. The Declarations are historic documents of Third-World nationalism.

It has sometimes been said that if the western captains and kings depart there will be a vacuum! Therefore, when the French withdrew after their abortive attempt to retake Vietnam, the Americans filled the vacuum. When the British relinquish their so-called 'East of Suez' role, their imperial role thousands of miles from Britain, there is supposed to be a vacuum in the areas from which they have removed their military presence. In fact, however, there seems to be the opposite of a vacuum in Vietnam. All the weight of American bombs and shells and soldiers and much else previously unknown to man has failed to provide even a few cubic feet of 'vacuum' in Vietnam. There seems to be something in all this which is not only ridiculous and dishonest, but also alien to the spirit of the Western political tradition which is most worth continuing. Western culture and authority is only one of the regional traditions of culture and authority in the modern world. The Vietnamese, for example, are a nation with a tradition of civilized living and national identity longer than that of a major Western nation like the French. Can one really believe that Asians, for example, who in China and Vietnam are doing very much better under total independence than they ever did under Western tutelage, need the presence of the West so much that as one imperial power withdraws another white nation must fill that role? Is the 'vacuum' theory foolish and ridiculous because it is simply dishonest? Or is the overweening pretentiousness of the efforts to universalize the 'Western' presence the work of those who do not know what the true greatness of Western culture and values is?

A profound and unrelenting self-searching seems to be called for; when the Vietnamese nationalists asserted their independence from the Japanese and successfully resisted a French come-back was there anything which the West brought to fill the 'vacuum' which the Vietnamese have either wanted or needed? One searches in the whole apparatus of the 'West' in Asia and finds the 'puppet' rulers and forms of 'government'; the strategic hamlets; the 'pacification' campaigns; the napalm, the supersize bombs and chemical and biological weapons of destruction; the practice of burning out the homes and livelihood of whole dissident communities of villages and towns; the 'hunting', capture, torture and killing of patriots; the obscene ingenuity of the calculation behind the use of the anti-personnel cluster bombs. Is there in all this any of the compassion, any of the respect for human freedom or for the sanctity of human life, any of the sense of shame – in which Western humanistic values originated? By all the standards of the genuine Western tradition this is an example of atrocious international conduct. It is the work, surely, of people who are unaware of what the greatness of the West is.[9]

We need more than ever to consider if the tradition of democracy was developed in the Third World in the nationalist and national liberation movements rather than in colonialism and imperialism. The Chinese tradition, the Cuban tradition, the Vietnamese tradition, are in line with what are the democratic achievements of an earlier generations of Englishmen, or Dutchmen, or Frenchmen, or Americans. Does not the West as represented by President Johnson and his 'new Asia' need to withdraw to its homeland in order that its genuine representatives may rejoin their own tradition, which teaches that in the face of authontarianism and oppression and injustice 'rebellion is justified'?

Are those of us whose homes are in Europe or North America destroying our own heritage – have we destroyed it already beyond repair? – by seeking paths of thought and action which are utterly foreign, repugnant, to the real Western civilization, with its well-tried and authentic conception of man's need for freedom, of community, of justice and of the value of people? Is there not good

[9] Contrasted with the usual fanaticism of Western attitudes to Asian radicalism and revolution there is the sober wisdom of a conservative like Walter Lippmann, who is no less concerned for Western civilization than anyone else. Quotations from three of his articles in the *Herald Tribune* will suffice:

> The inwardness of our messianic policy is the unavowed (often formally disavowed) assumption that the old mission of the Western white man, which Europe can no longer afford to carry on, has devolved upon us . . . In attempting to apply (the) ideology of the world wars to the Asia of the 1960s – the President and Secretary Rusk are involving the United States in a mission which cannot be fulfilled because it is based on a pervasive fallacy. They have not taken truly into account the cataclysmic consequences of the collapse of the empires and of the decolonization of the enormous masses of the Asian continent. We have, quite certainly, a great historic mission to perform in the Pacific and in Asia. But it cannot be performed by invading the continent of Asia and it is preposterous to think that we can regulate and determine the course of the revolutionary upheaval through which the people of Asia are fated to pass. Our task is to coexist peaceably and helpfully with them while they find their way. ('The Fallacy of U.S. Asian Policy', 19 November 1966.)

> . . . Among our great mistakes in Southeast Asia has been the reckless use of words. It is our own propaganda which has taught the world, and particularly the small allies, that the outcome in Vietnam was the 'test' of American courage, good faith, idealism and power. ('China and the Dominoes', 20 January 1967.)

> President Johnson has allowed the issue of the Vietnam war to become a test of whether the United States is to continue to be a military power on the Asian mainland. The President is acting through a puppet regime in Saigon supported by troops and enormous sea and air power . . . ('Collision Course in Asia', 24 May 1967.)

reason to place the unspeakable cruelty, the deception, the political chicanery, the greed, and the racialism manifested in Euramenca's attempt to dominate the Third World within another tradition than that to which Socrates, Voltaire, Thomas Paine, and Lincoln belong?

Should not the attempts at Western dominance of the World be brought to an end in order that people in Europe and North America can try to save, and revive, what is authentic in their own great tradition? Perhaps then the West will produce something contemporary which non-Westerners would be glad to use in order to enhance their own freedom and enrich their own lives. But, first, much of the promise of human enrichment, which is to be found in the creative work of scientists, inventors, thinkers, statesmen, artists, and others in the West remains yet as promise only of social justice, democracy, humanism, the joy of living and working, and peace *within Europe and North America*; cities have become places that cannot be lived in; extreme inequalities of wealth, social influence and political power degrade affluent societies; abiding and satisfying human relationships are often not available at any price; participation in political decision-making has become an empty formality; racial discrimination is growing; significant, intelligent and properly informed community-wide discussion of live and relevant moral, social and political issues aiming at the truth – the very foundation of democracy – are almost non-existent. Perhaps the enemies of the West are not those outside the gates; perhaps they are the people who are subverting the entire tradition from the seats of power. Intelligent people in the non-Western world are amazed at the cruelty, moral insensitiveness, ignorance and pretentiousness of Westerners who justify the continued attempts by Europe and North America to manage and control the whole world.[10]

The chorus of 'Yankee, Go Home' throughout the world – which becomes a serious matter when China and Vietnam resolve to exclude all foreign domination and privilege – may be a good thing in the long run. It is no shame to recognize that the American way

[10] Would it be fair to assume that if the Federal Bureau of Investigation and similar agencies were not too busy harassing or killing political dissenters at home and abroad it might have had cause to report fewer than that 3,250,000 'serious crimes' – and an eleven per cent increase over the 1965 figure for murders, rapes, robberies and assaults – which it reported for 1966? (*The Guardian*, 11 August 1967). If the United States were not spending at the rate of nearly 1,500 dollars per family a year for military purposes, would it not cease to be a country in which about fifty million people, equivalent to the total population of Britain, were living below the poverty line? (See *Poverty in America*. Edited by Louis A. Ferman, Joyce L. Kornbluh and Alan Haber. Ann Arbor. University of Michigan Press, 1966, pp. 1-81).

of life is not the model for the world and that it shows best in the soil in which it is grown. The notion that this is 'the American century' is a mischievous and misleading one. It is also no disgrace to recognize that European culture, for all its greatness, belongs to Europe; that it is a regional, not a universal culture. As part of a truly universal humanism European and American cultures need to be complemented by other modes of experience, the authentic insights of other peoples. There will be other gains. Even the most benevolent Westerners who impose themselves abroad tend to affect a superiority to other peoples and to despise or patronize them, and thus to cut themselves off from reality; they are deprived of the knowledge that comes to all of us from knowing ourselves in the mirror of other people. The end of Western domination, and a revival of the Western tradition in Europe and America, can help people in the West in the long run to learn to love Asians, Latin Americans and Africans, and to respect them, rather than to patronize and oppress them. They will thus come to have enough imagination to understand that the peoples of the Southern hemisphere are not simply more or less recalcitrant pupils learning the American or European way of life, people who willy-nilly live in extensions of America or Europe; but rather, that they can live and grow, mature and flower only in their own soil and climate.

The delights of the Maoists in seeing expelled from any part of the Third World the 'imperialism' and neo-colonialism' of the West has sometimes been taken as a challenge which needs to be met by counter-measures. But the expulsion of the Western presence from China alerts us to the danger that the unwelcome Western military, economic and political intrusions may lead in the long run to the rejection by the greater part of mankind of even what is good in Western culture.

4. *Are we being educated to live in the world of our time?*

One has cause to wonder if too many of the people who are helping to form the consciousness of those of us who have to live on into the twenty-first century are regretting, even resenting, the rapid passing of much that the pace of change has made untenable. Professor Herbert Butterfield of Cambridge University has reminded us that even the thirties now seem 'archaic' to us.[11] Consequently those who under the guise of scholarship are still firing verbal shots

[11] *The Present State of Historical Scholarship* (Cambridge: Cambridge University Press, 1965), p. 11.

in battles fought long ago have a bias and motivation which is not easily discernible to people who are living in the very different world of the sixties.

Younger people are, before they can take a dispassionate view of the world around them, conscripted to take part in a battle which they are told is going on. This battle is sometimes described as 'a battle for the hearts and minds of men'. They are thus heavily committed to a certain view of what the shape of the world and of world society is, what the boundaries are, where the dangers and where the safe places are; they are committed to an explanation of the sequence of events, causes and effects, human interactions, which have led to the present. But whether or not they are being initiated into a world of fantasy or of facts they have little opportunity of finding out until they rebel. A set of powerful symbols is used to engage their intellectual and emotional commitment in a big way.

The next stage, the manipulation of moral and emotional reactions, becomes even more terrifying to the observer, as it is manifested most clearly in attitudes to what the West is doing to the Vietnamese. Is it not true, one wonders, that the sense of human feeling and solidarity from which a moral sense partly arises is now so manipulated as to work selectively? That is, that all commendable moral considerations are suspended in dealings with selected races and nations?

Morally responsible action becomes impossible when we do not know (do not have cognition of) the context in which we are called upon to make decisions which express our free choices and affect the conduct and welfare, possibly the lives, of other men, women and children. Do our school education, our works of scholarship and our reference books, and our mass communications media give us an accurate picture of the shape and dimensions of the social reality of which we are a part? Rather, do they not form in our intellects and imaginations a conception which is built up of details in the wrong order and place, with non-facts included, and from which essential parts are missing? If the map of socio-historical reality is constructed out of such a series of fictitious reference points, we will be wrapped up in ideology and will in time be cut off from the real world, and our 'subjective' world and the 'objective' world will have little relation to each other.

There are possibly enough reasons why we are motivated not to take cognisance of what is out there in the world of persons and things – the actual causes and the actual effects, the omissions and the commissions, the apprehensions and the expectations, the gestures and the meanings. We sometimes do not want to know because our 'pretend-world' which we may be manipulated into conceiving suits our purposes. Anyone who has tried to displace such conceptions with the undisputed facts of history and geography and experienced the resistance will know how hard it is to dislodge fantasies with mere facts.

The effects of the brainwashing that goes on is that events, persons and things in reference to which we must make responsible moral decisions are not identifiably *there* in the consciousness of a large part of the community; they are not there in the culture. For example, most of the facts that provide a good and rational sociological explanation for Arab nationalism and its expression, or East Asian revolutions, or Latin American peasant insurgency, are not conceivable even by some experts on these matters.

In addition to the facts to which we refer our thoughts and actions, there are the feelings with which we apprehend those details of fact or what we imagine to be fact. The way we are moved, and the extent to which we are moved normally by the world outside of ourselves is partly decided by the culture of the society of which we are a part. But education, in the sense not of initiation but of the disciplining and sharpening of our perceptions and faculties so that we are in rational contact with objective reality, must teach us to respond to what the elements of the world outside are rather than to just 'emote' regardless of what we are responding to. The view of the world propagated by the army of reporters, commentators and the rest tends to condition us to respond emotionally to certain events, ideas, persons or groups, things and so on *in a given way*. We are *sentimentally* sorry or angry or loyal or hostile.

One abdicates moral freedom when one is under the spell of this kind of propaganda. To put it in general, everyday terms, when we are subtly conditioned in a laboratory situation to hate what is lovable, or to flee or attack what is harmless, to feel admiration for what is repulsive, it is not highly dangerous. But when our reactions and impulses are at variance with the actual qualities of things in the actual world in which we have to live and make responsible decisions which may more or less be momentous, we are incapable of free action; we would make as many ethical blunders as the mistakes we would make if we lived amidst people and things which were, unknown to us, made or masked to appear very different from what they really were. How, in that situation, could we act in a rational and human way? Enemies who are out to destroy us can appear as friends, and friends as enemies; cruelty appears as goodwill, and goodwill as cruelty. And our press and politicians tell us who the 'good boys' and causes are and who the 'bad boys' and causes are.

A false picture of the world, a wrong evaluation of and 'feel' for people and things, when to these is added a confusion about the way actions are to be evaluated as right or wrong, good or bad, kind or cruel, life-promoting or life-destroying, just or unjust, moral responsibility becomes very difficult. It becomes impossible when the notion is successfully propagated that there is no such thing as moral responsibility – whether one is robbing the weak, or torturing children, or slandering the noble or killing historic communities for political reasons, or in furtherance of the national interest.

The problem here is not the erosion of a set of fixed or absolute moral standards. The deification of a set of moral norms which were the creation of an earlier society results in the obstruction of the history-making and humanizing responsibility which every generation has. It is therefore good that there is much greater freedom now to re-examine taboos and prescriptions and prohibitions which we have inherited. But in the interaction between persons playing different roles, and also between human groups and nations, freedom of responsible moral choice is abdicated when 'anything goes'. It is present when people evaluate social-ethical norms in terms of whether or not some action (a protest, an attack, an 'exposure', an attempt at persuasion, help, obstruction, etc) hinders or promotes physical well-being (whether that may be), hinders or helps 'progress' towards independence, increases or relieves the burdens of the oppressed, etc. But when the pursuit of 'interests' becomes a norm it is empty of ethical content. When power or success becomes its own justification it is meaningless as a standard. One of the reasons why the brainwashing of people in the West today prevents the growth of a sense of responsibility in international conduct is the bogus pretence that *real-politik* is all there is to international affairs.

Another reason is the fact that hypocrisy has become the tradition in the international conduct of such nations as Britain and the United States. In less democratic times clap-trap of the kind current today – the free world, the civilizing mission, 'raising the cost of aggression', 'the honouring of solemn international obligations' – was common. Events and evidence were audaciously fabricated. And fictitious accounts of what had happened were given. But all that was in diplomatic exchanges between the governments. Today, as one can easily show, such hypocrisies and cynical fictions are the stock-in-trade of parsons, scholars and journalists, and are consented to by large masses of people. When pressed to talk about standards, people will readily admit to using multiple standards.[12]

The confusion about standards in the minds of many people makes them part of a moral universe which is at odds with the real world in which European and American military power and economic pressure are exercised. For the greater part of the social reality in our global society is one in which different kinds of international or intergroup or interclass action are evaluated fairly precisely. The Chinese and the Vietnamese are speaking a moral language which has precise and profound meaning. It is not rhetoric. Our ability to communicate with China is involved here. And, in any case, in any circumstances, is not the hypocrisy and the humbug bearable only in a fantasy world? For in the real world outside us it is an objective fact that collective human actions do (and do recognizably) create or destroy, enrich or impoverish, retard or promote progress, save life or kill, relieve or increase suffering. A sound education – which must include the sensitive reading of the great tragedies of Western literature – can sharpen our perceptions and introduce us to reality.

One of the reasons why people are getting more and more ignorant about the context in which their moral responsibility as a nation or race is exercised is the absence of a truly universal intellectual community. Neither in the United States nor in Britain, for instance, is there a centre of research and discussion or a serious journal which even approaches being a focus for the questions, the issues, the problems, the aspirations and achievements of different peoples. The intellectual *milieu* provided by the universities only

[12] Brigadier General Hugh B. Hester, in an article, wrote that 'China does not occupy a foot of any other country's territory nor does she have a single military man upon foreign soil. Yet the U.S. government, . . . has thousands of bases on other people's soil, a government whose President boasted . . . in 1964 that the U.S. had 344 anti-guerilla teams in 49 countries'. (*National Guardian*, 5 March 1966.) The European scholar, J. B. Duroselle, in his *From Wilson to Roosevelt* (London: Chatto & Windus, 1963), refers to the American tradition of transforming 'a conquest into a "mission", an intervention into "punishment of the wicked", a war into a "crusade".' Professor Van Alstyne has written: '. . . It might be pointed out that American foreign policy has a vocabulary all its own, consciously – even ostentatiously – sidestepping the use of terms that even hint at aggression or imperial domination, and taking refuge in abstract formulae, stereotyped phrases, and idealistic cliches that explain nothing. Phrases like "Monroe Doctrine", "no entangling alliances", "good neighbour policy", "Truman doctrine", "Eisenhower doctrine", strew the pages of American history but throw little light on the dynamics of American foreign policy . . . There is a strong pharasaical flavour about American diplomacy, easily detected abroad, but generally unrecognized at home.' (*The Rising American Empire*, p. 7.) Who would deny that one must be true to one's friends, honour one's international obligations, keep one's word, resist aggression, defend freedom and show that aggression does not pay? To moralize is one thing; to be truthful, relevant and morally just is another.

reinforces the false notion that non-Western people outside Euramerica are intellectually a lower order of being, and cannot supply any of the intellectual needs of a true intellectual community in the modern world. In other words, we have still to see research and teaching institutions (including publications) which are truly open and responsive to mankind. Nor has the great potential of radio been realized anywhere in the world for serious, critical thinking of this kind.

We must note here, too, the publication and use of seemingly authentic works of scholarship about the contemporary world under the sponsorship of state organizations of political propaganda, for example, the United States Information Agency and the Central Intelligence Agency. The strategy of this is to flood the academic libraries with political polemic masquerading as scholarship, and thus to ensure that the false picture of the world and of contemporary world history is too firmly established to make genuine scholarship or sensible viewpoints seem plausible.

To bemoan the fact that sensibilities have been dulled and that minds have been filled with trash is not enough. What can be done to restore what has been lost?

And finally, one of the beliefs which stands most in the way of a more sane, rational and morally responsible attitude to the world of our time is the belief that conformity is good and what is called 'alienation' is bad. Is it true that it is the rebels and revolutionaries who are those who do not know how to fit into human society? Or is it likely that those who have conformed best are those who have yet to 'join the human race?' There are assumptions in our thinking about these questions which are closely related to our world view: that, for example, social stability, and what makes for stability, are better that social instability and what makes for social instability. Are not all societies at some time or another the better off for experiencing some forms of instability?

Is it correct that in certain circumstances 'to rebel is justified', that sometimes truth may be with the non-conforming minority? What is 'the consensus' in Europe and America and how can it be produced? Is it not in fact produced without any significant community-wide discussion of issues?

We have already noted that there is plain and systematic lying about the contemporary world by what are supposed to be the community's means of 'information' or self-information. Intelligent people will find this offensive and corrupt. But what reasons can we give for saying that such corruption of supposedly democratic social institutions is to be condemned or brought to an end? Do our children, and their elders who seek the knowledge they need to live responsibly, have a right to the truth? If they do, what does it mean for us to be told the truth about any matter? More specifically, what does it mean in regard to questions in which our relations with other communities or other races are concerned? On the other hand, where true knowledge, sane attitudes and the training in making fine moral discriminations may lead to considerable deviation from the consensus (about the national interest), is it 'wrong' to secure the conformity of 'the people' by progressively limiting and tricking their perceptions of reality, manipulating their emotional responses and attitudes, and conditioning their moral choices? The demand that there should be conformity, that the consensus should be respected, that the decencies must be respected, that the national security should not be endangered by the spread of a sense of insecurity about the established order, that one must not rock the boat, that one must not be controversial, that extremism should be avoided, that one should not manifest signs of 'immaturity' by 'deviant' behaviour or signs of 'alienation' – all these seem to express little more than the wishes of the conservatives, of those who will never have it so good if there was social change.[13]

Everyone – the 'new man' more than all others – must take responsibility for the implications of national and international policies. How he, or the group or organization which he helps to create, act is an important matter. But it seems to be true that to call things by their right name, to relate oneself to what is going on, to have the right attitude, to make the correct evaluation, is always an acute dilemma, and particularly so when there is a revolutionary situation. China, or rather East Asia, is in a revolutionary situation. And the whole world (partly because of what has happened in China, in Vietnam, in Cuba, in Tanzania and elsewhere, and partly because of the refusal of the poor elsewhere to tolerate the oppression, the subhuman conditions and the indignity of their existence) has now moved irreversibly into a revolutionary situation. All of us are being forced to make choices; but we are pretending that we do not have to do so.

One of the most painful choices which willy-nilly all of us – and particularly the intellectuals, the politicians and the political activists

[13] It is interesting to observe how a man of the highest integrity and intelligence, like Dr Martin Luther King, has over the years removed from his eyes the scales which have prevented his eyes from seeing the realities of his own national community. The implications of his address at New York's Riverside Church in April 1967, published in the May 1967 issue of *Ramparts* under the title 'Declaration of Independence from the War in Vietnam', shows how 'dangerous' true knowledge of social reality can be.

– are now making is: which of the two sides must be dispossessed, of material well-being, of office, of power, of liberty, perhaps of education, perhaps even of life, in order that the other either remain in possession or take possession of these. The dilemma may not be of our own making; but because man in our generation, as in every other generation, is a maker of history, we are making a choice. The choice between the large American corporations and the impoverished Latin American masses whose homeland supplies these few corporations with enormous wealth is a fairly simple ethical question (although it is true that most Americans, including Christians, have made the other choice). But the struggle between landlords and their armies and tenants and labourers and their armies poses more extreme choices. Behind revolutionary and counter-revolutionary policies there may be the question: shall this one die that these may live? Can we answer? Have we been educated to answer questions of this kind which *must* be answered? For those of us involved personally, through friends, relations, pupils, colleagues, and co-religionists, the intellectual, emotional and moral burden of the choices can sometimes be too great to bear. Nevertheless, we give consent to or withhold consent from choices which are nominally made on our behalf.

But the kind of a world in which we must take adult responsibilities is this kind of a world, not one of cowboys and Indians. Is it not true that most of us are not only badly informed about the shape of the world we live in, and how it came into being, but also intellectually, emotionally and morally far from being mature enough to cope with the problems of a very difficult world? If it is, what can we do about it?

These considerations are only a few of the many that are relevant when we try to solve the 'problem' which the rise of Maoist China poses for us. There are others which are just as important. We have to seek a satisfactory explanation for the prevalence on a massive scale of poverty, hunger and ignorance in the world of which we are a part. We have reason to ask if there is any creative role for the middle class to play in the kind of world which is emerging. We have to work out the price it is worth paying for true democracy within and among nations. And so on.

But we need to be careful not to make the challenge of China the excuse for theoretical exercises in social ethics or social philosophy. To keep ourselves on a practical and realistic level will prove to be difficult enough, without our becoming abstract and speculative. Before we can decide what we will or will not do about the mythical Yellow Peril, what we will or will not be made to do by others who decide in what causes our money, our skills and our lives will be spent, we need to know more than we are now allowed to know; we also need to do more than we now are encouraged or permitted to do.

We do not even know what is the point of no return from a war against a quarter of mankind. Can such a war be made an impossibility, at least in our own life-time? Or will the verbal and intellectual assaults on China be followed through by decisions and actions of military and political powers over whom we have no control. Do we have time left to understand what China's resurgence means for us? These questions are not rhetorical; they express our ignorance, and the recognition of our ignorance on a matter of what appears to be of great importance. One can only hope that it is not too late for us to act for ourselves. What those who want – for 'good' reasons or bad – to destroy 'Red' China will be destroying is much more than just China itself.

Suggestions for Further Reading

Books

Alstyne, Richard van. *The Rising American Empire* (London: Oxford University Press, 1960)

Buchanan, Keith. *The Chinese People and the Chinese Earth* (London: George Bell, 1966)

Blaustein, Albert P. *Fundamental Legal Documents of Communist China* (South Hackensack: Rothman & Co., 1962)

Ch'en, Jerome. *Mao and the Chinese Revolution* (London: Oxford University Press, 1965)

Chen Yi. *Vice-Premier Chen Yi Answers Questions Put by Correspondents* (Peking: The Foreign Languages Press, 1966)

Debray, Regis. *Revolution in the Revolution?* (New York: The Monthly Review Press, 1967)

Dumont, Rene. *Lands Alive* (New York: The Monthly Review Press, 1965)

Douglas, Bruce. Ed. *The Rise of China* (Special Issue of *The Student World* Vol. LX No. 1. Geneva: World Student Christian Federation, 1967)

Eckstein, Alexander. *Communist China's Economic Growth and Foreign Trade. Implications for U.S. Foreign Policy* (New York: McGraw-Hill, 1966)

Epstein, Israel. *From Opium War to Liberation* (Peking: The Foreign Languages Press, 1964)

Fanon, Frantz. *The Wretched of the Earth* (Trans. by Constance Farrington. Preface by Jean-Paul Sartre. (London: MacGibbon & Kee, 1965)

Feber, Walter Le. *The New Empire* (Ithaca: Cornell University Press, 1963)

Fleming, D. F. *The Cold War and Its Origins 1917-1960*, 2 vols (New York: Doubleday, 1961)

Fitzgerald, C. P. *The Birth of Communist China* (London: Penguin, 1964)

Forman, Harrison. *Report from Red China* (London: Hale, 1947)

Gittings, John. *The Role of the Chinese Army* (London: Oxford University Press, 1967)

Greene, Felix. *A Curtain of Ignorance* (New York: Doubleday, 1964)

Gelder, Stuart. *The Chinese Communists* (London: Gollancz, 1946)

Han Suyin: *The Crippled Tree*; *The Mortal Flower* (London: Cape, 1965, 1966)

Hinton, William. *Fanshen* (New York: The Monthly Review Press, 1966)

Johnson, Chalmers A. *Peasant Nationalism and Communist Power; the Emergence of Revolutionary China 1937-45* (Stanford University Press, 1953)

Lattimore, Owen. *From China Looking Outward* (Leeds University Press, 1964)

Lin Piao. *Long Live the Victory of People's War* (Peking: The Foreign Languages Press, 1965)

Lutz, Jessie. Ed. *Christian Missions in China – Evangelists of What?* (New York: Heath, 1965)

Mao Tse Tung, *Selected Works*, 4 vols. (Peking: The Foreign Languages Press, 1965)

——. *On the Correct Handling of Contradictions Among the People* (Peking: The Foreign Languages Press, 1957)

Myrdal, Jan. *Report From a Chinese Village* (London: Heinemann, 1965; Penguin 1967)

People's Republic of China, *U.S. Aggression Has no Bounds and the Counter to Aggressions Has no Bounds* (Peking: The Foreign Languages Press, 1966)

——. *People of the World, Unite, for the Complete, Thorough, Total and Resolute Prohibition and Destruction of Nuclear Weapons* (Peking: The Foreign Languages Press, 1963)

——. Afro-Asian Solidarity Against Imperialism (Peking: The Foreign Languages Press, 1964)

Romein, Jan. *The Asian Century* (London: Allen & Unwin, 1962)

Snow, Edgar. *Red Star Over China* (London: Gollancz, 1937)

——. *Journey to the Beginning* (London: Gollancz, 1959)

——. *The Other Side of the River* (London: Gollancz, 1963; New York: Random House, 1962)

Stein, Gunther. *The Challenge of Red China* (London: Pilot Press, 1945)

Schram, Stuart. *The Political Thought of Mao Tse Tung* (New York: Praeger, 1964)

Sun Yat Sen. *San Min Chu I*. Trans. by Frank Price (*Calcutta*: 1942)

Tawney, R. H. *Land and Labour in China* (London: Allen & Unwin, 1932)

United States Government. *United States Relations With China* (Washington: U.S. State Department, 1949)

Wilson, Dick. *A Quarter of Mankind* (London: Weidenfeld & Nicolson, 1966)

Worsley, Peter. *The Third World* (London: Weidenfeld & Nicolson, 1964)

Journals

Peking Review (Peking)
Eastern Horizon (Hong Kong)
Summary of World Broadcasts (B.B.C. Monitoring service)
Far Eastern Economic Review (Hong Kong)

Index